THE AVENGERS
IRON MAN

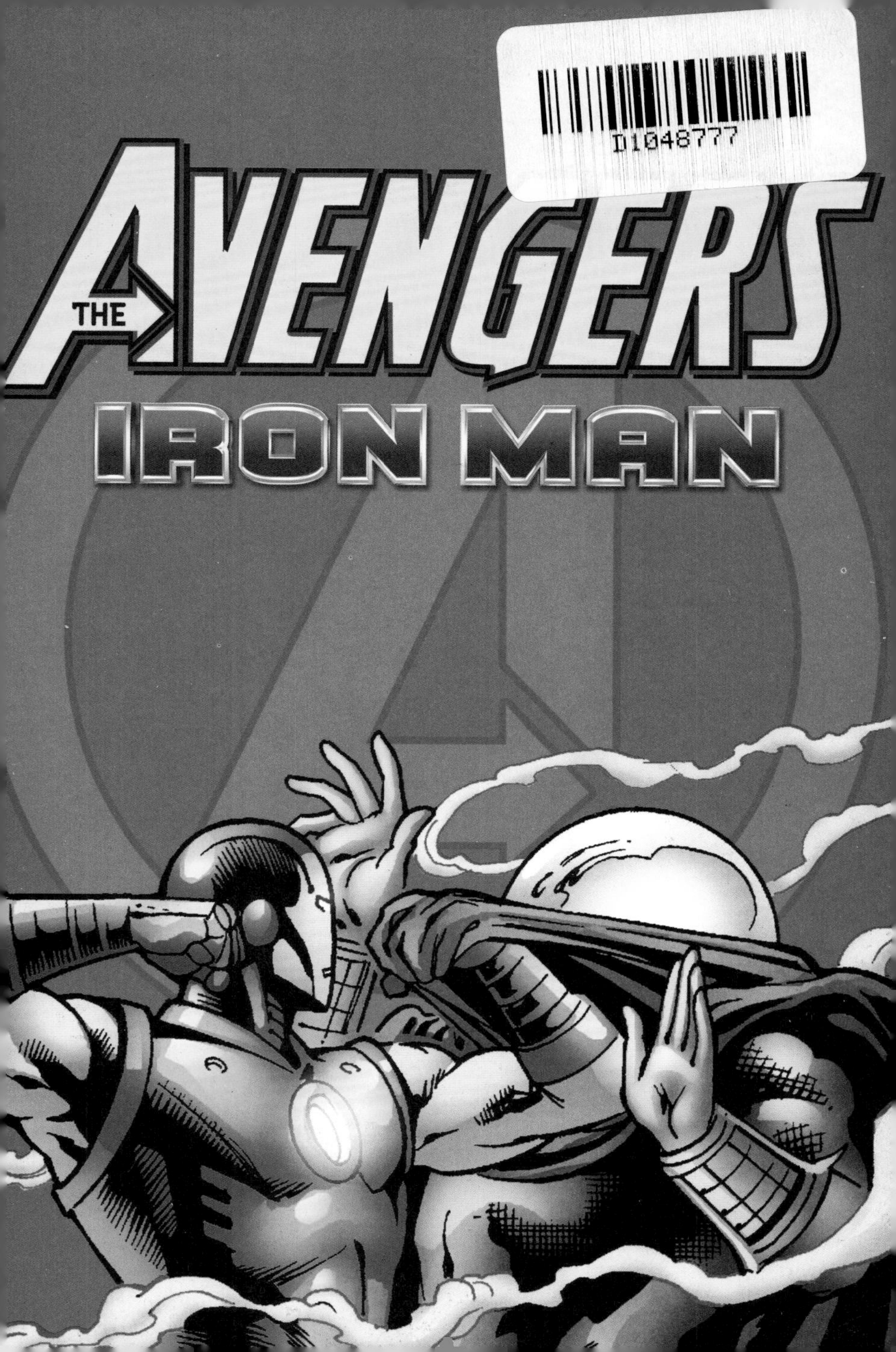

THE AVENGERS
IRON MAN

Writer: Paul Tobin
Penciler: Ronan Cliquet
Inker: Amilton Santos

Colorist: Sotocolor
Letterer: Dave Sharpe
Cover Artist: Clayton Henry
with Guru eFX and Brad Anderson
Assistant Editor: Michael Horwitz
Editor: Nathan Cosby

Captain America created by Joe Simon & Jack Kirby

Collection Editor: Cory Levine
Editorial Assistants: James Emmett & Joe Hochstein
Assistant Editors: Alex Starbuck & Nelson Ribeiro
Editors, Special Projects: Jennifer Grünwald & Mark D. Beazley
Senior Editor, Special Projects: Jeff Youngquist
Senior Vice President of Sales: David Gabriel

Editor in Chief: Joe Quesada
Publisher: Dan Buckley
Executive Producer: Alan Fine

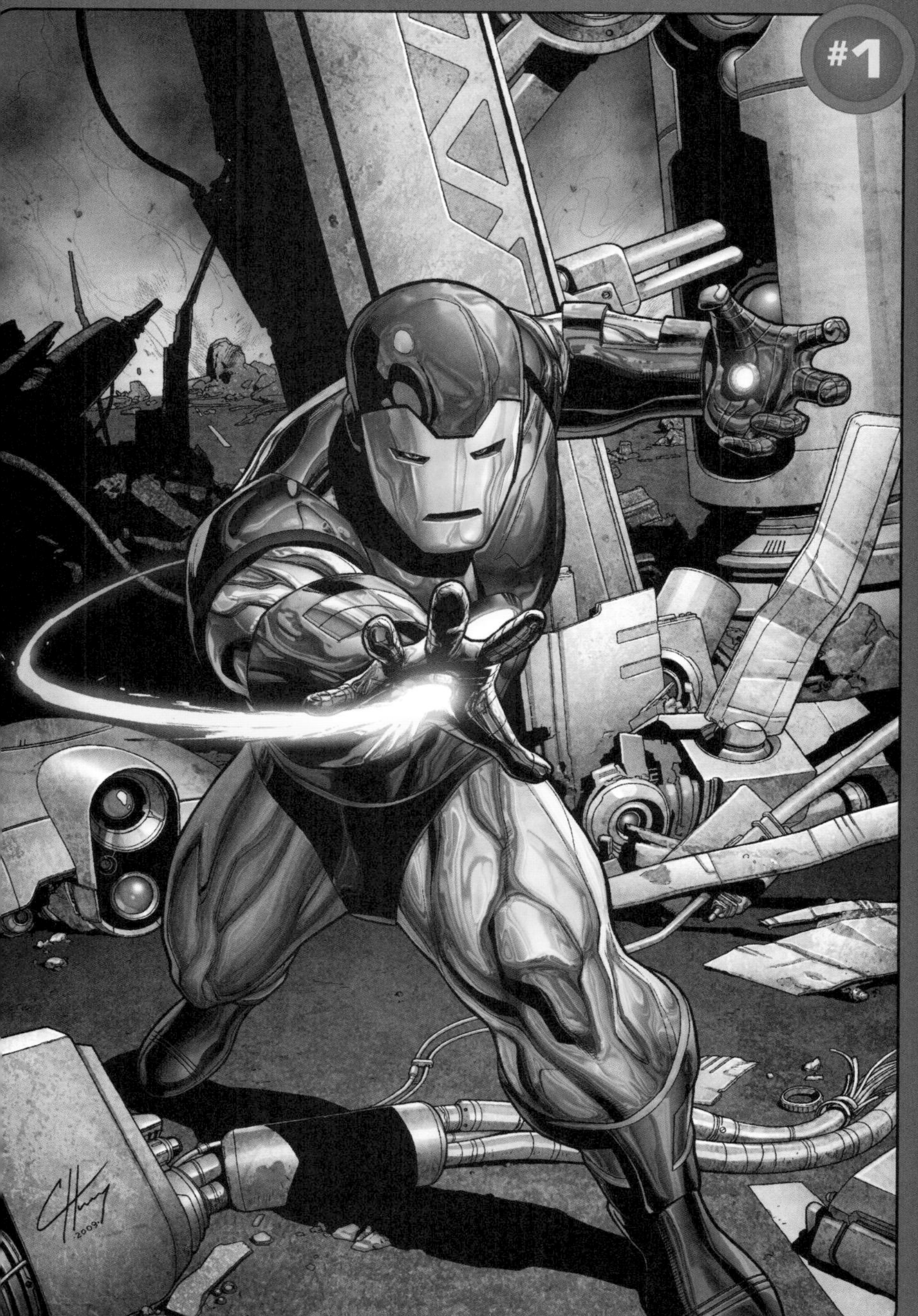
#1
2009

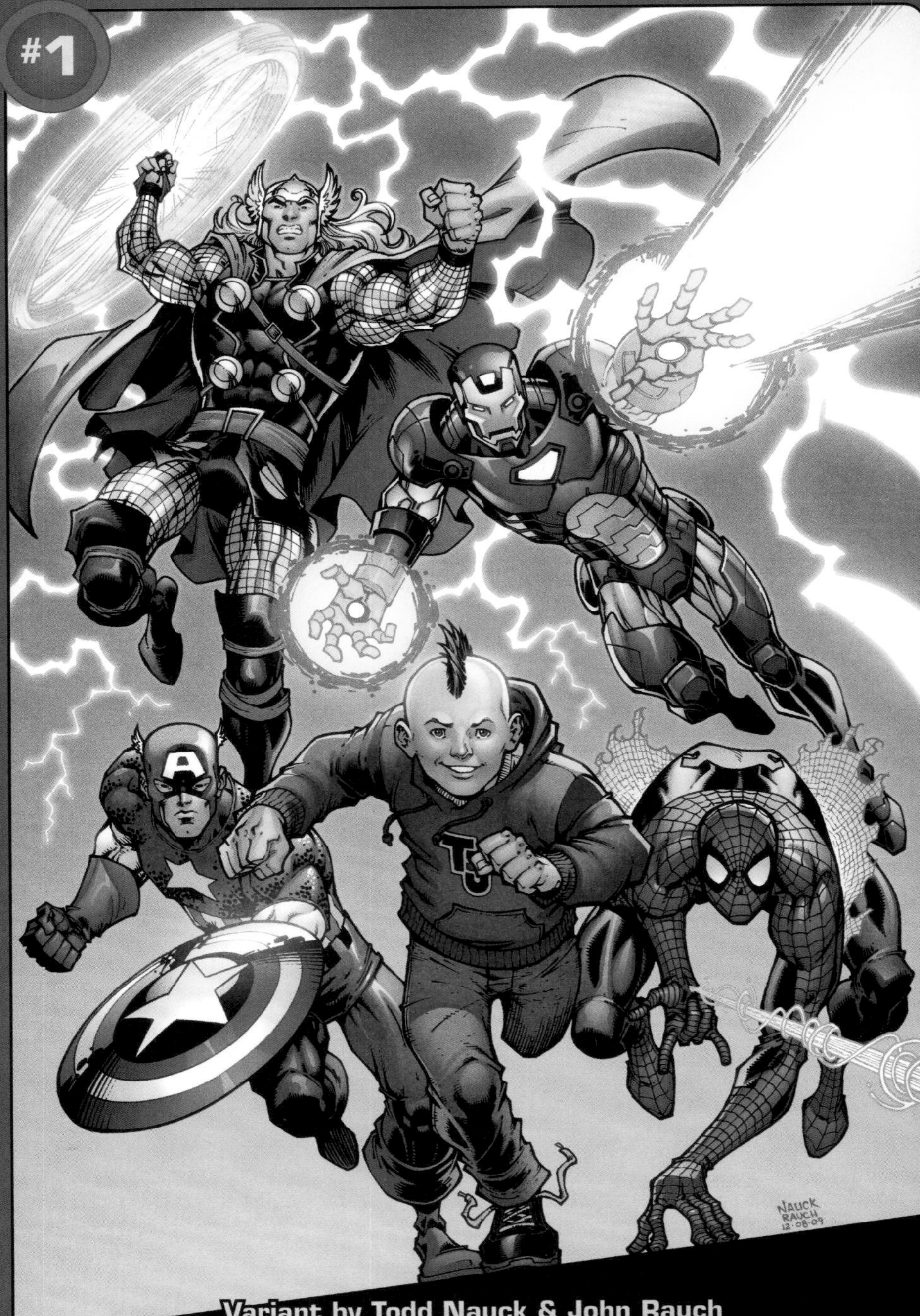
#1
NAUCK
RAUCH
12·08·09

Variant by Todd Nauck & John Rauch

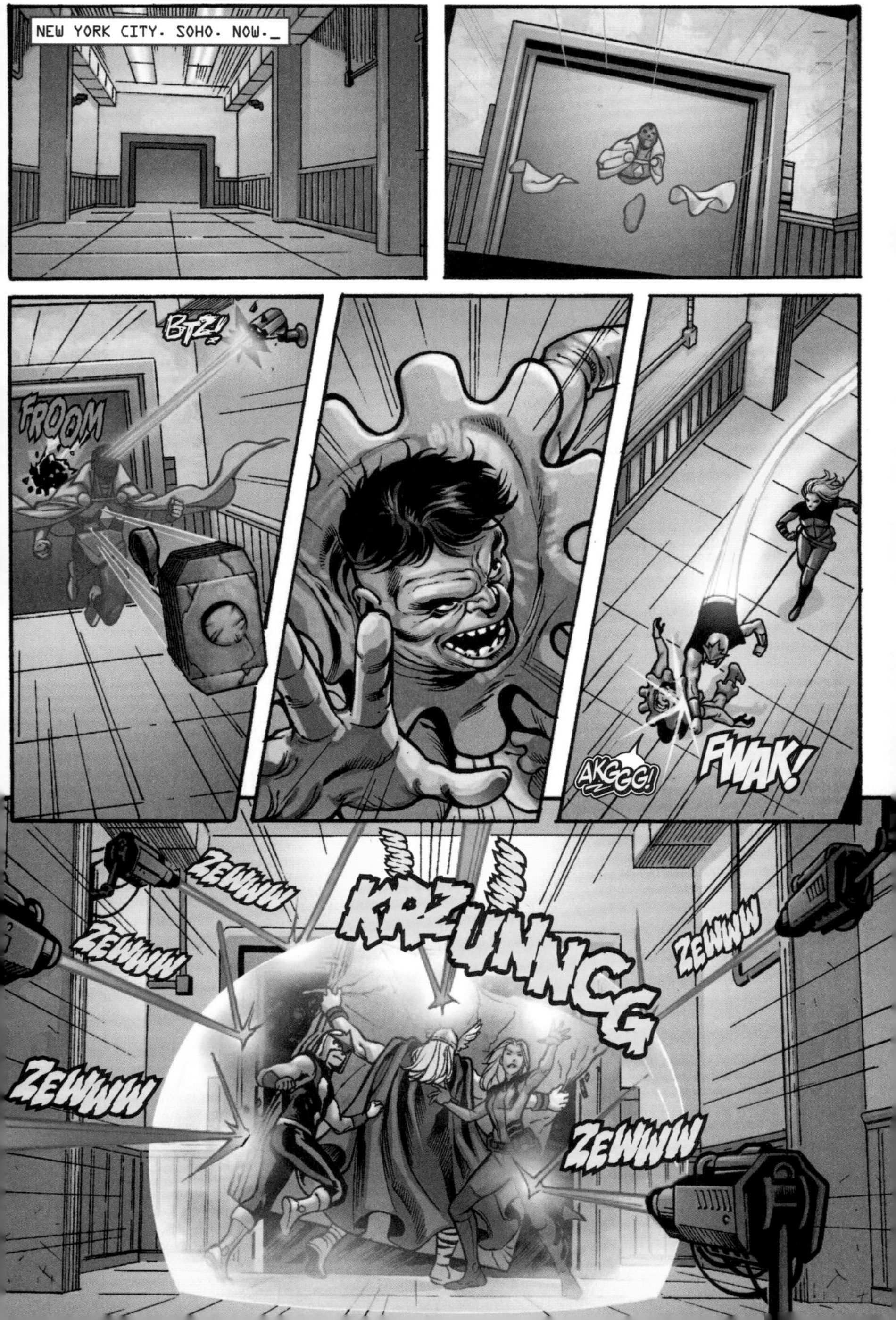
NEW YORK CITY. SOHO. NOW._
BTZ!
FROOM
AKGGG!
FWAK!
ZEWWW
ZEWWW
KRZUNNCG
ZEWWW
ZEWWW
ZEWWW

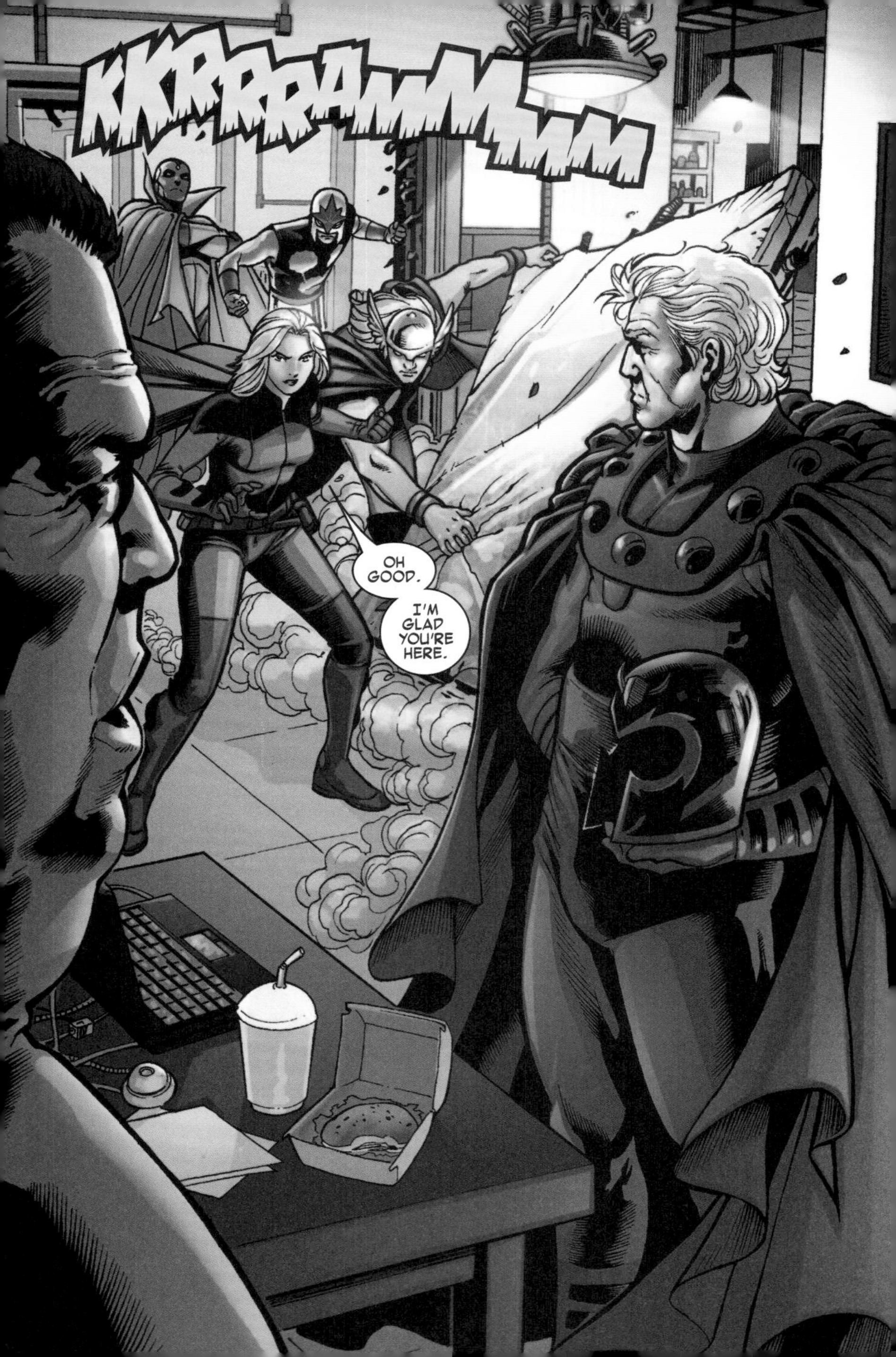
KKRRRAMMMMM
OH GOOD.
I'M GLAD YOU'RE HERE.

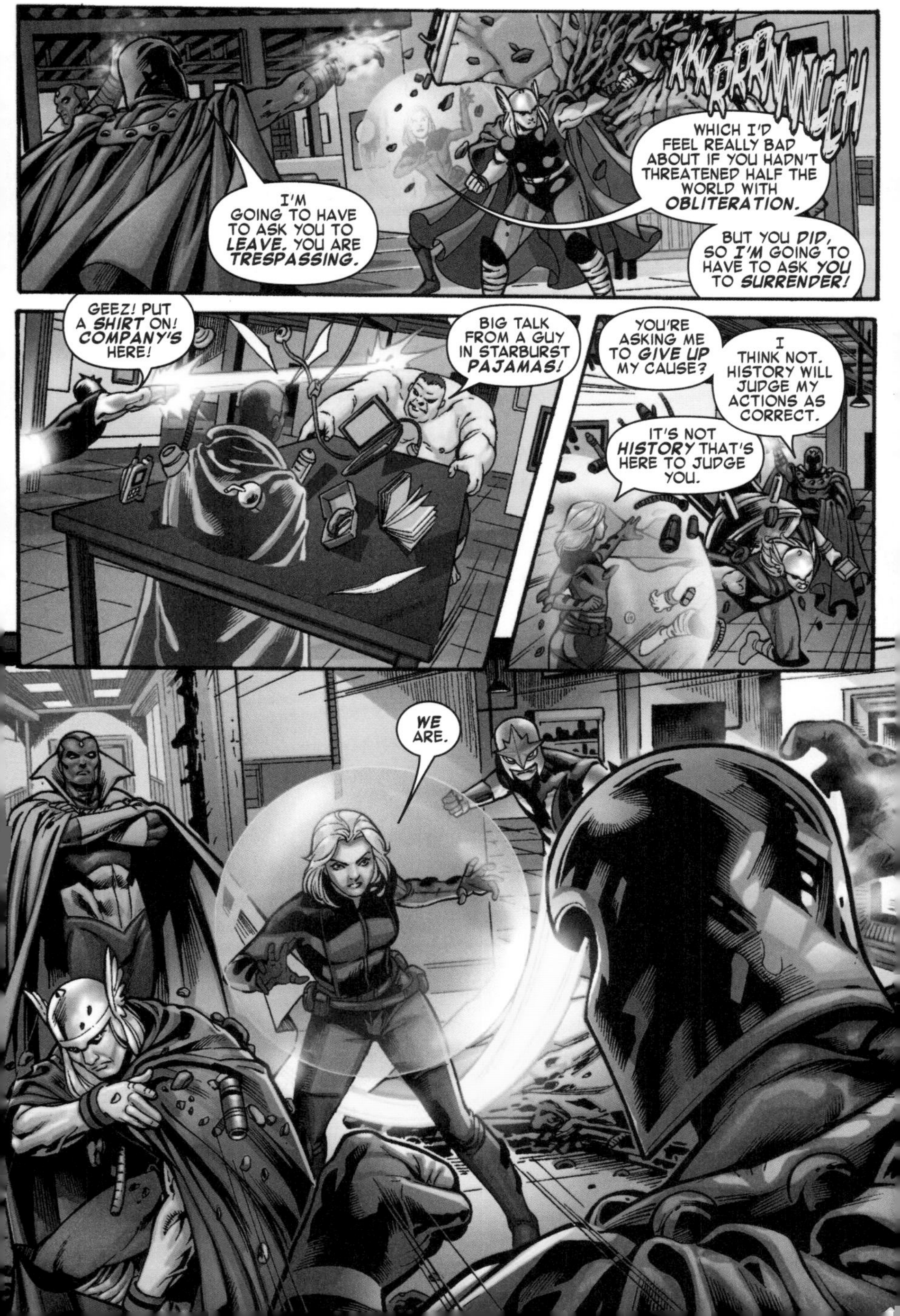
KKKRRRNNNCH
I'M GOING TO HAVE TO ASK YOU TO LEAVE. YOU ARE TRESPASSING.
WHICH I'D FEEL REALLY BAD ABOUT IF YOU HADN'T THREATENED HALF THE WORLD WITH OBLITERATION.
BUT YOU DID, SO I'M GOING TO HAVE TO ASK YOU TO SURRENDER!
GEEZ! PUT A SHIRT ON! COMPANY'S HERE!
BIG TALK FROM A GUY IN STARBURST PAJAMAS!
YOU'RE ASKING ME TO GIVE UP MY CAUSE?
I THINK NOT. HISTORY WILL JUDGE MY ACTIONS AS CORRECT.
IT'S NOT HISTORY THAT'S HERE TO JUDGE YOU.
WE ARE.

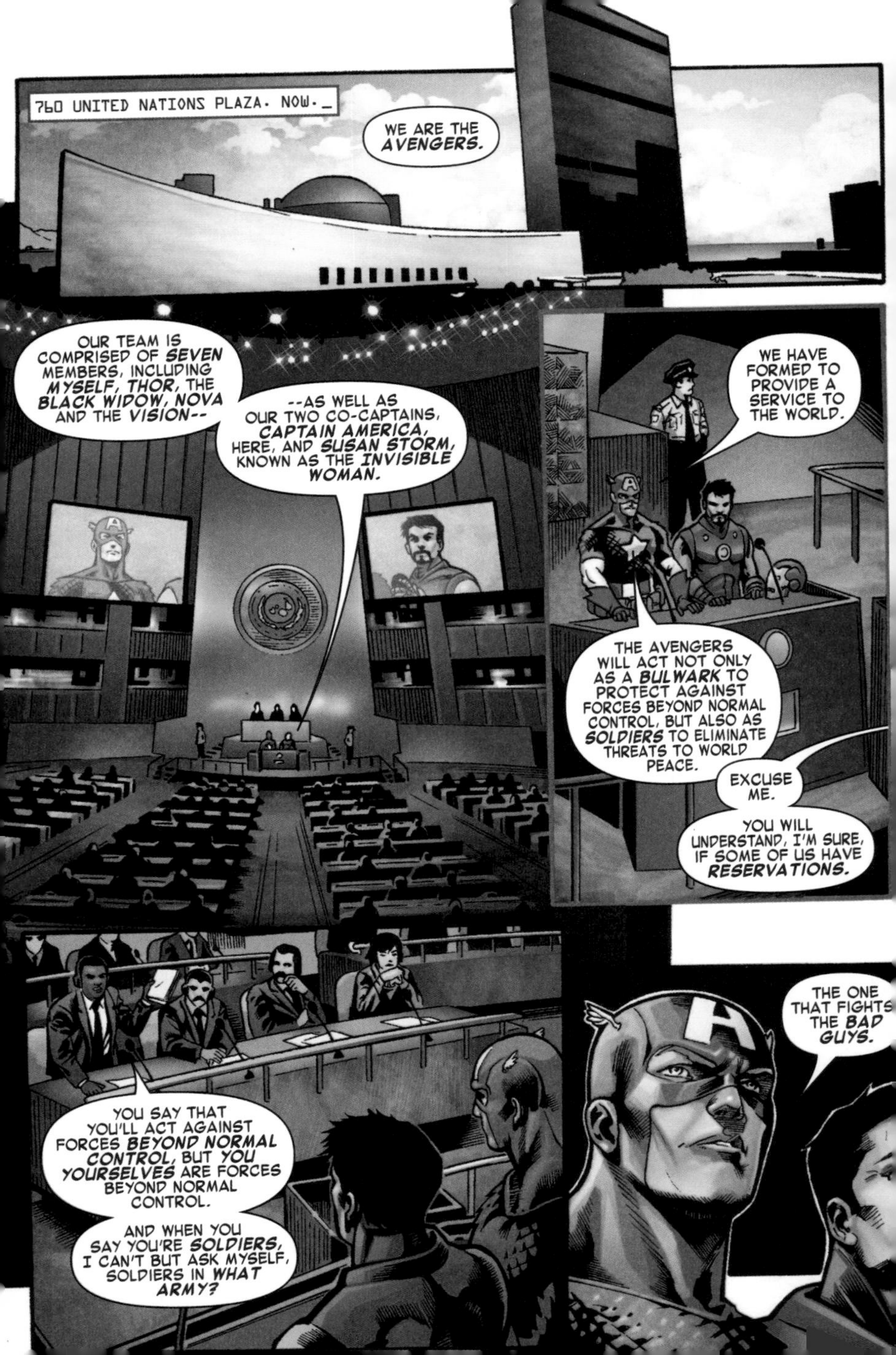
760 UNITED NATIONS PLAZA. NOW._
WE ARE THE AVENGERS.
OUR TEAM IS COMPRISED OF SEVEN MEMBERS, INCLUDING MYSELF, THOR, THE BLACK WIDOW, NOVA AND THE VISION--
--AS WELL AS OUR TWO CO-CAPTAINS, CAPTAIN AMERICA, HERE, AND SUSAN STORM, KNOWN AS THE INVISIBLE WOMAN.
WE HAVE FORMED TO PROVIDE A SERVICE TO THE WORLD.
THE AVENGERS WILL ACT NOT ONLY AS A BULWARK TO PROTECT AGAINST FORCES BEYOND NORMAL CONTROL, BUT ALSO AS SOLDIERS TO ELIMINATE THREATS TO WORLD PEACE.
EXCUSE ME.
YOU WILL UNDERSTAND, I'M SURE, IF SOME OF US HAVE RESERVATIONS.
YOU SAY THAT YOU'LL ACT AGAINST FORCES BEYOND NORMAL CONTROL, BUT YOU YOURSELVES ARE FORCES BEYOND NORMAL CONTROL.
AND WHEN YOU SAY YOU'RE SOLDIERS, I CAN'T BUT ASK MYSELF, SOLDIERS IN WHAT ARMY?
THE ONE THAT FIGHTS THE BAD GUYS.

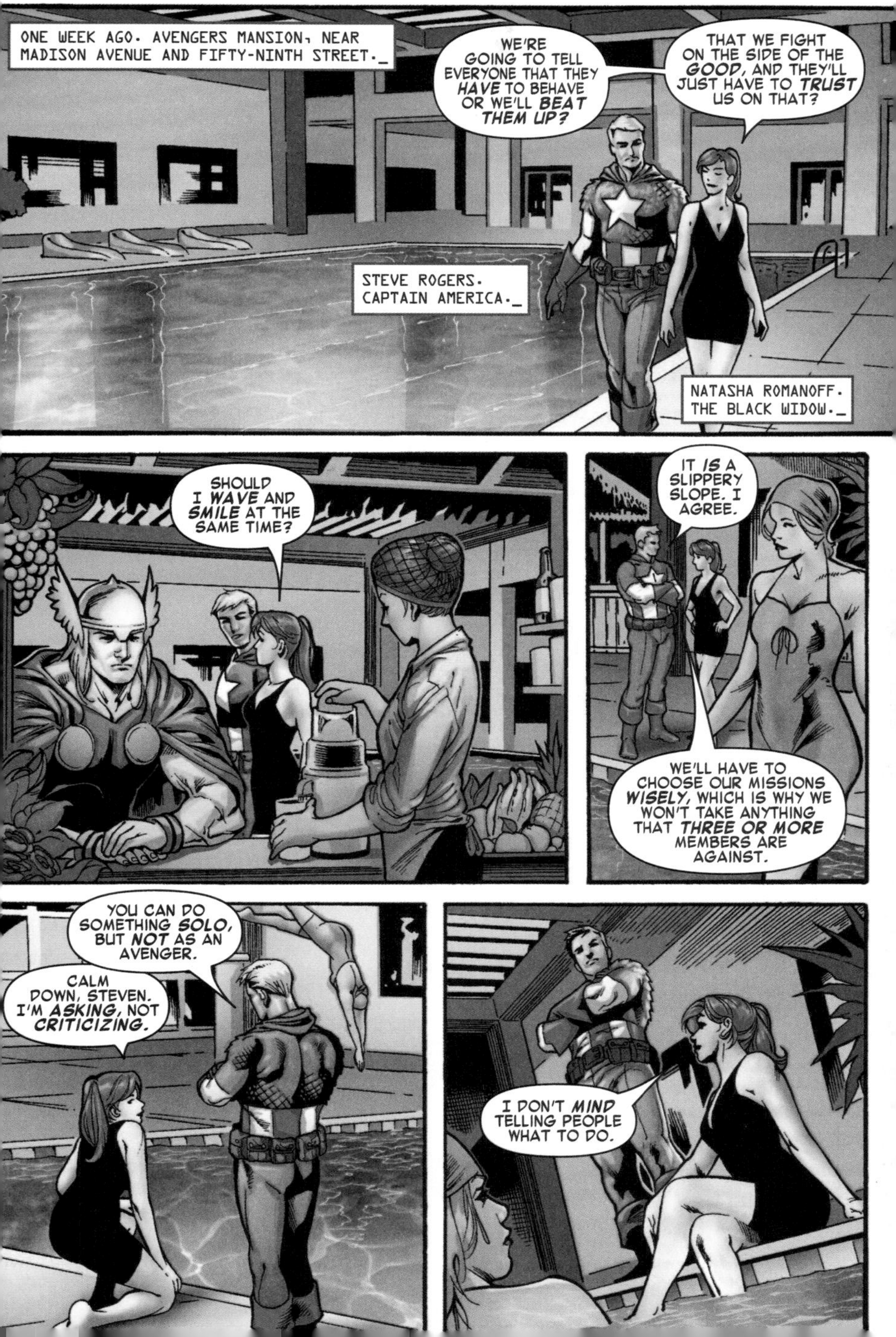
ONE WEEK AGO. AVENGERS MANSION, NEAR MADISON AVENUE AND FIFTY-NINTH STREET._
WE'RE GOING TO TELL EVERYONE THAT THEY HAVE TO BEHAVE OR WE'LL BEAT THEM UP?
THAT WE FIGHT ON THE SIDE OF THE GOOD, AND THEY'LL JUST HAVE TO TRUST US ON THAT?
STEVE ROGERS. CAPTAIN AMERICA._
NATASHA ROMANOFF. THE BLACK WIDOW._
SHOULD I WAVE AND SMILE AT THE SAME TIME?
IT IS A SLIPPERY SLOPE. I AGREE.
WE'LL HAVE TO CHOOSE OUR MISSIONS WISELY, WHICH IS WHY WE WON'T TAKE ANYTHING THAT THREE OR MORE MEMBERS ARE AGAINST.
YOU CAN DO SOMETHING SOLO, BUT NOT AS AN AVENGER.
CALM DOWN, STEVEN. I'M ASKING, NOT CRITICIZING.
I DON'T MIND TELLING PEOPLE WHAT TO DO.

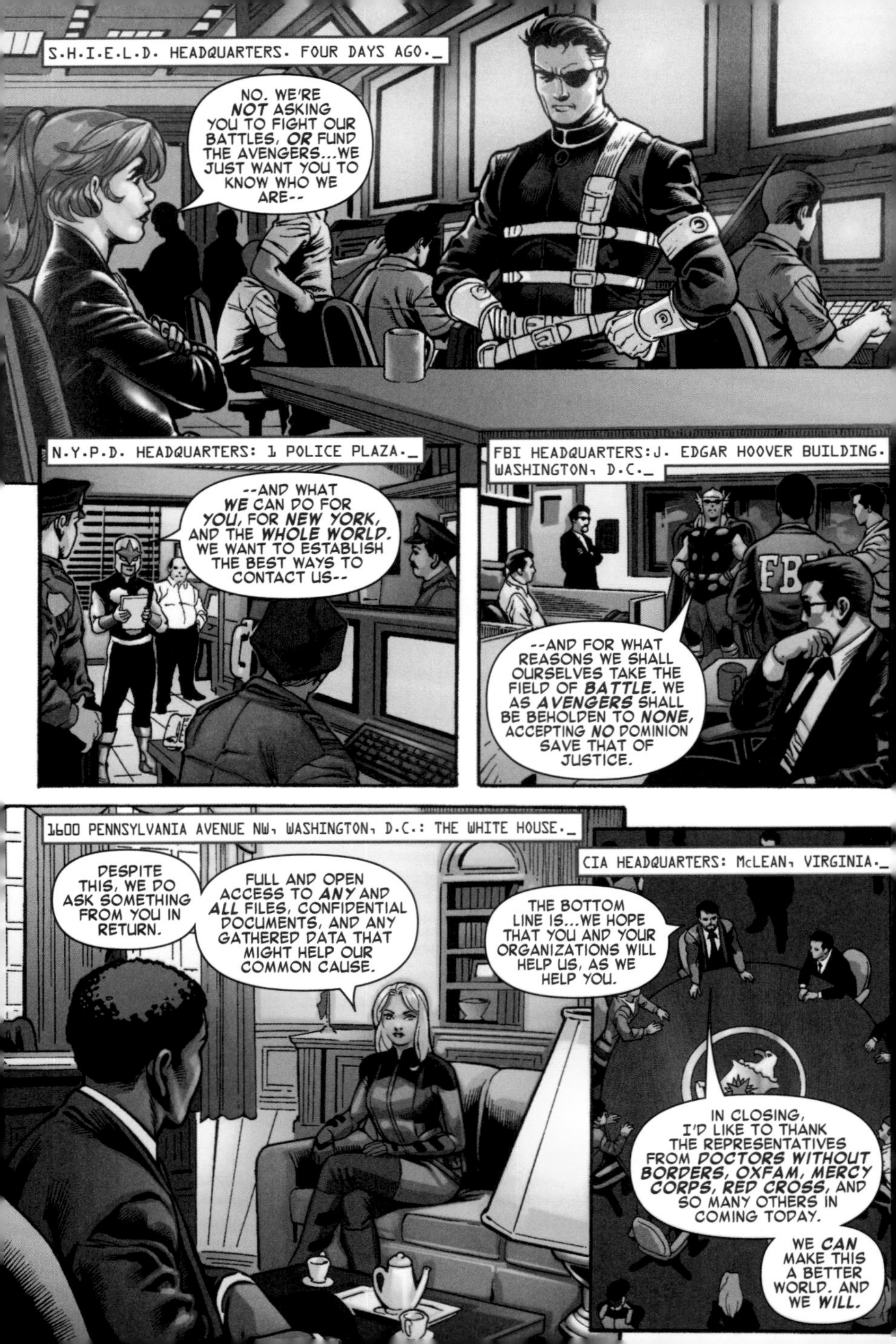
S.H.I.E.L.D. HEADQUARTERS. FOUR DAYS AGO._
NO. WE'RE NOT ASKING YOU TO FIGHT OUR BATTLES, OR FUND THE AVENGERS...WE JUST WANT YOU TO KNOW WHO WE ARE--
N.Y.P.D. HEADQUARTERS: 1 POLICE PLAZA._
--AND WHAT WE CAN DO FOR YOU, FOR NEW YORK, AND THE WHOLE WORLD. WE WANT TO ESTABLISH THE BEST WAYS TO CONTACT US--
FBI HEADQUARTERS: J. EDGAR HOOVER BUILDING. WASHINGTON, D.C._
--AND FOR WHAT REASONS WE SHALL OURSELVES TAKE THE FIELD OF BATTLE. WE AS AVENGERS SHALL BE BEHOLDEN TO NONE, ACCEPTING NO DOMINION SAVE THAT OF JUSTICE.
1600 PENNSYLVANIA AVENUE NW, WASHINGTON, D.C.: THE WHITE HOUSE._
DESPITE THIS, WE DO ASK SOMETHING FROM YOU IN RETURN.
FULL AND OPEN ACCESS TO ANY AND ALL FILES, CONFIDENTIAL DOCUMENTS, AND ANY GATHERED DATA THAT MIGHT HELP OUR COMMON CAUSE.
CIA HEADQUARTERS: McLEAN, VIRGINIA._
THE BOTTOM LINE IS...WE HOPE THAT YOU AND YOUR ORGANIZATIONS WILL HELP US, AS WE HELP YOU.
IN CLOSING, I'D LIKE TO THANK THE REPRESENTATIVES FROM DOCTORS WITHOUT BORDERS, OXFAM, MERCY CORPS, RED CROSS, AND SO MANY OTHERS IN COMING TODAY.
WE CAN MAKE THIS A BETTER WORLD. AND WE WILL.

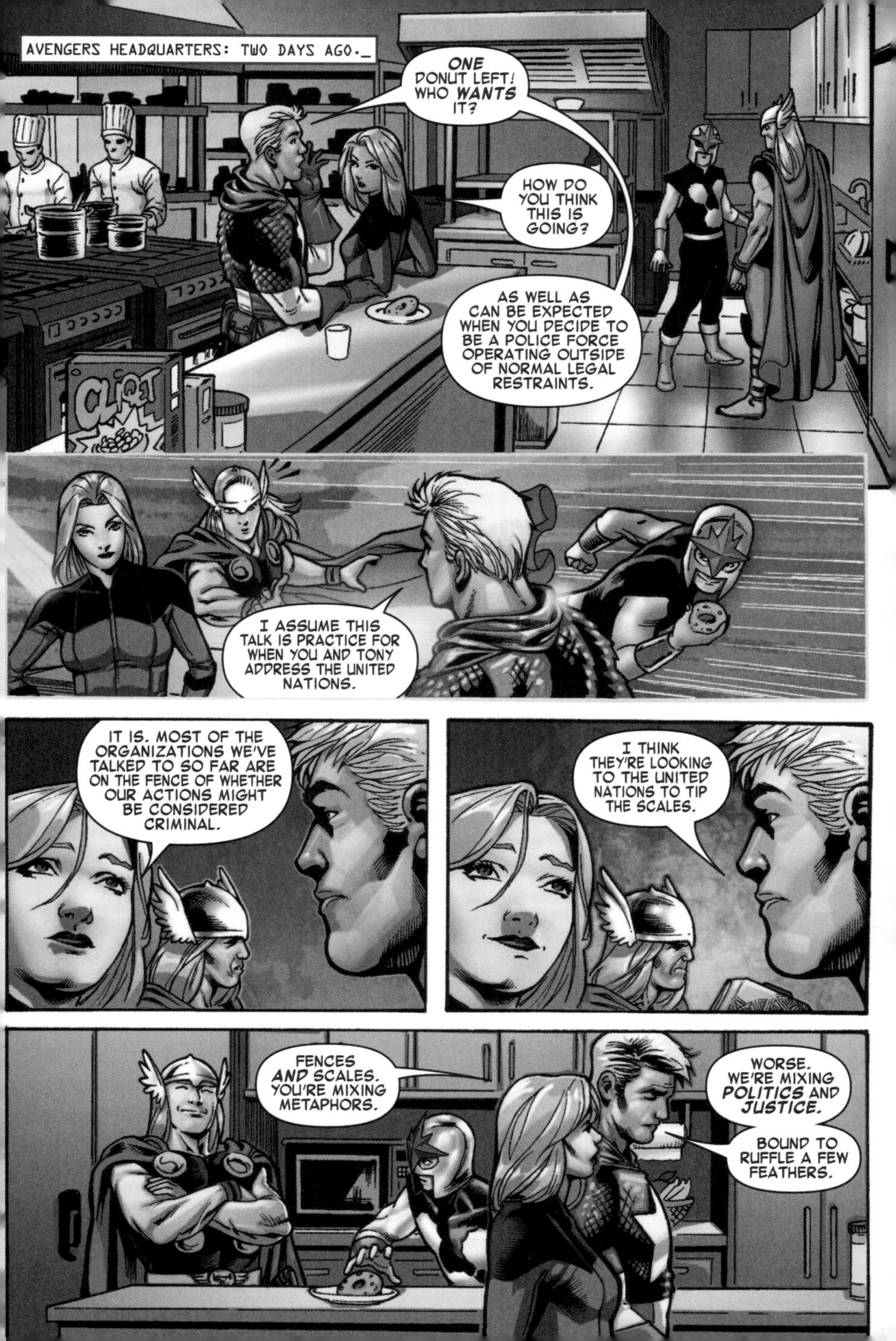
AVENGERS HEADQUARTERS: TWO DAYS AGO._
ONE DONUT LEFT! WHO WANTS IT?
HOW DO YOU THINK THIS IS GOING?
AS WELL AS CAN BE EXPECTED WHEN YOU DECIDE TO BE A POLICE FORCE OPERATING OUTSIDE OF NORMAL LEGAL RESTRAINTS.
I ASSUME THIS TALK IS PRACTICE FOR WHEN YOU AND TONY ADDRESS THE UNITED NATIONS.
IT IS. MOST OF THE ORGANIZATIONS WE'VE TALKED TO SO FAR ARE ON THE FENCE OF WHETHER OUR ACTIONS MIGHT BE CONSIDERED CRIMINAL.
I THINK THEY'RE LOOKING TO THE UNITED NATIONS TO TIP THE SCALES.
FENCES AND SCALES. YOU'RE MIXING METAPHORS.
WORSE. WE'RE MIXING POLITICS AND JUSTICE.
BOUND TO RUFFLE A FEW FEATHERS.

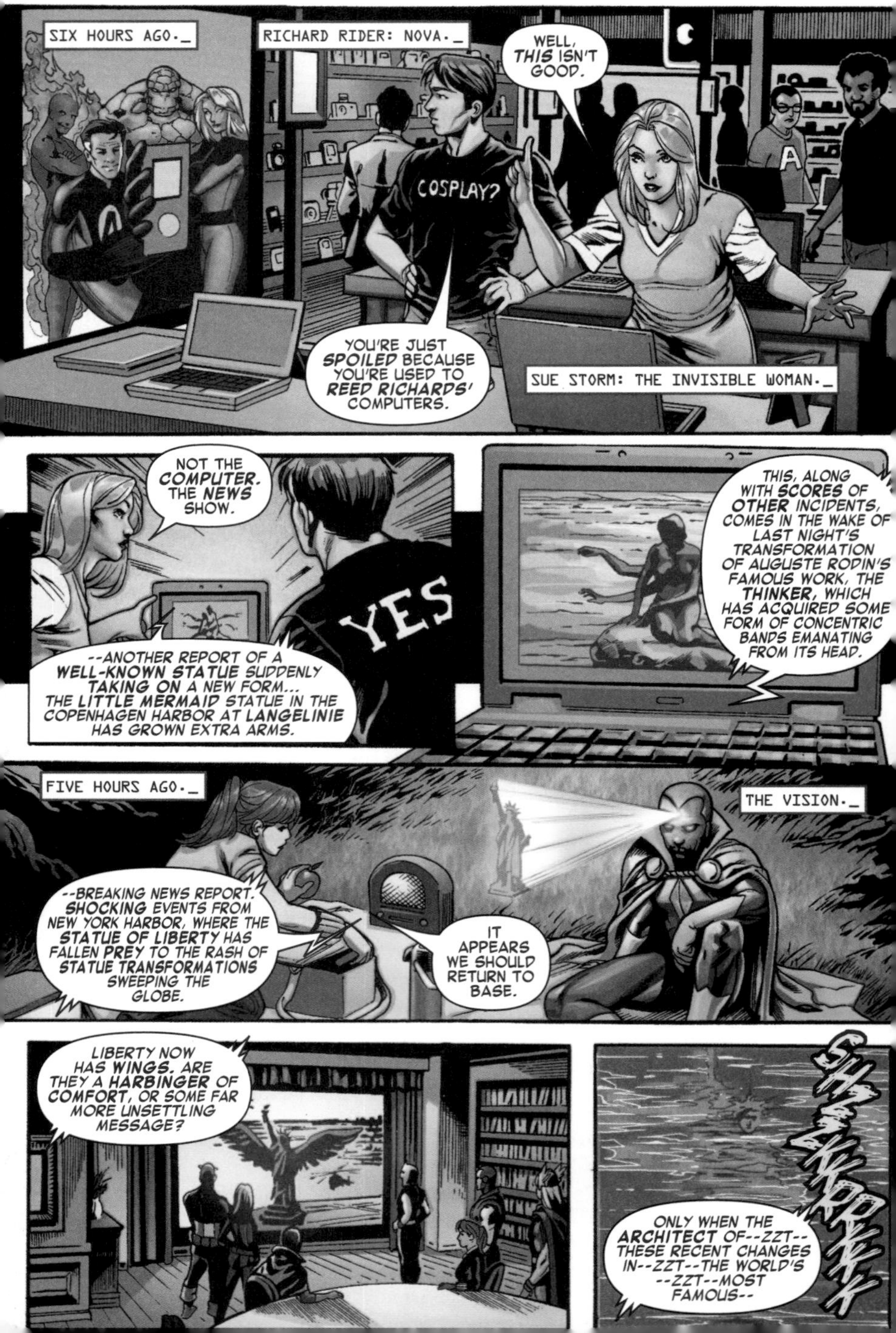
SIX HOURS AGO._
RICHARD RIDER: NOVA._
WELL, THIS ISN'T GOOD.
COSPLAY?
YOU'RE JUST SPOILED BECAUSE YOU'RE USED TO REED RICHARDS' COMPUTERS.
SUE STORM: THE INVISIBLE WOMAN._
NOT THE COMPUTER. THE NEWS SHOW.
YES
--ANOTHER REPORT OF A WELL-KNOWN STATUE SUDDENLY TAKING ON A NEW FORM... THE LITTLE MERMAID STATUE IN THE COPENHAGEN HARBOR AT LANGELINIE HAS GROWN EXTRA ARMS.
THIS, ALONG WITH SCORES OF OTHER INCIDENTS, COMES IN THE WAKE OF LAST NIGHT'S TRANSFORMATION OF AUGUSTE RODIN'S FAMOUS WORK, THE THINKER, WHICH HAS ACQUIRED SOME FORM OF CONCENTRIC BANDS EMANATING FROM ITS HEAD.
FIVE HOURS AGO._
THE VISION._
--BREAKING NEWS REPORT. SHOCKING EVENTS FROM NEW YORK HARBOR, WHERE THE STATUE OF LIBERTY HAS FALLEN PREY TO THE RASH OF STATUE TRANSFORMATIONS SWEEPING THE GLOBE.
IT APPEARS WE SHOULD RETURN TO BASE.
LIBERTY NOW HAS WINGS. ARE THEY A HARBINGER OF COMFORT, OR SOME FAR MORE UNSETTLING MESSAGE?
SHHKRRKK
ONLY WHEN THE ARCHITECT OF--ZZT-- THESE RECENT CHANGES IN--ZZT--THE WORLD'S --ZZT--MOST FAMOUS--

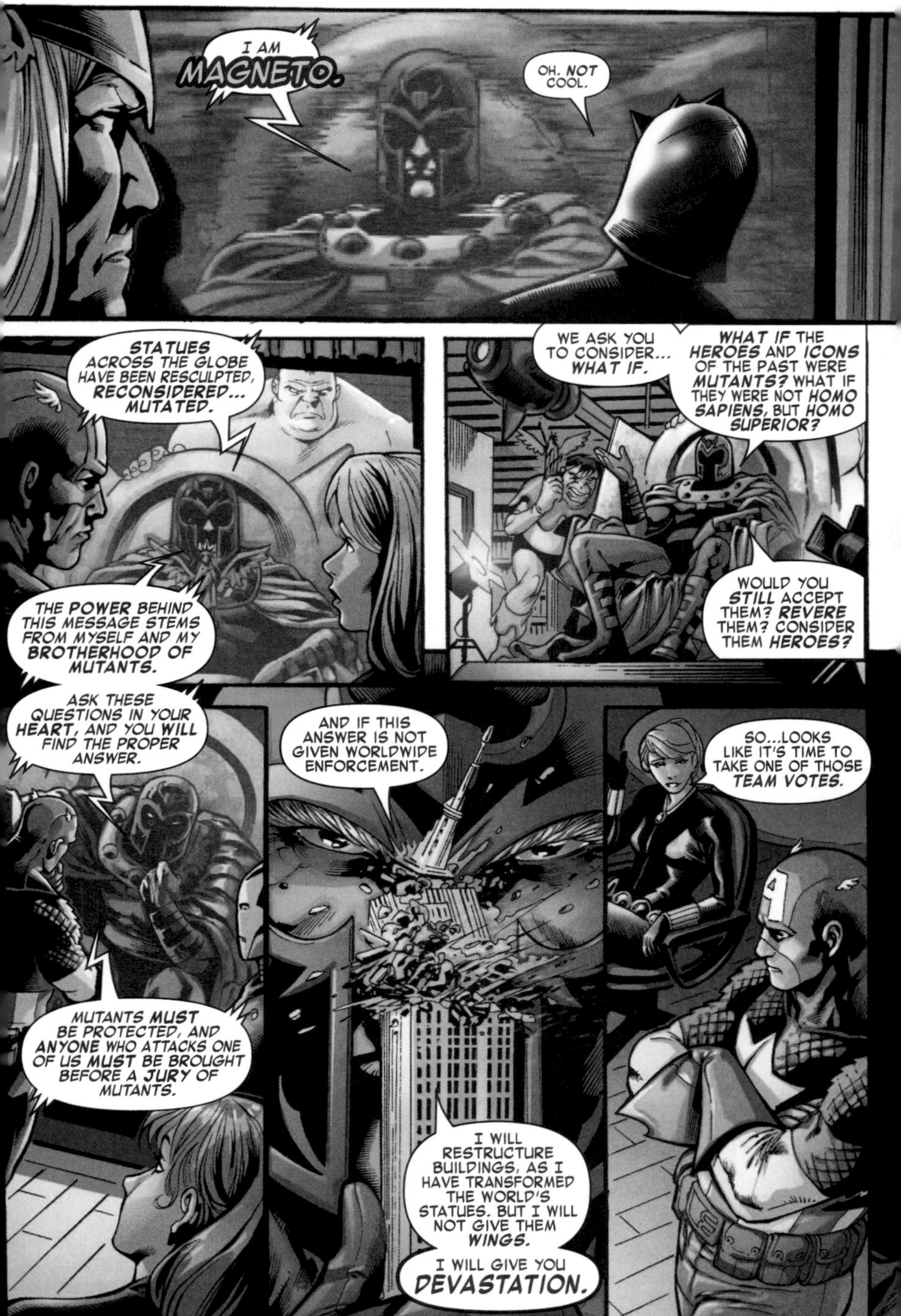
I AM MAGNETO.
OH. NOT COOL.
STATUES ACROSS THE GLOBE HAVE BEEN RESCULPTED, RECONSIDERED... MUTATED.
THE POWER BEHIND THIS MESSAGE STEMS FROM MYSELF AND MY BROTHERHOOD OF MUTANTS.
WE ASK YOU TO CONSIDER... WHAT IF.
WHAT IF THE HEROES AND ICONS OF THE PAST WERE MUTANTS? WHAT IF THEY WERE NOT HOMO SAPIENS, BUT HOMO SUPERIOR?
WOULD YOU STILL ACCEPT THEM? REVERE THEM? CONSIDER THEM HEROES?
ASK THESE QUESTIONS IN YOUR HEART, AND YOU WILL FIND THE PROPER ANSWER.
MUTANTS MUST BE PROTECTED, AND ANYONE WHO ATTACKS ONE OF US MUST BE BROUGHT BEFORE A JURY OF MUTANTS.
AND IF THIS ANSWER IS NOT GIVEN WORLDWIDE ENFORCEMENT.
I WILL RESTRUCTURE BUILDINGS, AS I HAVE TRANSFORMED THE WORLD'S STATUES. BUT I WILL NOT GIVE THEM WINGS.
I WILL GIVE YOU DEVASTATION.
SO...LOOKS LIKE IT'S TIME TO TAKE ONE OF THOSE TEAM VOTES.

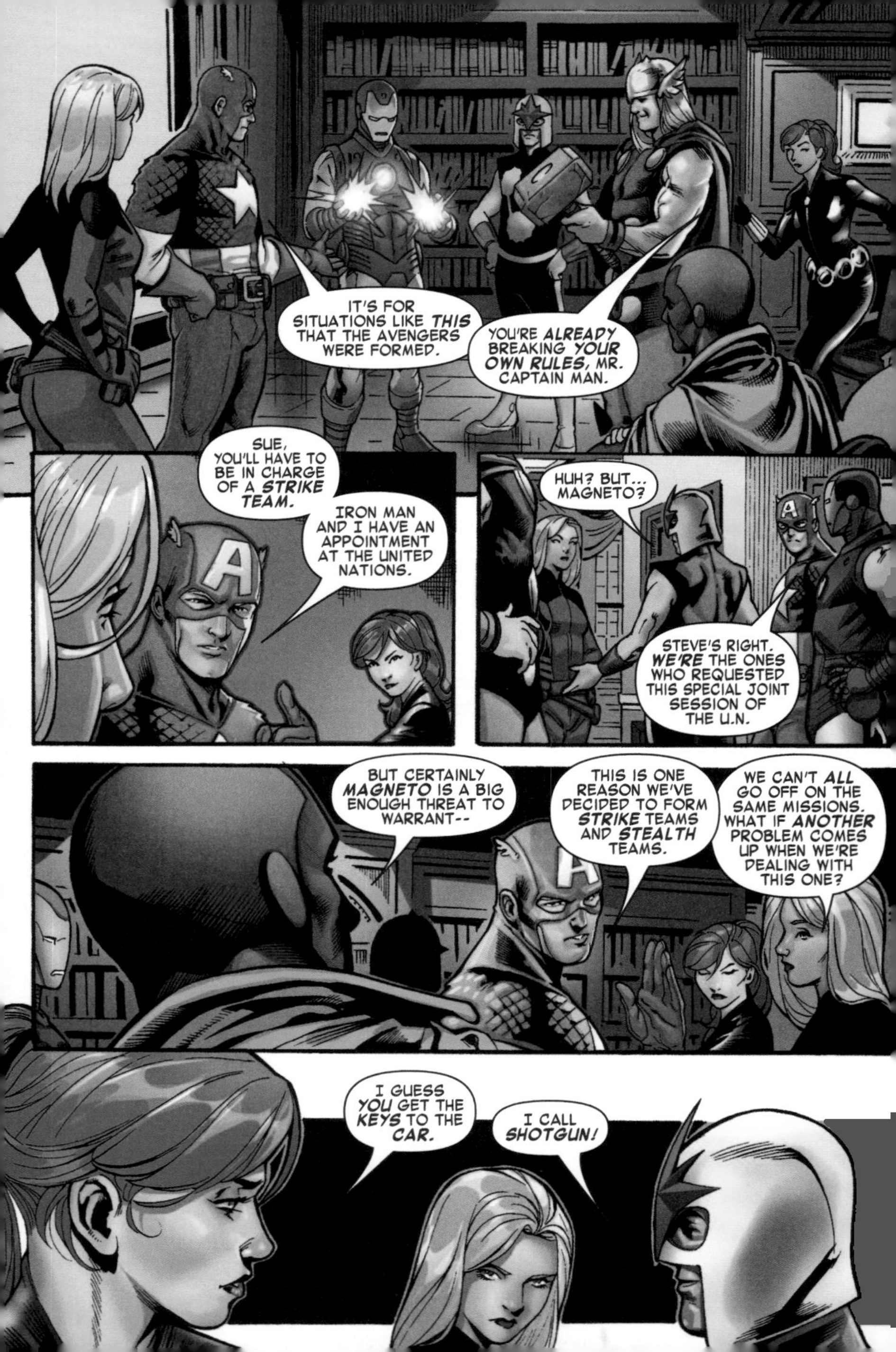
IT'S FOR SITUATIONS LIKE THIS THAT THE AVENGERS WERE FORMED.
YOU'RE ALREADY BREAKING YOUR OWN RULES, MR. CAPTAIN MAN.
SUE, YOU'LL HAVE TO BE IN CHARGE OF A STRIKE TEAM.
IRON MAN AND I HAVE AN APPOINTMENT AT THE UNITED NATIONS.
HUH? BUT... MAGNETO?
STEVE'S RIGHT. WE'RE THE ONES WHO REQUESTED THIS SPECIAL JOINT SESSION OF THE U.N.
BUT CERTAINLY MAGNETO IS A BIG ENOUGH THREAT TO WARRANT--
THIS IS ONE REASON WE'VE DECIDED TO FORM STRIKE TEAMS AND STEALTH TEAMS.
WE CAN'T ALL GO OFF ON THE SAME MISSIONS. WHAT IF ANOTHER PROBLEM COMES UP WHEN WE'RE DEALING WITH THIS ONE?
I GUESS YOU GET THE KEYS TO THE CAR.
I CALL SHOTGUN!

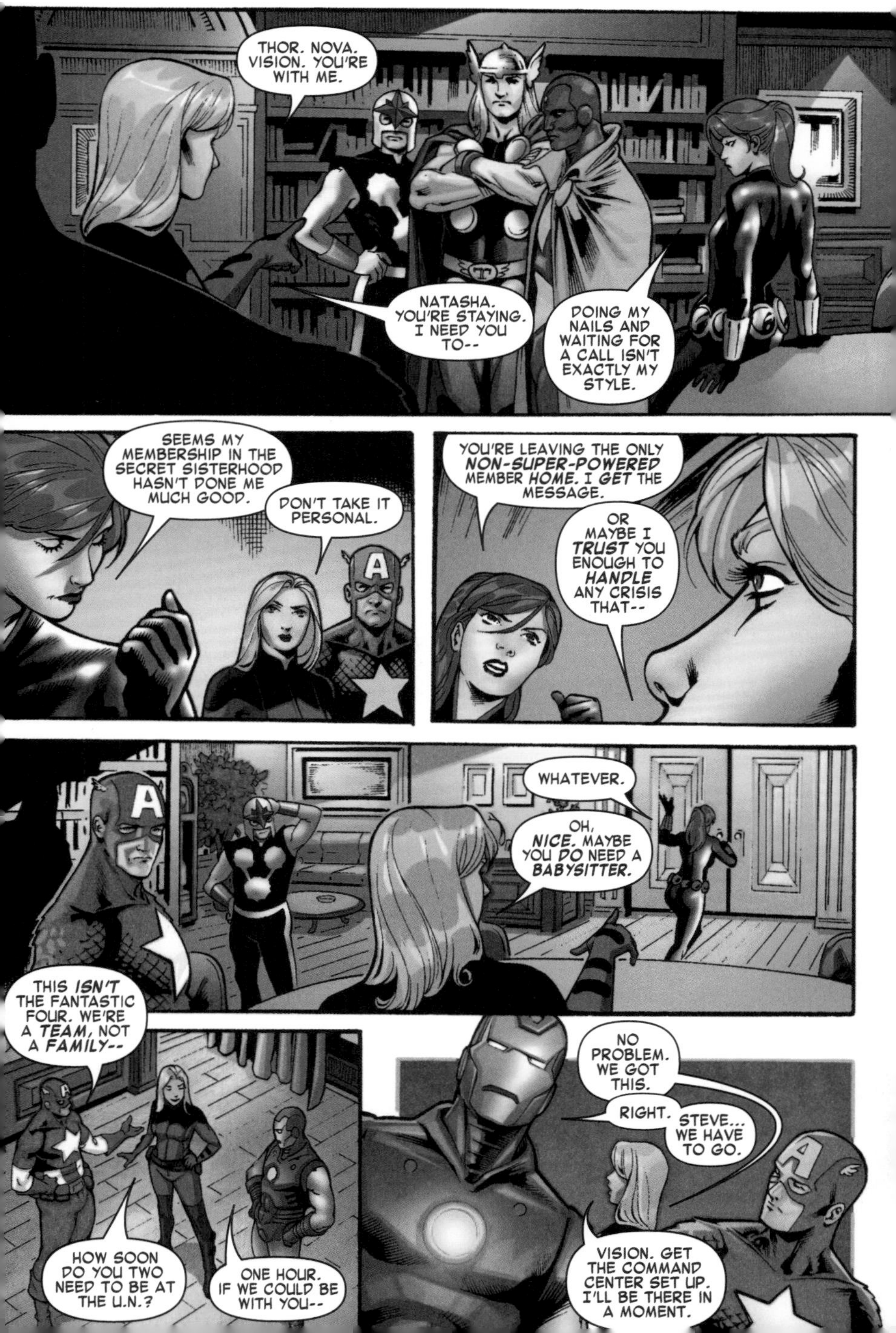
THOR. NOVA. VISION. YOU'RE WITH ME.
NATASHA. YOU'RE STAYING. I NEED YOU TO--
DOING MY NAILS AND WAITING FOR A CALL ISN'T EXACTLY MY STYLE.
SEEMS MY MEMBERSHIP IN THE SECRET SISTERHOOD HASN'T DONE ME MUCH GOOD.
DON'T TAKE IT PERSONAL.
YOU'RE LEAVING THE ONLY NON-SUPER-POWERED MEMBER HOME. I GET THE MESSAGE.
OR MAYBE I TRUST YOU ENOUGH TO HANDLE ANY CRISIS THAT--
WHATEVER.
OH, NICE. MAYBE YOU DO NEED A BABYSITTER.
THIS ISN'T THE FANTASTIC FOUR. WE'RE A TEAM, NOT A FAMILY--
HOW SOON DO YOU TWO NEED TO BE AT THE U.N.?
ONE HOUR. IF WE COULD BE WITH YOU--
NO PROBLEM. WE GOT THIS.
RIGHT.
STEVE... WE HAVE TO GO.
VISION. GET THE COMMAND CENTER SET UP. I'LL BE THERE IN A MOMENT.

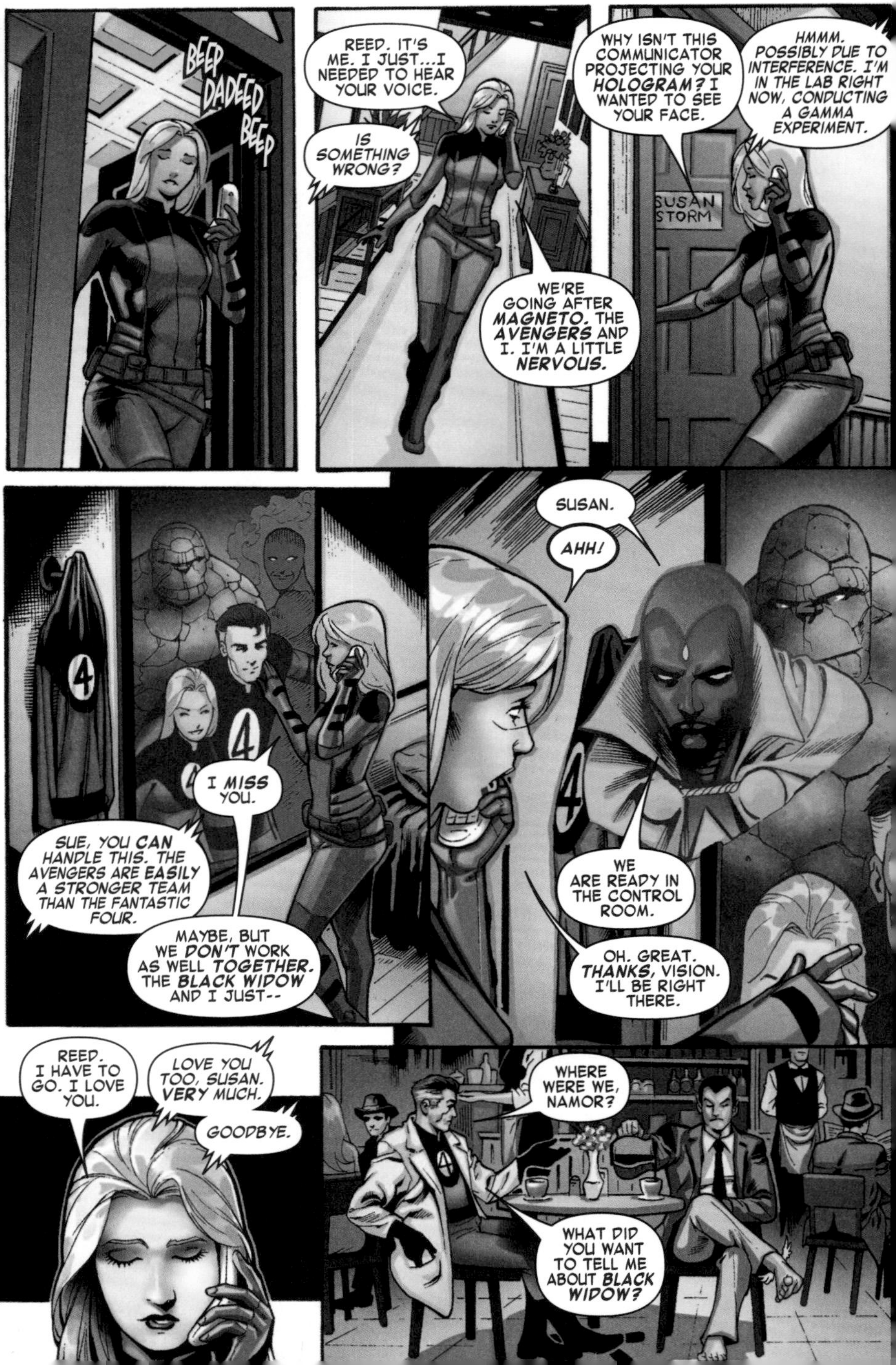
BEEP DADEED BEEP
REED. IT'S ME. I JUST...I NEEDED TO HEAR YOUR VOICE.
IS SOMETHING WRONG?
WE'RE GOING AFTER MAGNETO. THE AVENGERS AND I. I'M A LITTLE NERVOUS.
WHY ISN'T THIS COMMUNICATOR PROJECTING YOUR HOLOGRAM? I WANTED TO SEE YOUR FACE.
HMMM. POSSIBLY DUE TO INTERFERENCE. I'M IN THE LAB RIGHT NOW, CONDUCTING A GAMMA EXPERIMENT.
SUSAN STORM
I MISS YOU.
SUE, YOU CAN HANDLE THIS. THE AVENGERS ARE EASILY A STRONGER TEAM THAN THE FANTASTIC FOUR.
MAYBE, BUT WE DON'T WORK AS WELL TOGETHER. THE BLACK WIDOW AND I JUST--
SUSAN.
AHH!
WE ARE READY IN THE CONTROL ROOM.
OH. GREAT. THANKS, VISION. I'LL BE RIGHT THERE.
REED. I HAVE TO GO. I LOVE YOU.
LOVE YOU TOO, SUSAN. VERY MUCH.
GOODBYE.
WHERE WERE WE, NAMOR?
WHAT DID YOU WANT TO TELL ME ABOUT BLACK WIDOW?

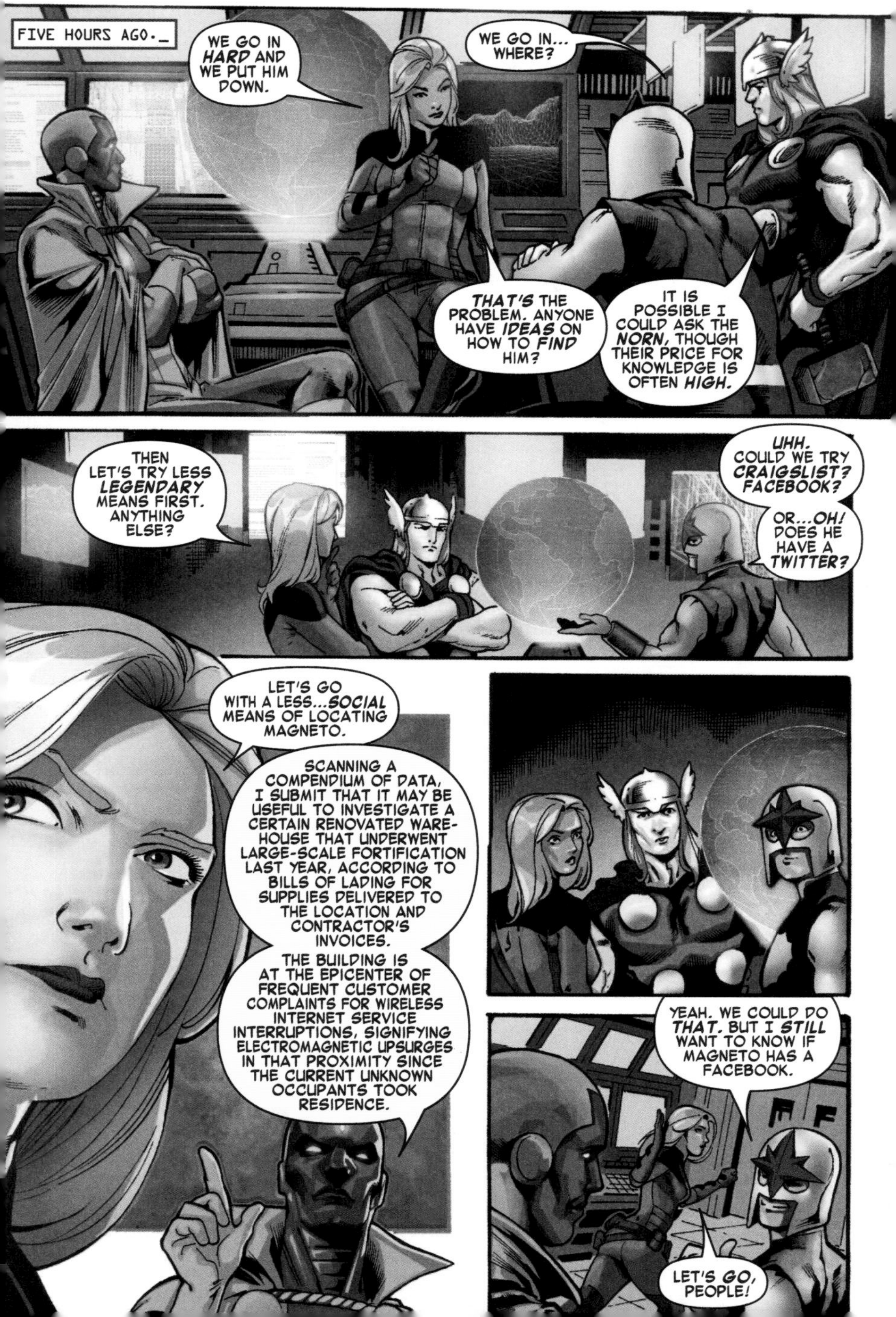
FIVE HOURS AGO._
WE GO IN HARD AND WE PUT HIM DOWN.
WE GO IN... WHERE?
THAT'S THE PROBLEM. ANYONE HAVE IDEAS ON HOW TO FIND HIM?
IT IS POSSIBLE I COULD ASK THE NORN, THOUGH THEIR PRICE FOR KNOWLEDGE IS OFTEN HIGH.
THEN LET'S TRY LESS LEGENDARY MEANS FIRST. ANYTHING ELSE?
UHH. COULD WE TRY CRAIGSLIST? FACEBOOK?
OR...OH! DOES HE HAVE A TWITTER?
LET'S GO WITH A LESS...SOCIAL MEANS OF LOCATING MAGNETO.
SCANNING A COMPENDIUM OF DATA, I SUBMIT THAT IT MAY BE USEFUL TO INVESTIGATE A CERTAIN RENOVATED WARE-HOUSE THAT UNDERWENT LARGE-SCALE FORTIFICATION LAST YEAR, ACCORDING TO BILLS OF LADING FOR SUPPLIES DELIVERED TO THE LOCATION AND CONTRACTOR'S INVOICES.
THE BUILDING IS AT THE EPICENTER OF FREQUENT CUSTOMER COMPLAINTS FOR WIRELESS INTERNET SERVICE INTERRUPTIONS, SIGNIFYING ELECTROMAGNETIC UPSURGES IN THAT PROXIMITY SINCE THE CURRENT UNKNOWN OCCUPANTS TOOK RESIDENCE.
YEAH. WE COULD DO THAT. BUT I STILL WANT TO KNOW IF MAGNETO HAS A FACEBOOK.
LET'S GO, PEOPLE!

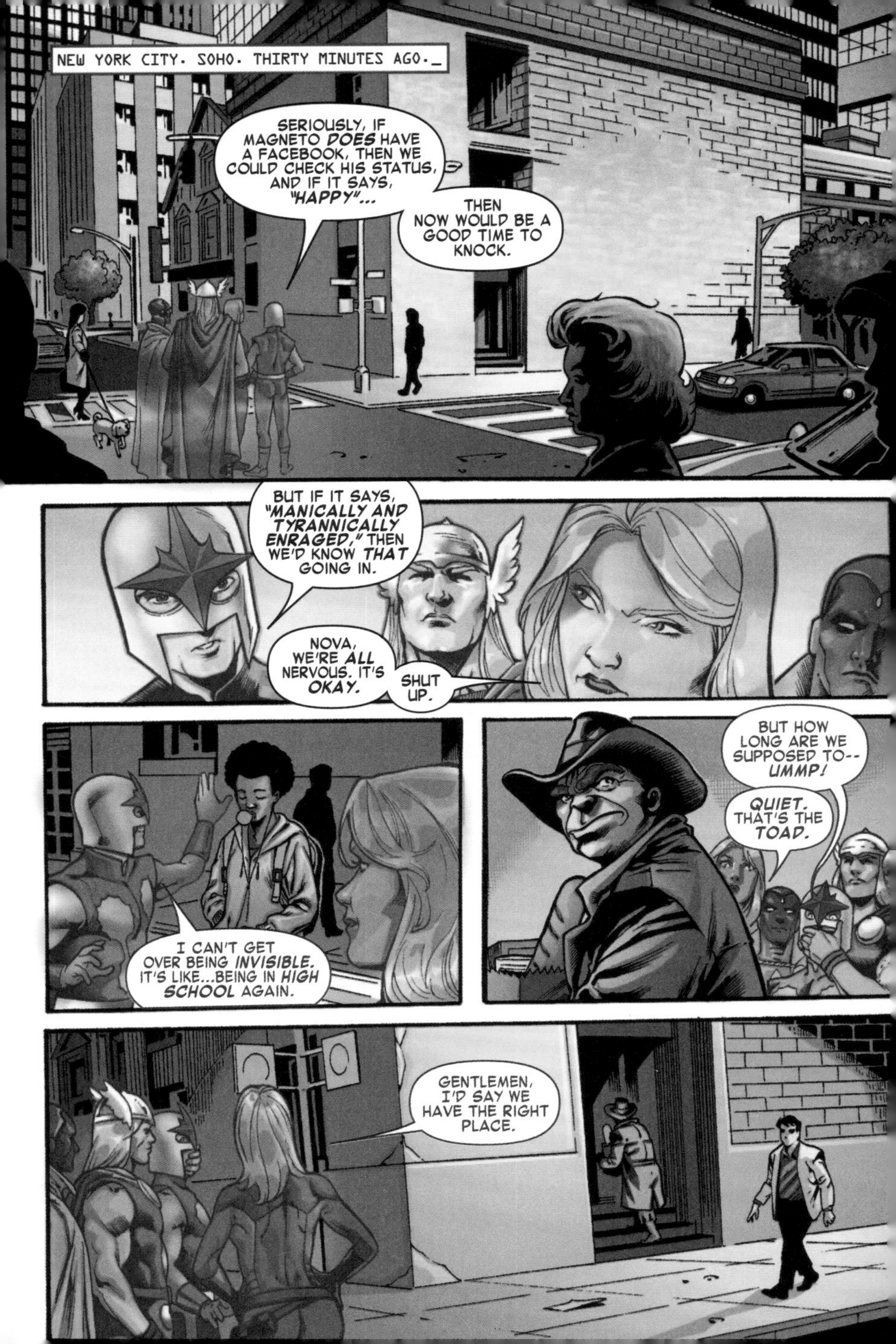
NEW YORK CITY. SOHO. THIRTY MINUTES AGO._
SERIOUSLY, IF MAGNETO *DOES* HAVE A FACEBOOK, THEN WE COULD CHECK HIS STATUS, AND IF IT SAYS, *"HAPPY"*...
THEN NOW WOULD BE A GOOD TIME TO KNOCK.
BUT IF IT SAYS, *"MANICALLY AND TYRANNICALLY ENRAGED,"* THEN WE'D KNOW *THAT* GOING IN.
NOVA, WE'RE *ALL* NERVOUS. IT'S *OKAY.*
SHUT UP.
I CAN'T GET OVER BEING *INVISIBLE.* IT'S LIKE...BEING IN *HIGH SCHOOL* AGAIN.
BUT HOW LONG ARE WE SUPPOSED TO-- *UMMP!*
QUIET. THAT'S THE *TOAD.*
GENTLEMEN, I'D SAY WE HAVE THE RIGHT PLACE.

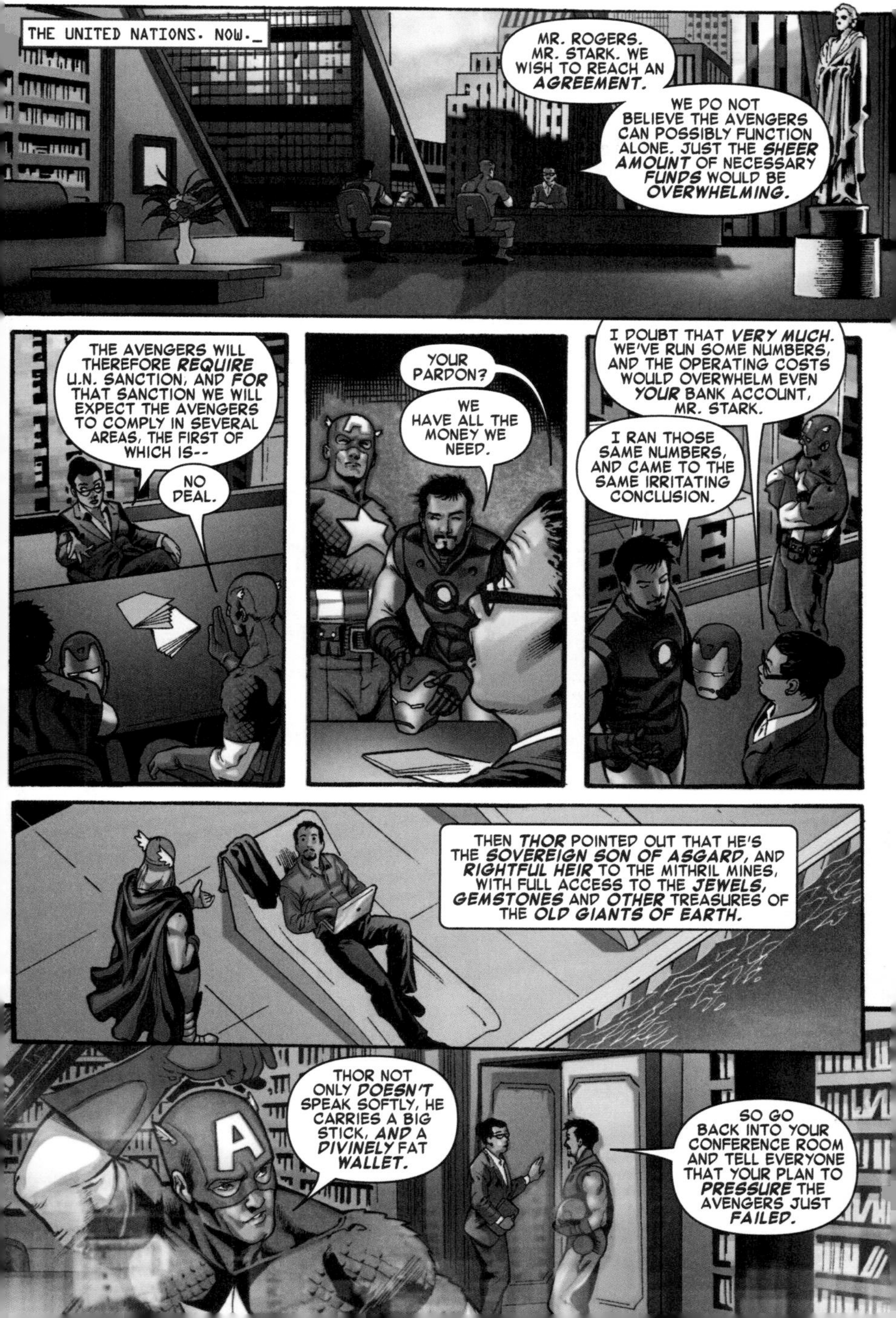
THE UNITED NATIONS. NOW._
MR. ROGERS. MR. STARK. WE WISH TO REACH AN AGREEMENT.
WE DO NOT BELIEVE THE AVENGERS CAN POSSIBLY FUNCTION ALONE. JUST THE SHEER AMOUNT OF NECESSARY FUNDS WOULD BE OVERWHELMING.
THE AVENGERS WILL THEREFORE REQUIRE U.N. SANCTION, AND FOR THAT SANCTION WE WILL EXPECT THE AVENGERS TO COMPLY IN SEVERAL AREAS, THE FIRST OF WHICH IS--
NO DEAL.
YOUR PARDON?
WE HAVE ALL THE MONEY WE NEED.
I DOUBT THAT VERY MUCH. WE'VE RUN SOME NUMBERS, AND THE OPERATING COSTS WOULD OVERWHELM EVEN YOUR BANK ACCOUNT, MR. STARK.
I RAN THOSE SAME NUMBERS, AND CAME TO THE SAME IRRITATING CONCLUSION.
THEN THOR POINTED OUT THAT HE'S THE SOVEREIGN SON OF ASGARD, AND RIGHTFUL HEIR TO THE MITHRIL MINES, WITH FULL ACCESS TO THE JEWELS, GEMSTONES AND OTHER TREASURES OF THE OLD GIANTS OF EARTH.
THOR NOT ONLY DOESN'T SPEAK SOFTLY, HE CARRIES A BIG STICK, AND A DIVINELY FAT WALLET.
SO GO BACK INTO YOUR CONFERENCE ROOM AND TELL EVERYONE THAT YOUR PLAN TO PRESSURE THE AVENGERS JUST FAILED.

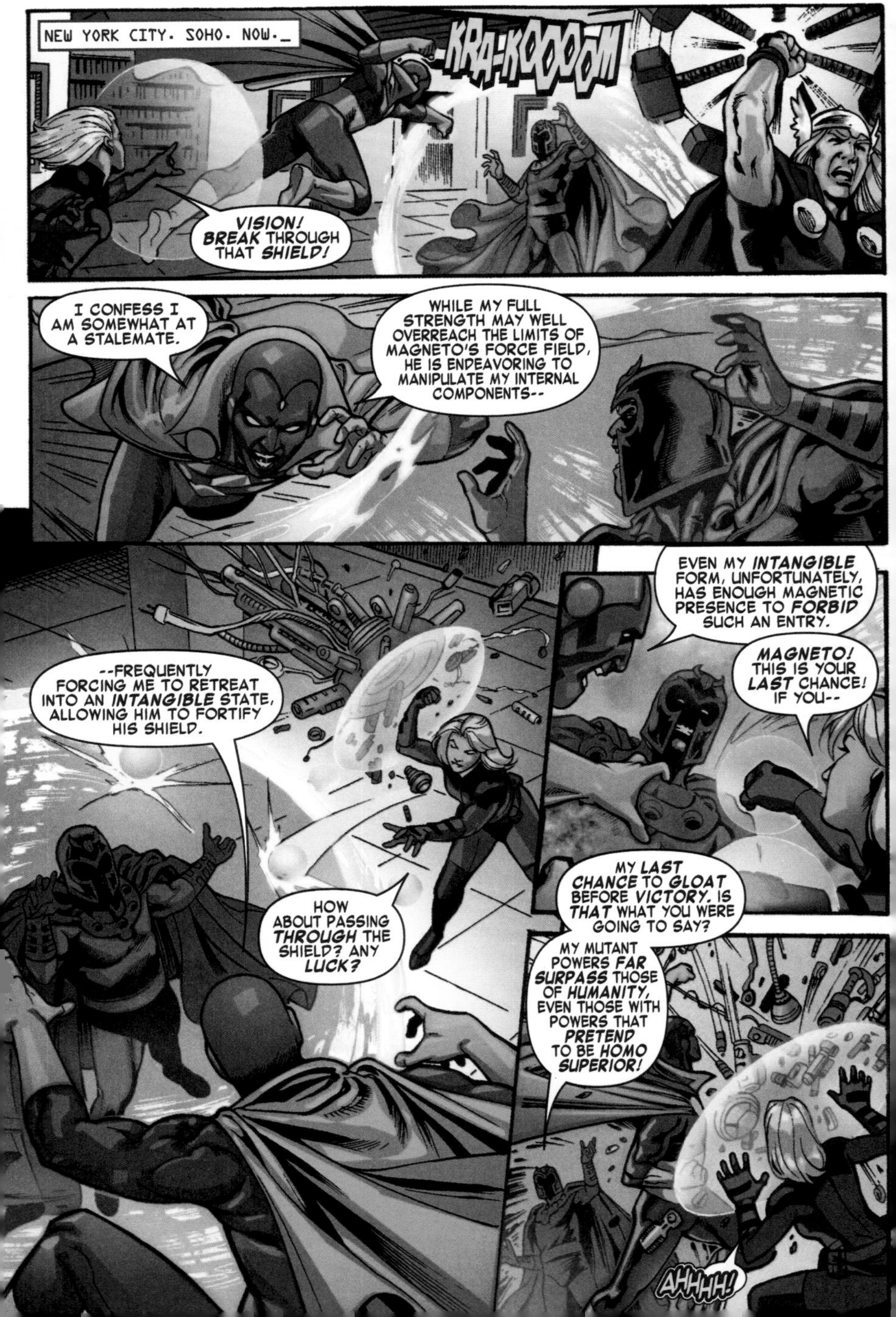
NEW YORK CITY. SOHO. NOW._
KRA-KOOOOM
VISION! BREAK THROUGH THAT SHIELD!
I CONFESS I AM SOMEWHAT AT A STALEMATE.
WHILE MY FULL STRENGTH MAY WELL OVERREACH THE LIMITS OF MAGNETO'S FORCE FIELD, HE IS ENDEAVORING TO MANIPULATE MY INTERNAL COMPONENTS--
--FREQUENTLY FORCING ME TO RETREAT INTO AN INTANGIBLE STATE, ALLOWING HIM TO FORTIFY HIS SHIELD.
HOW ABOUT PASSING THROUGH THE SHIELD? ANY LUCK?
EVEN MY INTANGIBLE FORM, UNFORTUNATELY, HAS ENOUGH MAGNETIC PRESENCE TO FORBID SUCH AN ENTRY.
MAGNETO! THIS IS YOUR LAST CHANCE! IF YOU--
MY LAST CHANCE TO GLOAT BEFORE VICTORY. IS THAT WHAT YOU WERE GOING TO SAY?
MY MUTANT POWERS FAR SURPASS THOSE OF HUMANITY, EVEN THOSE WITH POWERS THAT PRETEND TO BE HOMO SUPERIOR!
AHHHH!

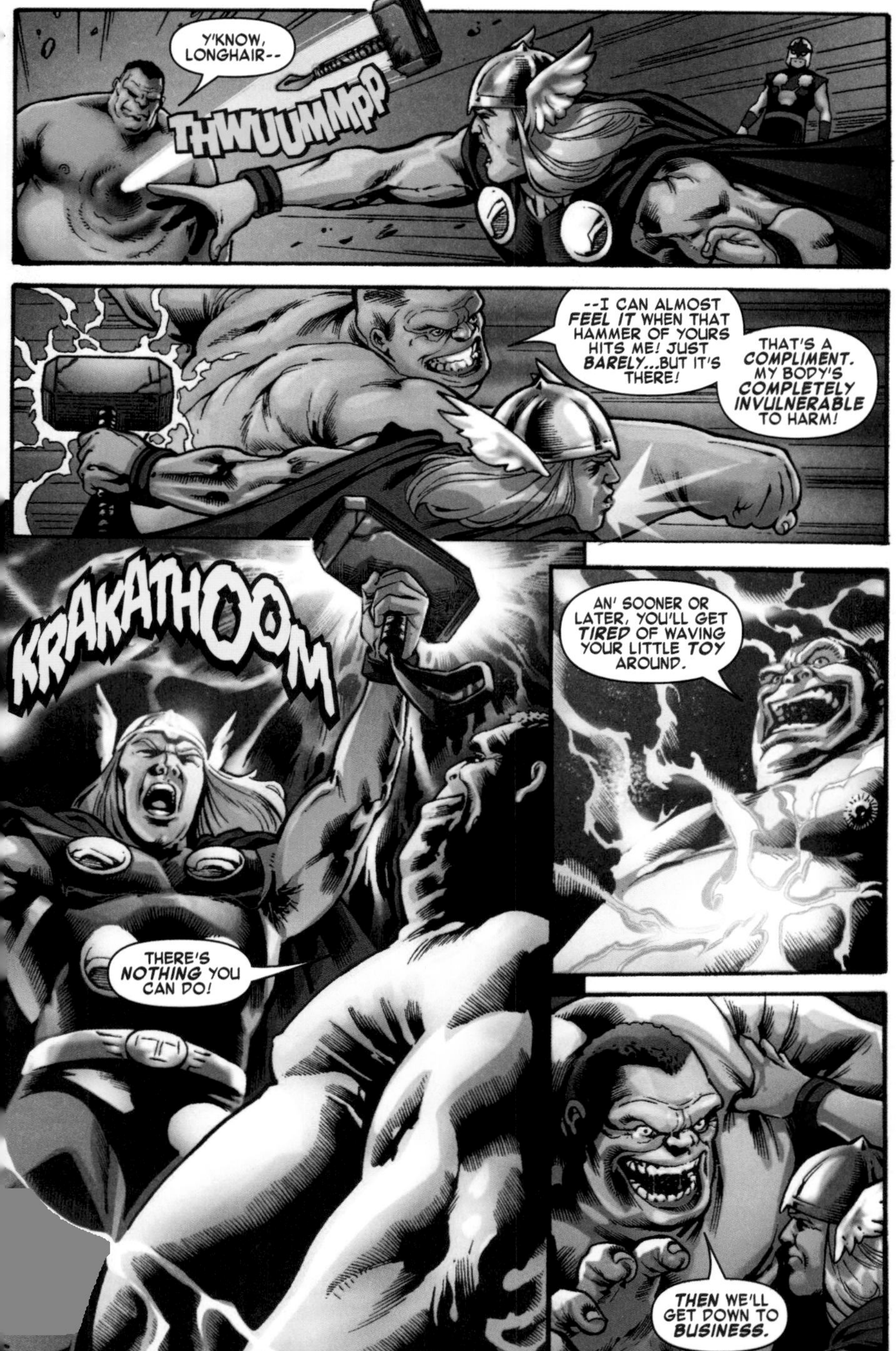

Y'KNOW, LONGHAIR--
THWUUMMPP
--I CAN ALMOST FEEL IT WHEN THAT HAMMER OF YOURS HITS ME! JUST BARELY...BUT IT'S THERE!
THAT'S A COMPLIMENT. MY BODY'S COMPLETELY INVULNERABLE TO HARM!
KRAKATHOOM
THERE'S NOTHING YOU CAN DO!
AN' SOONER OR LATER, YOU'LL GET TIRED OF WAVING YOUR LITTLE TOY AROUND.
THEN WE'LL GET DOWN TO BUSINESS.

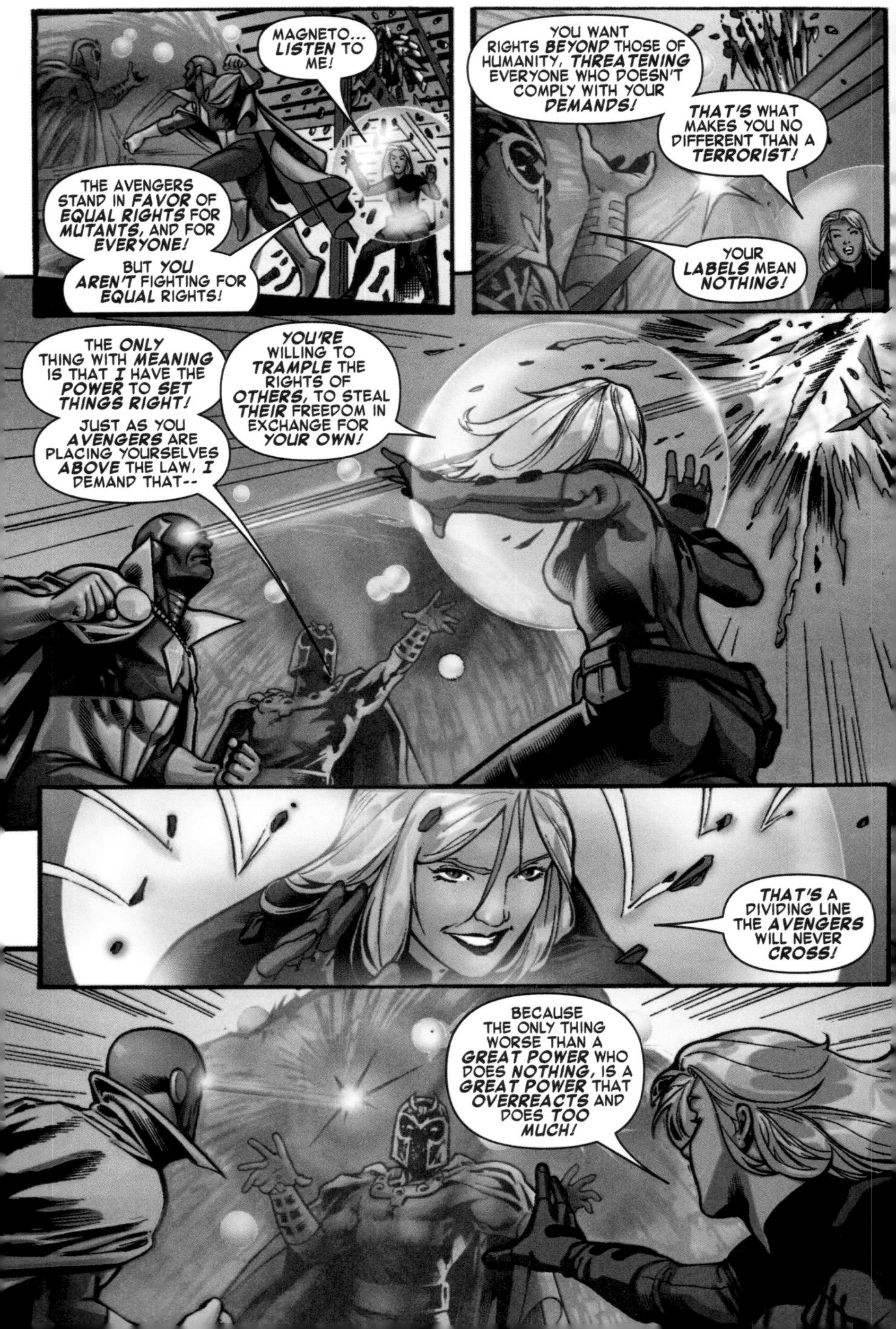
MAGNETO... LISTEN TO ME!
THE AVENGERS STAND IN FAVOR OF EQUAL RIGHTS FOR MUTANTS, AND FOR EVERYONE!
BUT YOU AREN'T FIGHTING FOR EQUAL RIGHTS!
YOU WANT RIGHTS BEYOND THOSE OF HUMANITY, THREATENING EVERYONE WHO DOESN'T COMPLY WITH YOUR DEMANDS!
THAT'S WHAT MAKES YOU NO DIFFERENT THAN A TERRORIST!
YOUR LABELS MEAN NOTHING!
THE ONLY THING WITH MEANING IS THAT I HAVE THE POWER TO SET THINGS RIGHT!
JUST AS YOU AVENGERS ARE PLACING YOURSELVES ABOVE THE LAW, I DEMAND THAT--
YOU'RE WILLING TO TRAMPLE THE RIGHTS OF OTHERS, TO STEAL THEIR FREEDOM IN EXCHANGE FOR YOUR OWN!
THAT'S A DIVIDING LINE THE AVENGERS WILL NEVER CROSS!
BECAUSE THE ONLY THING WORSE THAN A GREAT POWER WHO DOES NOTHING, IS A GREAT POWER THAT OVERREACTS AND DOES TOO MUCH!

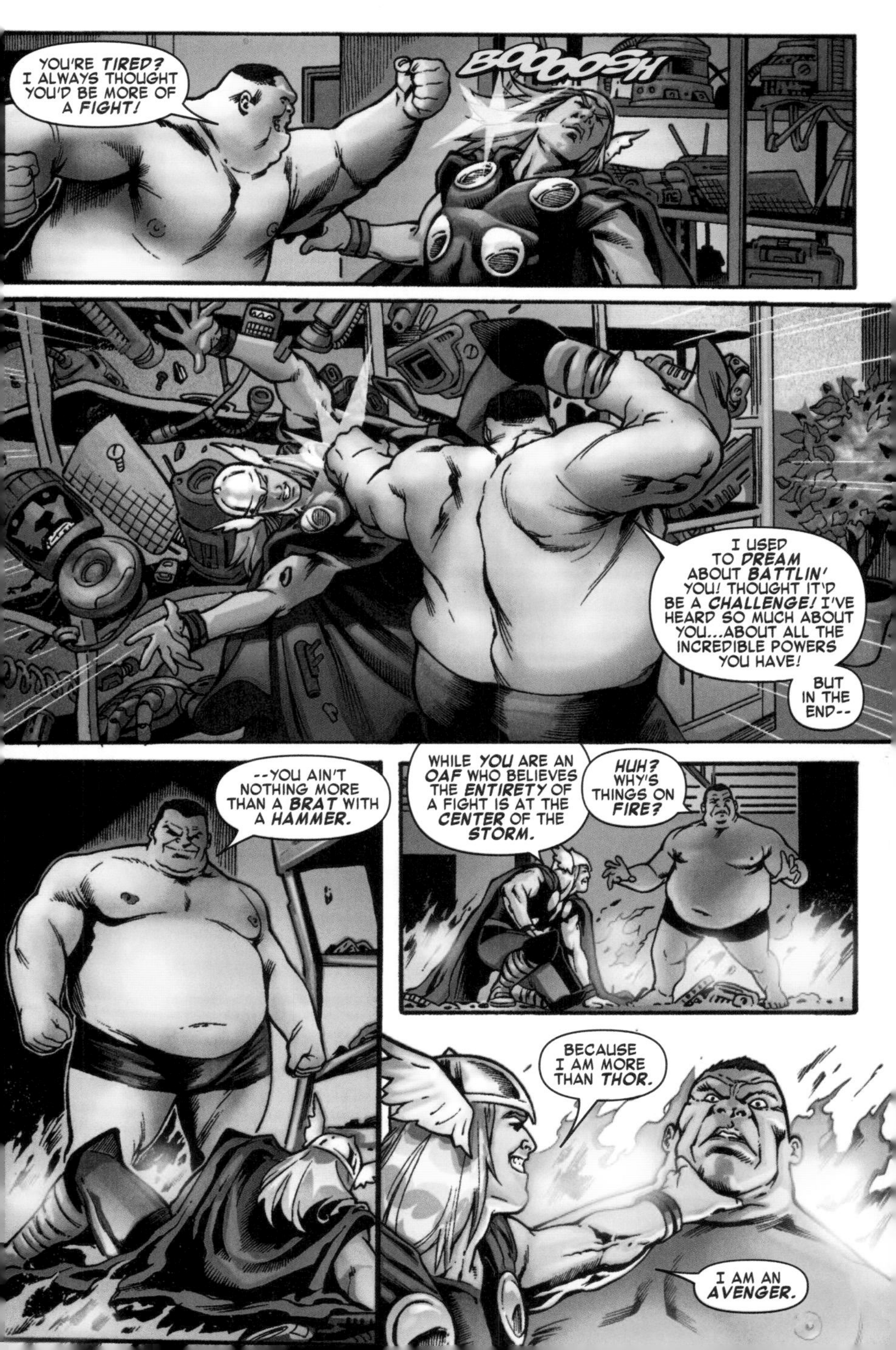

YOU'RE TIRED? I ALWAYS THOUGHT YOU'D BE MORE OF A FIGHT!
BOOOOOSH
I USED TO DREAM ABOUT BATTLIN' YOU! THOUGHT IT'D BE A CHALLENGE! I'VE HEARD SO MUCH ABOUT YOU...ABOUT ALL THE INCREDIBLE POWERS YOU HAVE!
BUT IN THE END--
--YOU AIN'T NOTHING MORE THAN A BRAT WITH A HAMMER.
WHILE YOU ARE AN OAF WHO BELIEVES THE ENTIRETY OF A FIGHT IS AT THE CENTER OF THE STORM.
HUH? WHY'S THINGS ON FIRE?
BECAUSE I AM MORE THAN THOR.
I AM AN AVENGER.

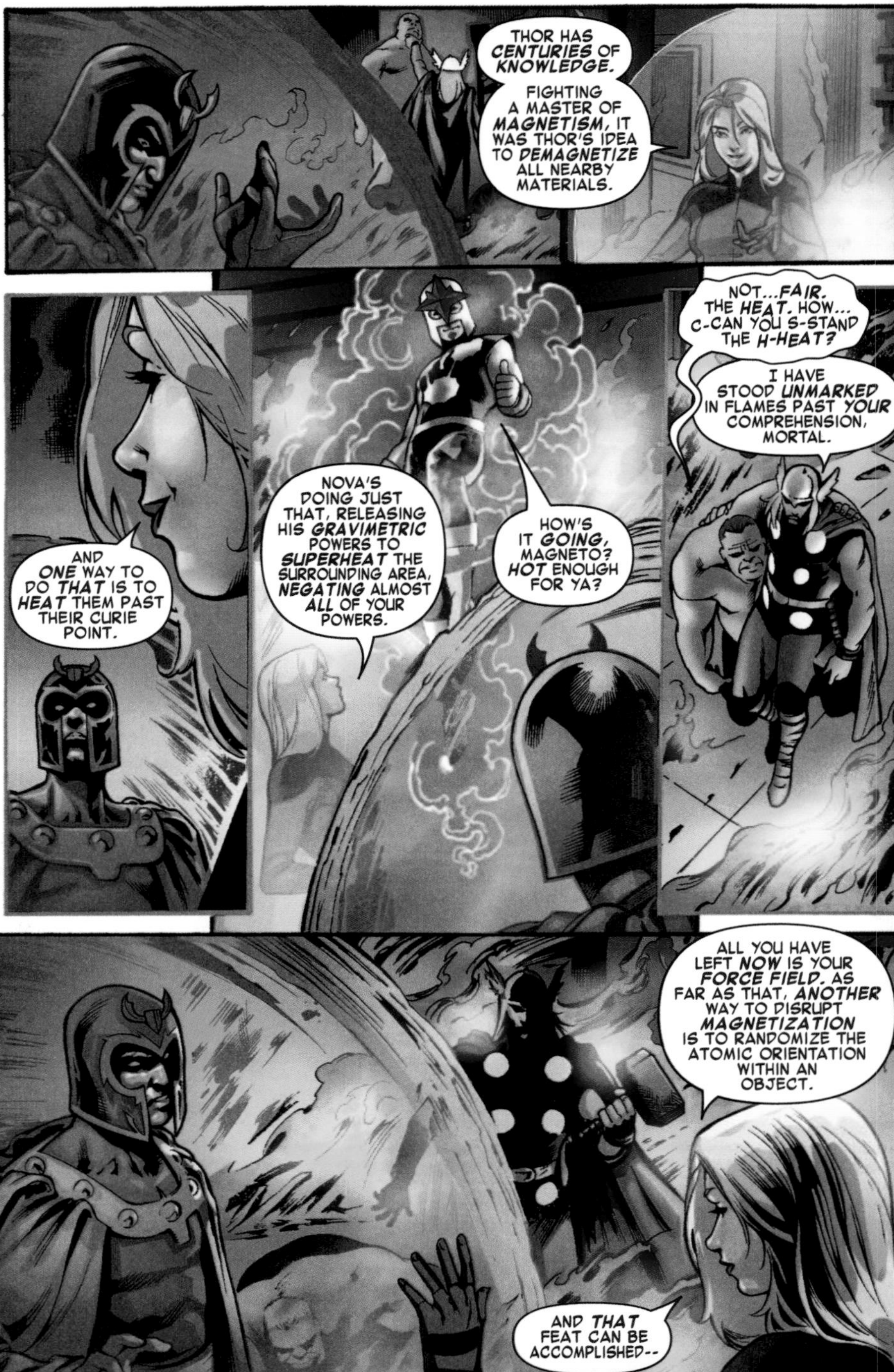
THOR HAS CENTURIES OF KNOWLEDGE.
FIGHTING A MASTER OF MAGNETISM, IT WAS THOR'S IDEA TO DEMAGNETIZE ALL NEARBY MATERIALS.
AND ONE WAY TO DO THAT IS TO HEAT THEM PAST THEIR CURIE POINT.
NOVA'S DOING JUST THAT, RELEASING HIS GRAVIMETRIC POWERS TO SUPERHEAT THE SURROUNDING AREA, NEGATING ALMOST ALL OF YOUR POWERS.
HOW'S IT GOING, MAGNETO? HOT ENOUGH FOR YA?
NOT...FAIR. THE HEAT. HOW... C-CAN YOU S-STAND THE H-HEAT?
I HAVE STOOD UNMARKED IN FLAMES PAST YOUR COMPREHENSION, MORTAL.
ALL YOU HAVE LEFT NOW IS YOUR FORCE FIELD. AS FAR AS THAT, ANOTHER WAY TO DISRUPT MAGNETIZATION IS TO RANDOMIZE THE ATOMIC ORIENTATION WITHIN AN OBJECT.
AND THAT FEAT CAN BE ACCOMPLISHED--

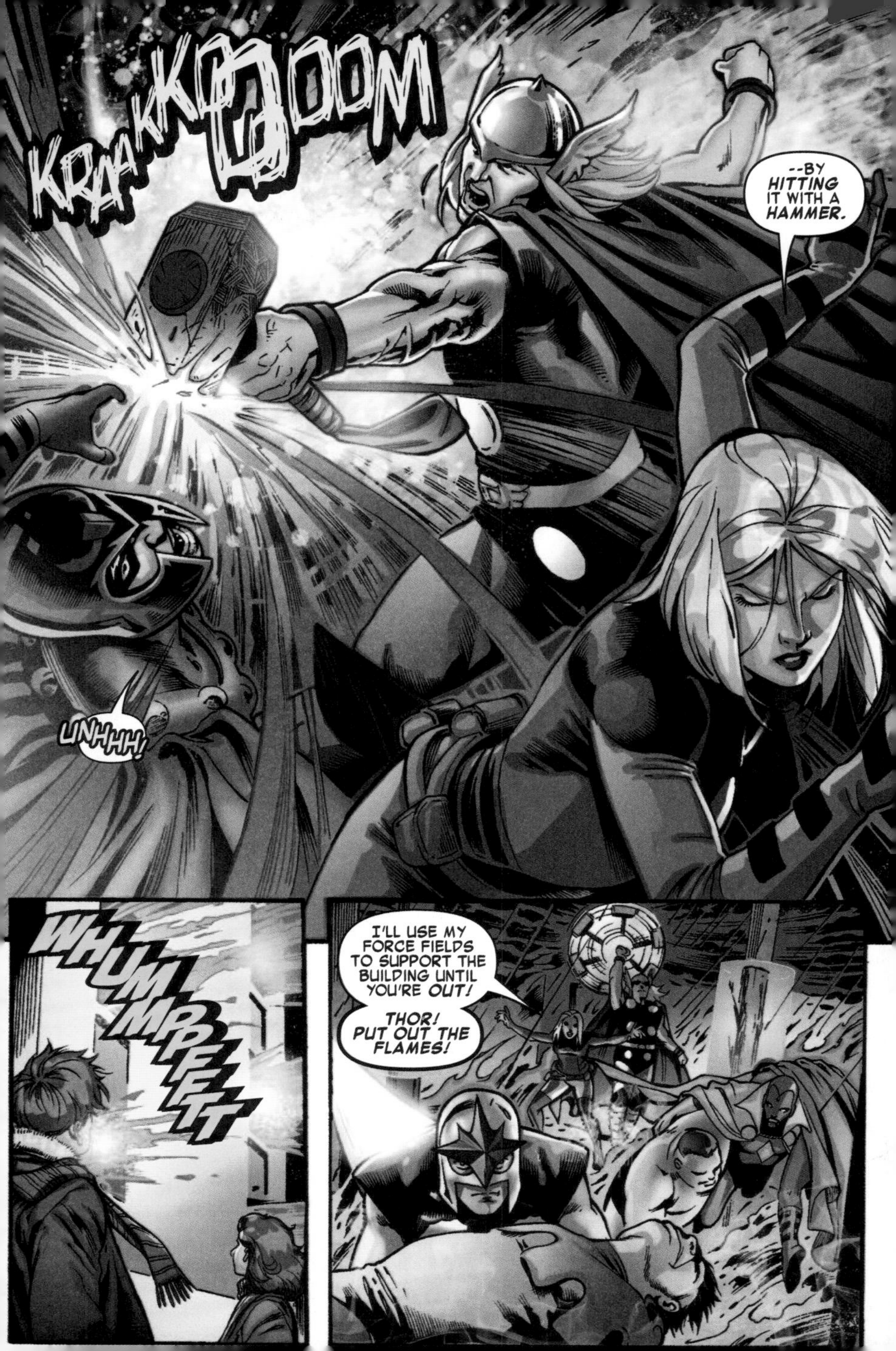
KRAAKKOOOOM
--BY HITTING IT WITH A HAMMER.
UNHHH!
WHUMMPFFTT
I'LL USE MY FORCE FIELDS TO SUPPORT THE BUILDING UNTIL YOU'RE OUT!
THOR! PUT OUT THE FLAMES!

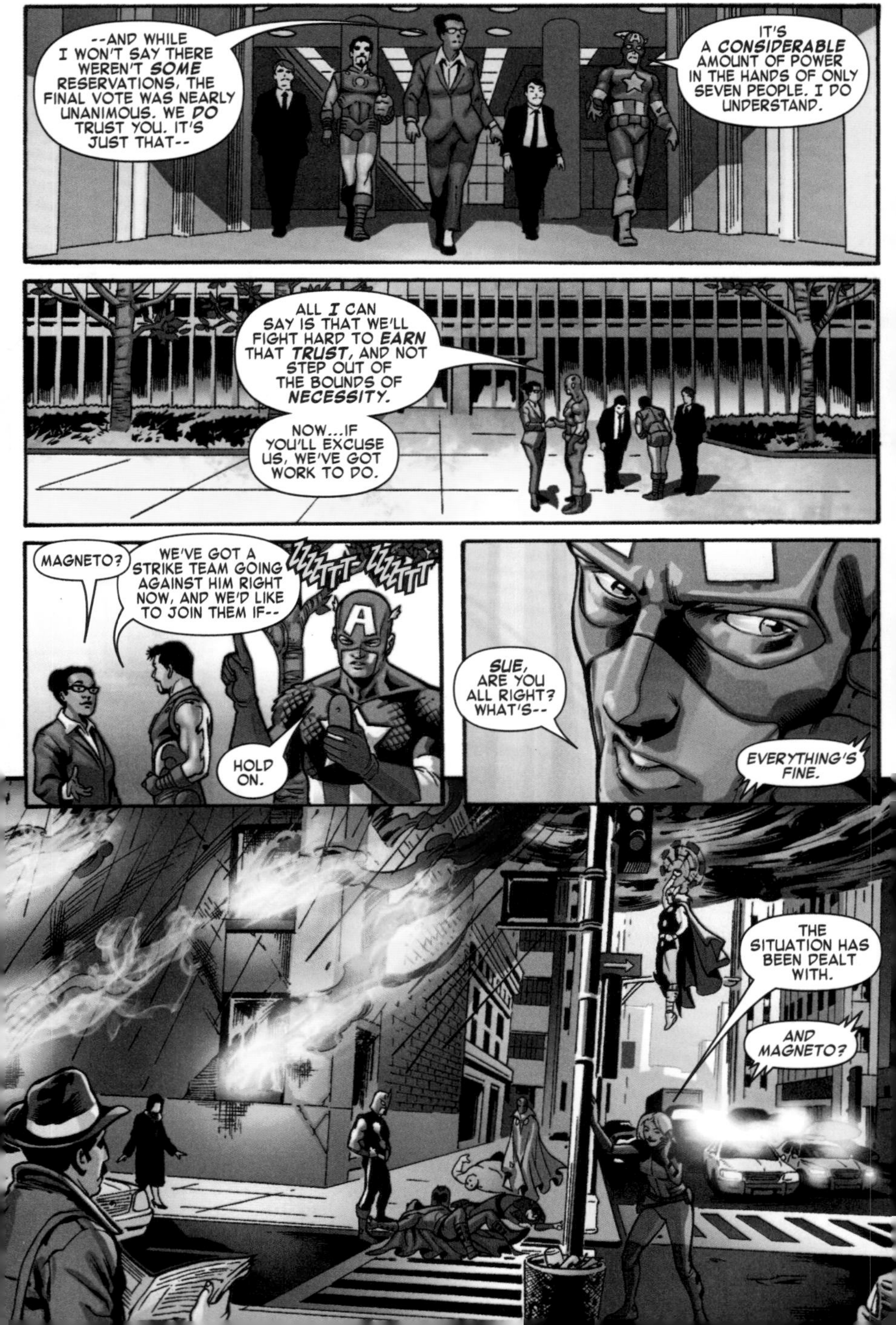
--AND WHILE I WON'T SAY THERE WEREN'T SOME RESERVATIONS, THE FINAL VOTE WAS NEARLY UNANIMOUS. WE DO TRUST YOU. IT'S JUST THAT--
IT'S A CONSIDERABLE AMOUNT OF POWER IN THE HANDS OF ONLY SEVEN PEOPLE. I DO UNDERSTAND.
ALL I CAN SAY IS THAT WE'LL FIGHT HARD TO EARN THAT TRUST, AND NOT STEP OUT OF THE BOUNDS OF NECESSITY.
NOW...IF YOU'LL EXCUSE US, WE'VE GOT WORK TO DO.
MAGNETO?
WE'VE GOT A STRIKE TEAM GOING AGAINST HIM RIGHT NOW, AND WE'D LIKE TO JOIN THEM IF--
ZZZTTT- ZZZTTT
HOLD ON.
SUE, ARE YOU ALL RIGHT? WHAT'S--
EVERYTHING'S FINE.
THE SITUATION HAS BEEN DEALT WITH.
AND MAGNETO?

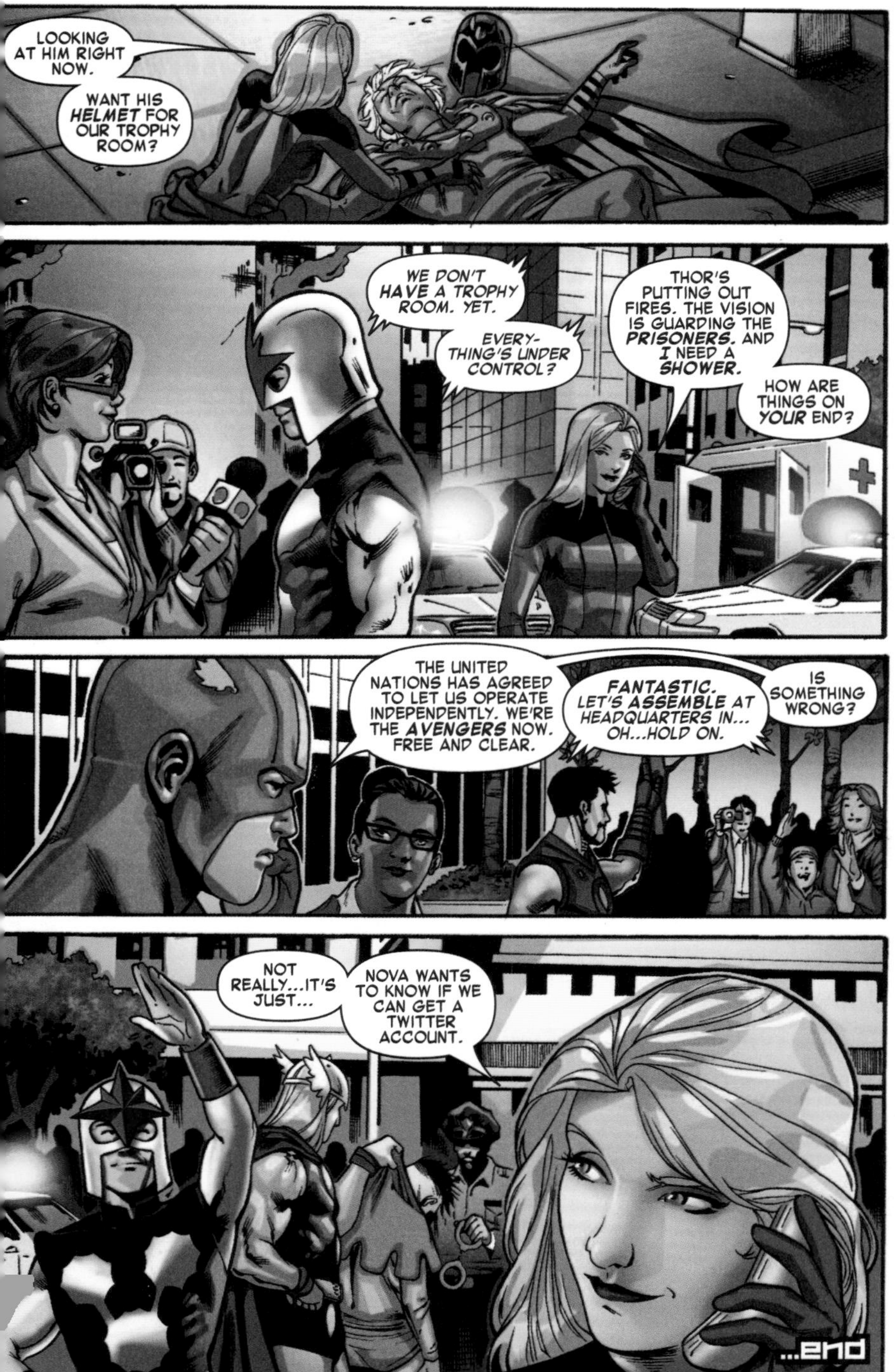
LOOKING AT HIM RIGHT NOW.
WANT HIS HELMET FOR OUR TROPHY ROOM?
WE DON'T HAVE A TROPHY ROOM. YET.
EVERYTHING'S UNDER CONTROL?
THOR'S PUTTING OUT FIRES. THE VISION IS GUARDING THE PRISONERS. AND I NEED A SHOWER.
HOW ARE THINGS ON YOUR END?
THE UNITED NATIONS HAS AGREED TO LET US OPERATE INDEPENDENTLY. WE'RE THE AVENGERS NOW. FREE AND CLEAR.
FANTASTIC. LET'S ASSEMBLE AT HEADQUARTERS IN... OH...HOLD ON.
...IS SOMETHING WRONG?
NOT REALLY...IT'S JUST...
NOVA WANTS TO KNOW IF WE CAN GET A TWITTER ACCOUNT.
...END

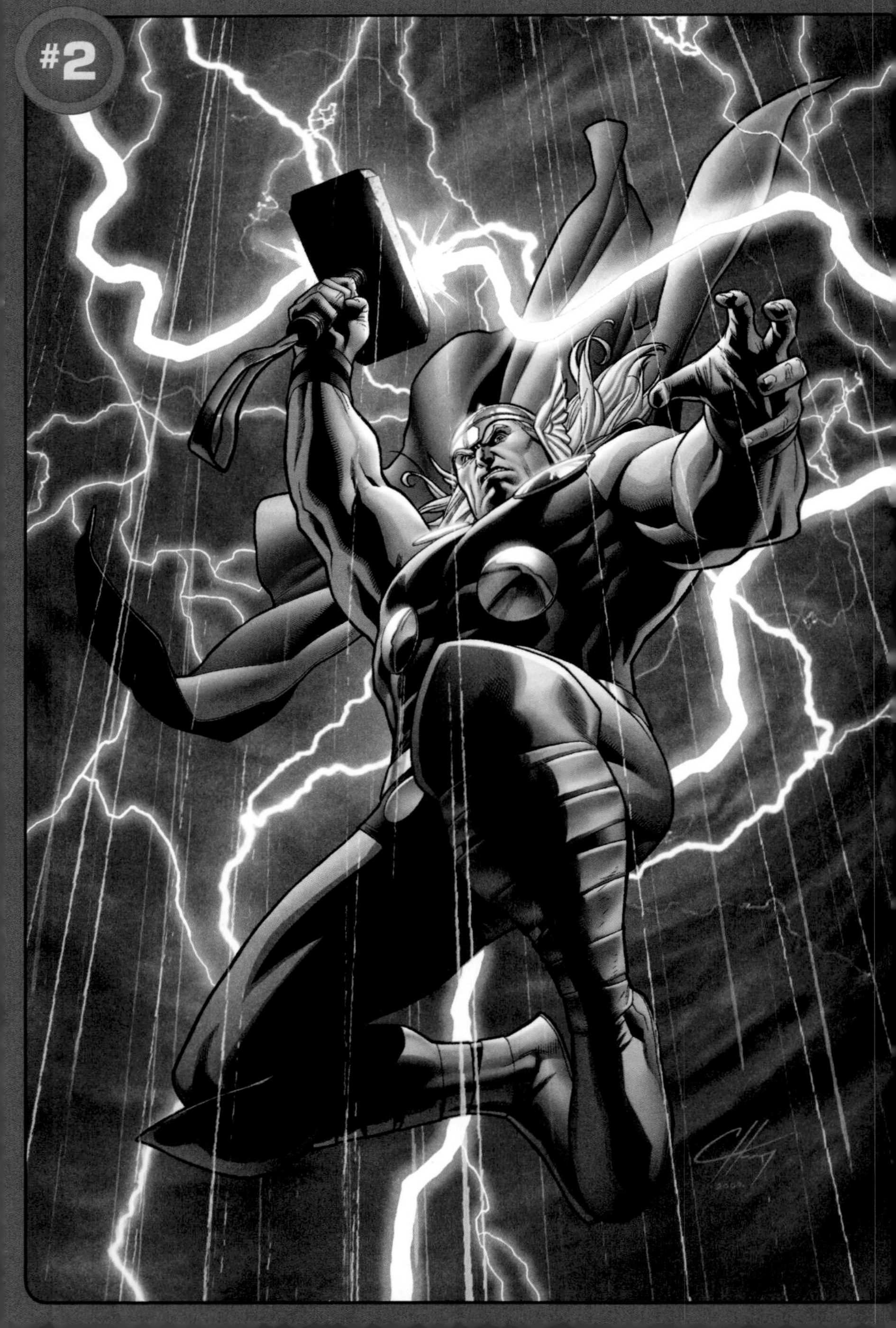
#2

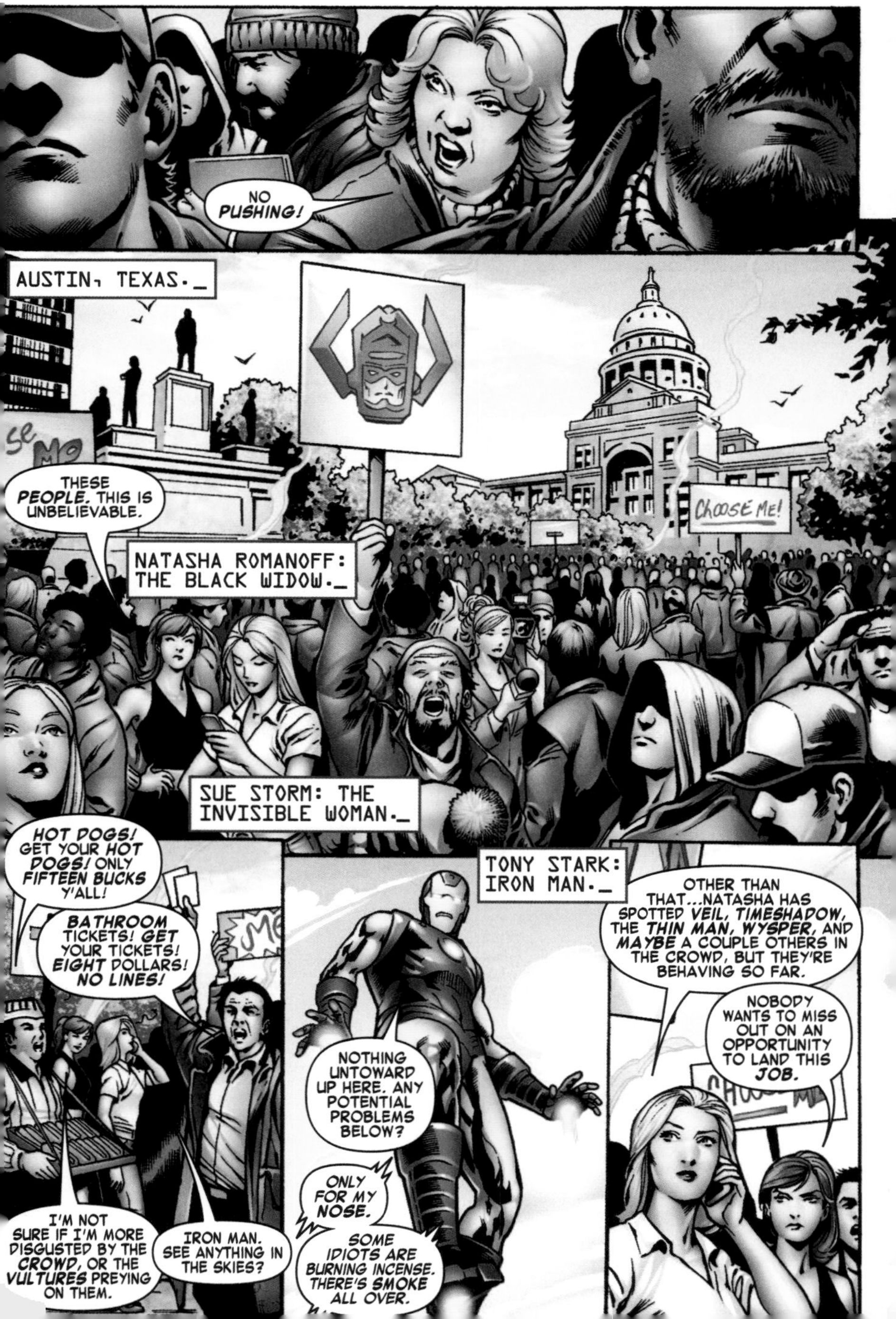
NO PUSHING!
AUSTIN, TEXAS.
CHOOSE ME!
THESE PEOPLE. THIS IS UNBELIEVABLE.
NATASHA ROMANOFF: THE BLACK WIDOW.
SUE STORM: THE INVISIBLE WOMAN.
HOT DOGS! GET YOUR HOT DOGS! ONLY FIFTEEN BUCKS Y'ALL!
BATHROOM TICKETS! GET YOUR TICKETS! EIGHT DOLLARS! NO LINES!
I'M NOT SURE IF I'M MORE DISGUSTED BY THE CROWD, OR THE VULTURES PREYING ON THEM.
IRON MAN. SEE ANYTHING IN THE SKIES?
TONY STARK: IRON MAN.
NOTHING UNTOWARD UP HERE. ANY POTENTIAL PROBLEMS BELOW?
ONLY FOR MY NOSE.
SOME IDIOTS ARE BURNING INCENSE. THERE'S SMOKE ALL OVER.
OTHER THAN THAT...NATASHA HAS SPOTTED VEIL, TIMESHADOW, THE THIN MAN, WYSPER, AND MAYBE A COUPLE OTHERS IN THE CROWD, BUT THEY'RE BEHAVING SO FAR.
NOBODY WANTS TO MISS OUT ON AN OPPORTUNITY TO LAND THIS JOB.

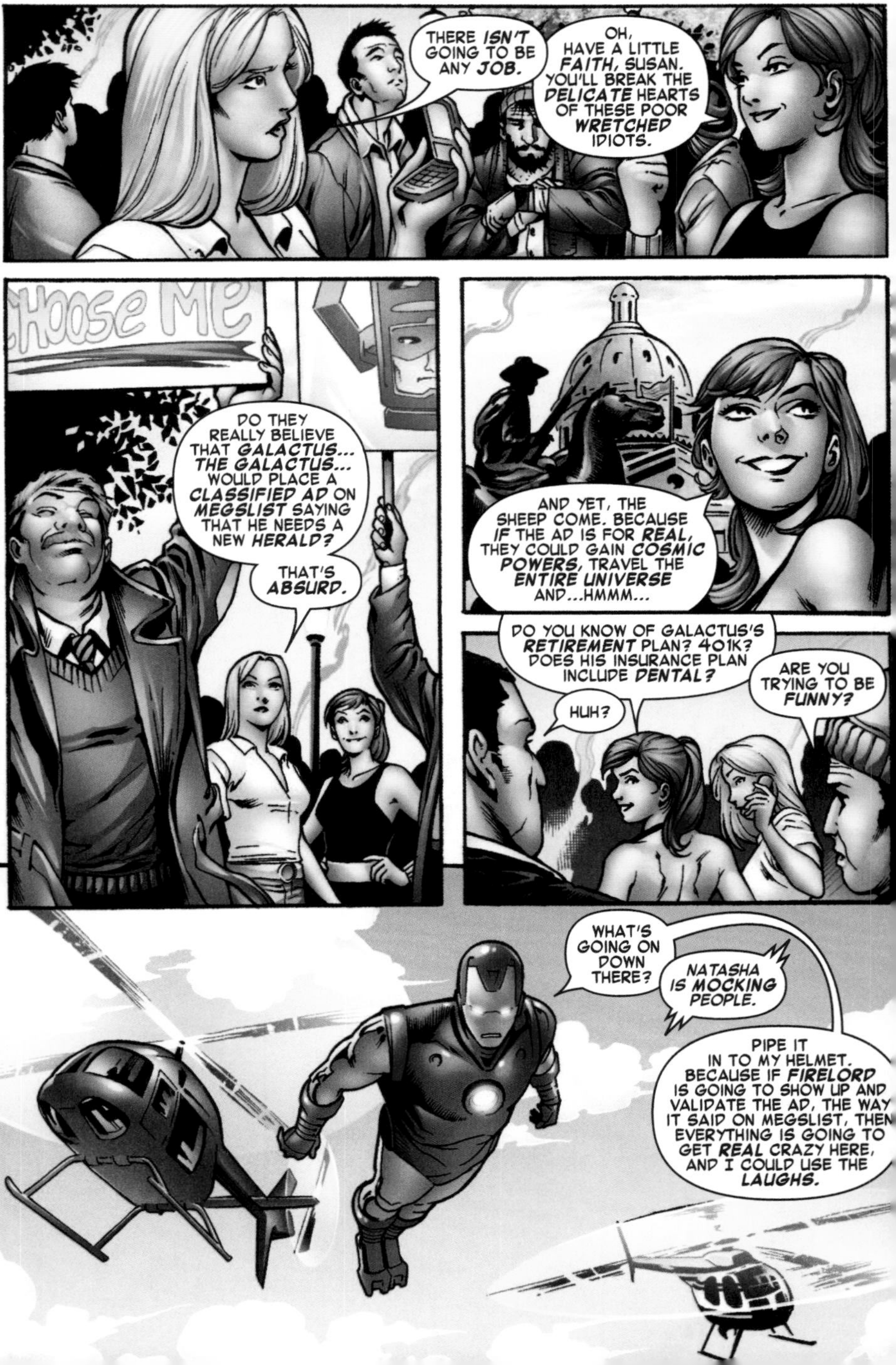
THERE ISN'T GOING TO BE ANY JOB.
OH, HAVE A LITTLE FAITH, SUSAN. YOU'LL BREAK THE DELICATE HEARTS OF THESE POOR WRETCHED IDIOTS.
CHOOSE ME
DO THEY REALLY BELIEVE THAT GALACTUS... THE GALACTUS... WOULD PLACE A CLASSIFIED AD ON MEGSLIST SAYING THAT HE NEEDS A NEW HERALD?
THAT'S ABSURD.
AND YET, THE SHEEP COME. BECAUSE IF THE AD IS FOR REAL, THEY COULD GAIN COSMIC POWERS, TRAVEL THE ENTIRE UNIVERSE AND...HMMM...
DO YOU KNOW OF GALACTUS'S RETIREMENT PLAN? 401K? DOES HIS INSURANCE PLAN INCLUDE DENTAL?
HUH?
ARE YOU TRYING TO BE FUNNY?
WHAT'S GOING ON DOWN THERE?
NATASHA IS MOCKING PEOPLE.
PIPE IT IN TO MY HELMET. BECAUSE IF FIRELORD IS GOING TO SHOW UP AND VALIDATE THE AD, THE WAY IT SAID ON MEGSLIST, THEN EVERYTHING IS GOING TO GET REAL CRAZY HERE, AND I COULD USE THE LAUGHS.

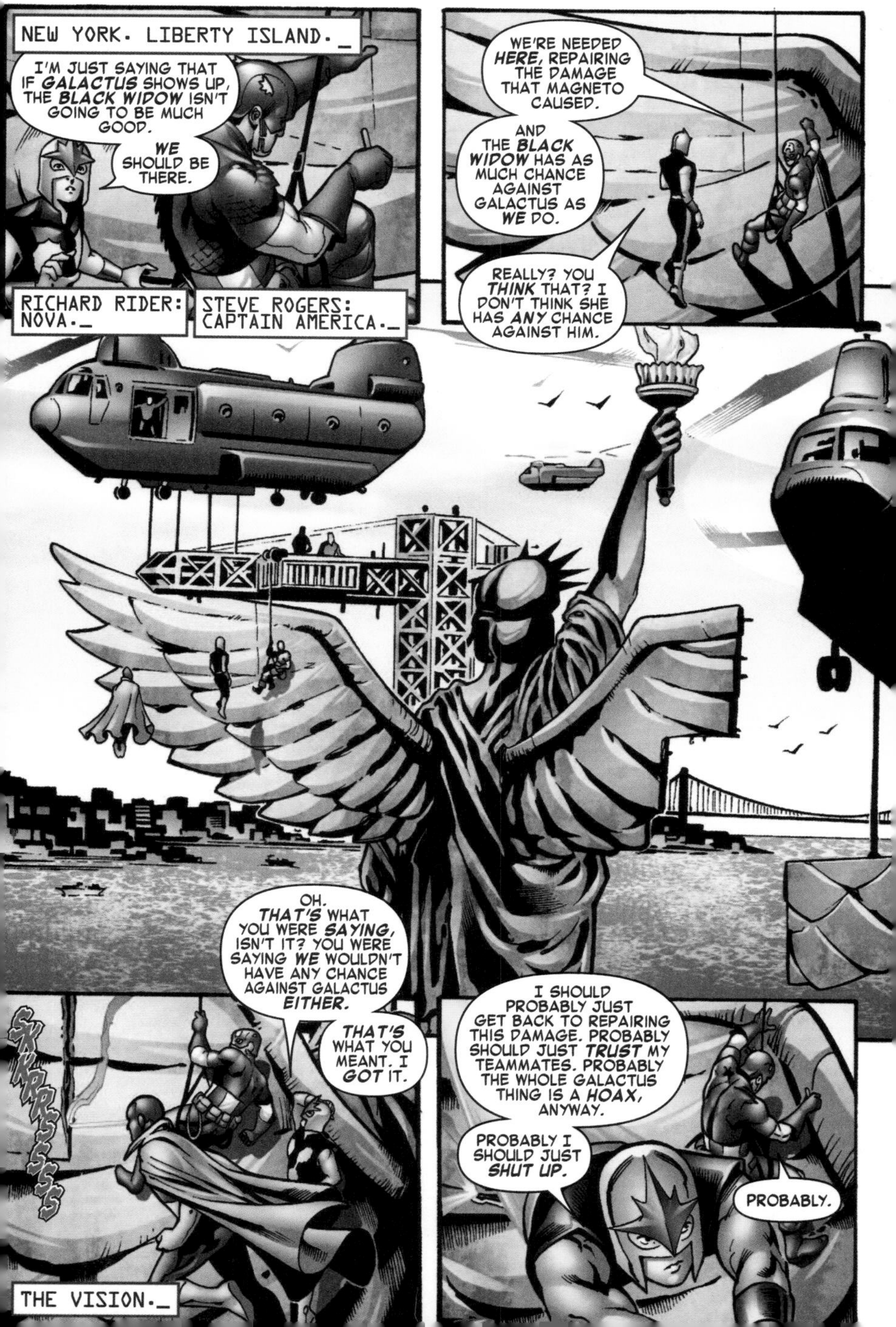
NEW YORK. LIBERTY ISLAND._
I'M JUST SAYING THAT IF GALACTUS SHOWS UP, THE BLACK WIDOW ISN'T GOING TO BE MUCH GOOD.
WE SHOULD BE THERE.
RICHARD RIDER: NOVA._
STEVE ROGERS: CAPTAIN AMERICA._
WE'RE NEEDED HERE, REPAIRING THE DAMAGE THAT MAGNETO CAUSED.
AND THE BLACK WIDOW HAS AS MUCH CHANCE AGAINST GALACTUS AS WE DO.
REALLY? YOU THINK THAT? I DON'T THINK SHE HAS ANY CHANCE AGAINST HIM.
OH. THAT'S WHAT YOU WERE SAYING, ISN'T IT? YOU WERE SAYING WE WOULDN'T HAVE ANY CHANCE AGAINST GALACTUS EITHER.
THAT'S WHAT YOU MEANT. I GOT IT.
SKRRSSSS
THE VISION._
I SHOULD PROBABLY JUST GET BACK TO REPAIRING THIS DAMAGE. PROBABLY SHOULD JUST TRUST MY TEAMMATES. PROBABLY THE WHOLE GALACTUS THING IS A HOAX, ANYWAY.
PROBABLY I SHOULD JUST SHUT UP.
PROBABLY.

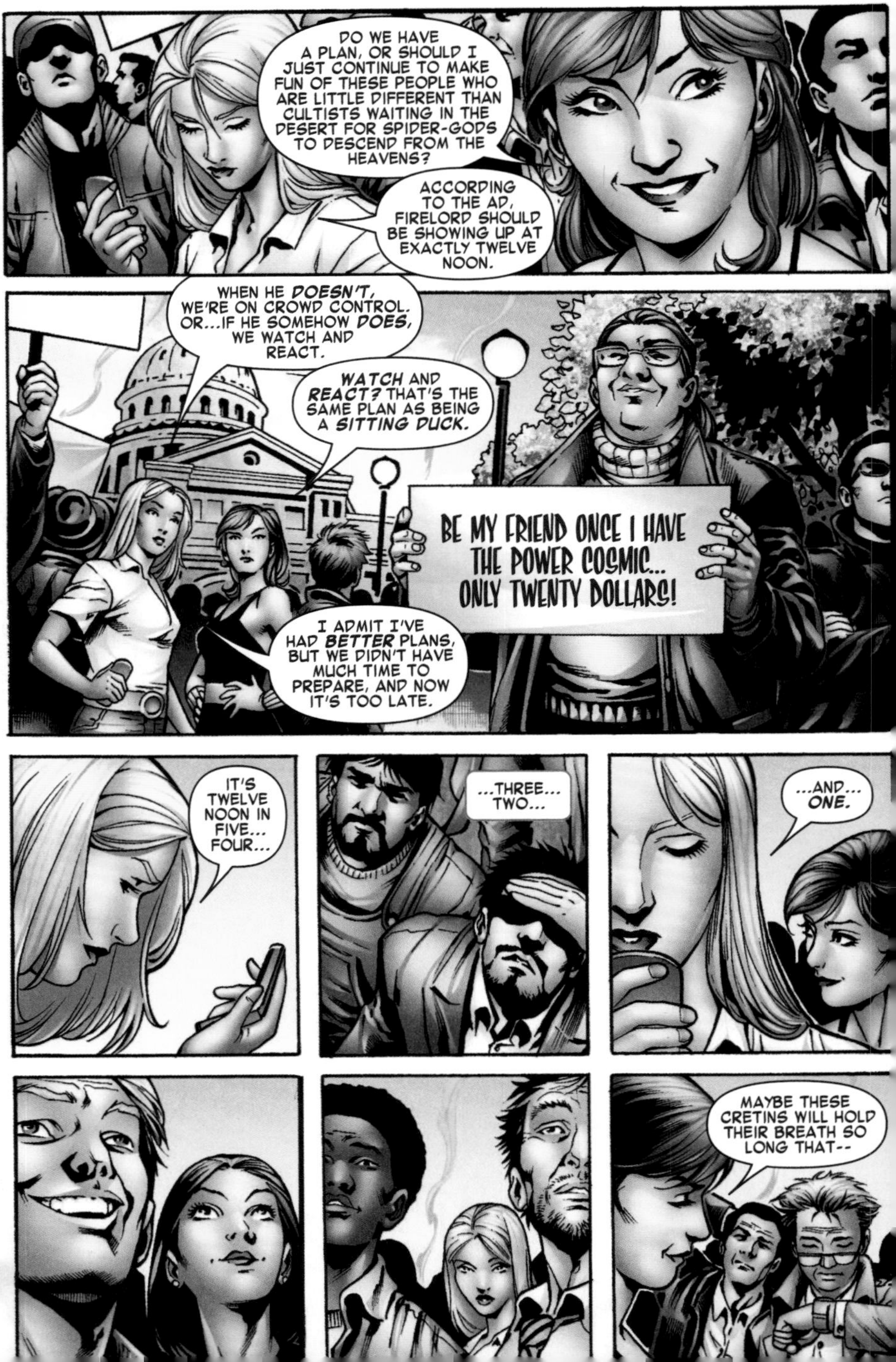

DO WE HAVE A PLAN, OR SHOULD I JUST CONTINUE TO MAKE FUN OF THESE PEOPLE WHO ARE LITTLE DIFFERENT THAN CULTISTS WAITING IN THE DESERT FOR SPIDER-GODS TO DESCEND FROM THE HEAVENS?
ACCORDING TO THE AD, FIRELORD SHOULD BE SHOWING UP AT EXACTLY TWELVE NOON.
WHEN HE DOESN'T, WE'RE ON CROWD CONTROL. OR...IF HE SOMEHOW DOES, WE WATCH AND REACT.
WATCH AND REACT? THAT'S THE SAME PLAN AS BEING A SITTING DUCK.
BE MY FRIEND ONCE I HAVE THE POWER COSMIC... ONLY TWENTY DOLLARS!
I ADMIT I'VE HAD BETTER PLANS, BUT WE DIDN'T HAVE MUCH TIME TO PREPARE, AND NOW IT'S TOO LATE.
IT'S TWELVE NOON IN FIVE... FOUR...
...THREE... TWO...
...AND... ONE.
MAYBE THESE CRETINS WILL HOLD THEIR BREATH SO LONG THAT--

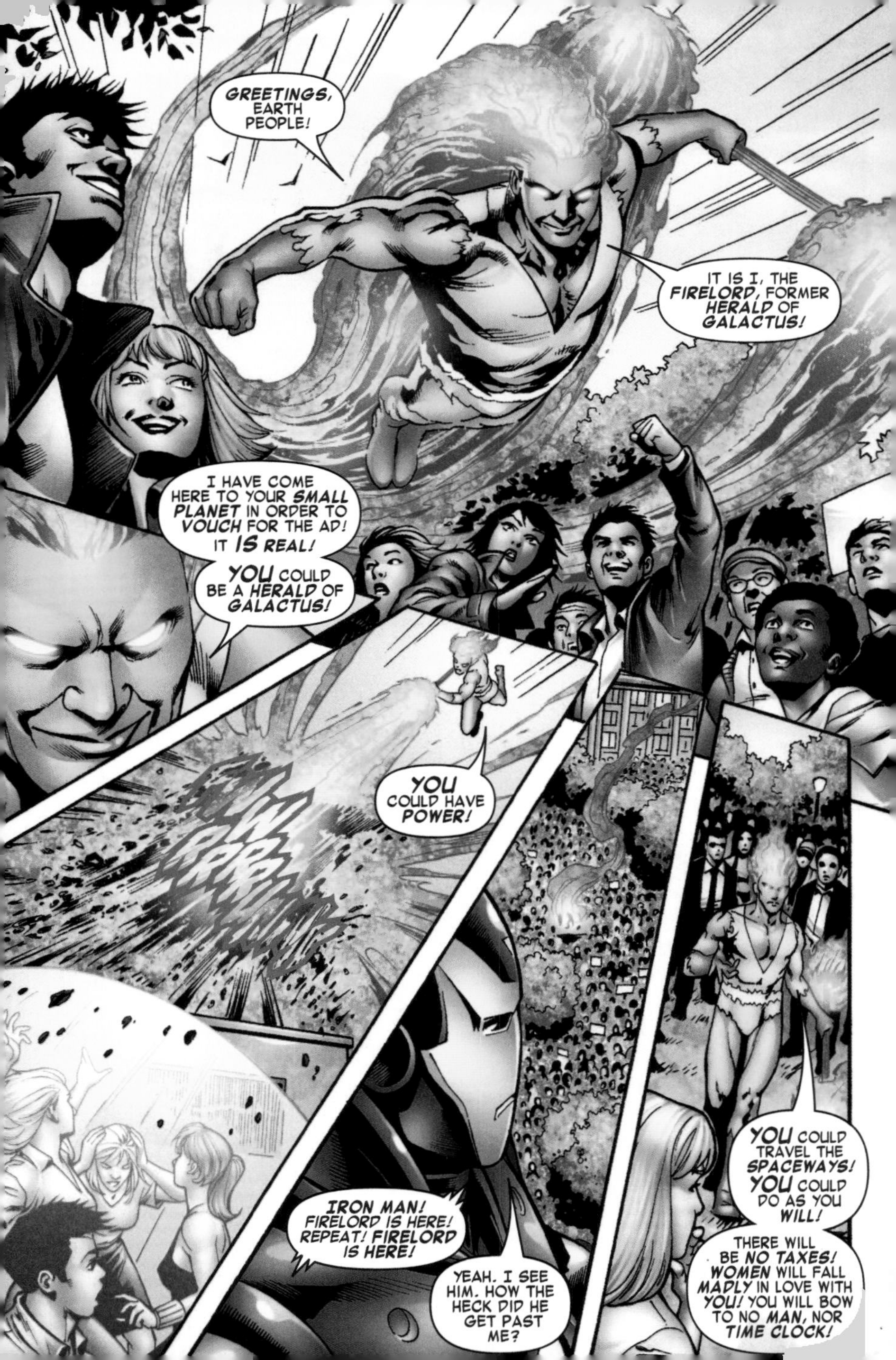
GREETINGS, EARTH PEOPLE!
IT IS I, THE FIRELORD, FORMER HERALD OF GALACTUS!
I HAVE COME HERE TO YOUR SMALL PLANET IN ORDER TO VOUCH FOR THE AD! IT IS REAL!
YOU COULD BE A HERALD OF GALACTUS!
YOU COULD HAVE POWER!
IRON MAN! FIRELORD IS HERE! REPEAT! FIRELORD IS HERE!
YEAH. I SEE HIM. HOW THE HECK DID HE GET PAST ME?
YOU COULD TRAVEL THE SPACEWAYS! YOU COULD DO AS YOU WILL!
THERE WILL BE NO TAXES! WOMEN WILL FALL MADLY IN LOVE WITH YOU! YOU WILL BOW TO NO MAN, NOR TIME CLOCK!

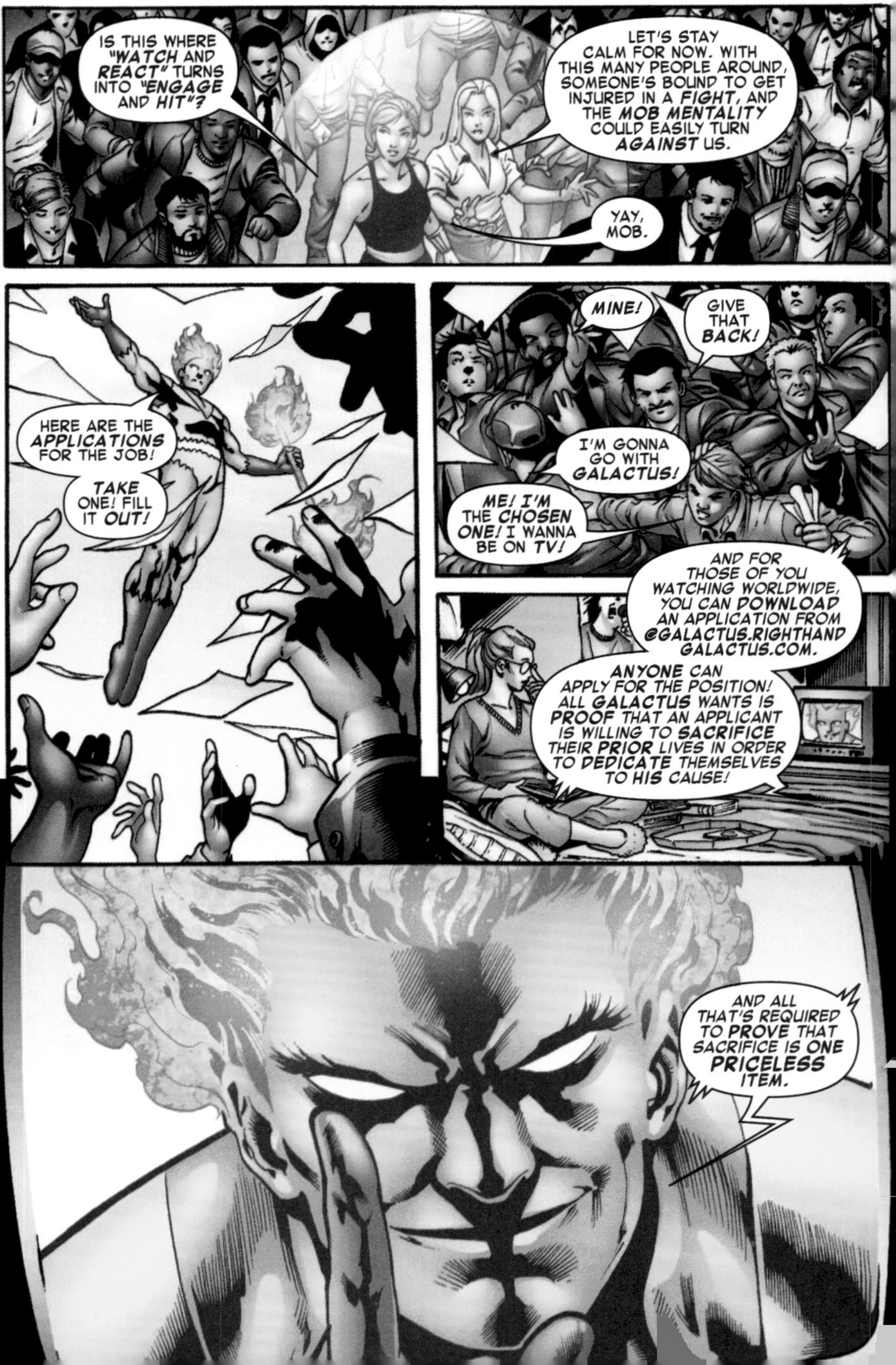
IS THIS WHERE "WATCH AND REACT" TURNS INTO "ENGAGE AND HIT"?
LET'S STAY CALM FOR NOW. WITH THIS MANY PEOPLE AROUND, SOMEONE'S BOUND TO GET INJURED IN A FIGHT, AND THE MOB MENTALITY COULD EASILY TURN AGAINST US.
YAY, MOB.
HERE ARE THE APPLICATIONS FOR THE JOB!
TAKE ONE! FILL IT OUT!
MINE!
GIVE THAT BACK!
I'M GONNA GO WITH GALACTUS!
ME! I'M THE CHOSEN ONE! I WANNA BE ON TV!
AND FOR THOSE OF YOU WATCHING WORLDWIDE, YOU CAN DOWNLOAD AN APPLICATION FROM @GALACTUS.RIGHTHAND GALACTUS.COM.
ANYONE CAN APPLY FOR THE POSITION! ALL GALACTUS WANTS IS PROOF THAT AN APPLICANT IS WILLING TO SACRIFICE THEIR PRIOR LIVES IN ORDER TO DEDICATE THEMSELVES TO HIS CAUSE!
AND ALL THAT'S REQUIRED TO PROVE THAT SACRIFICE IS ONE PRICELESS ITEM.

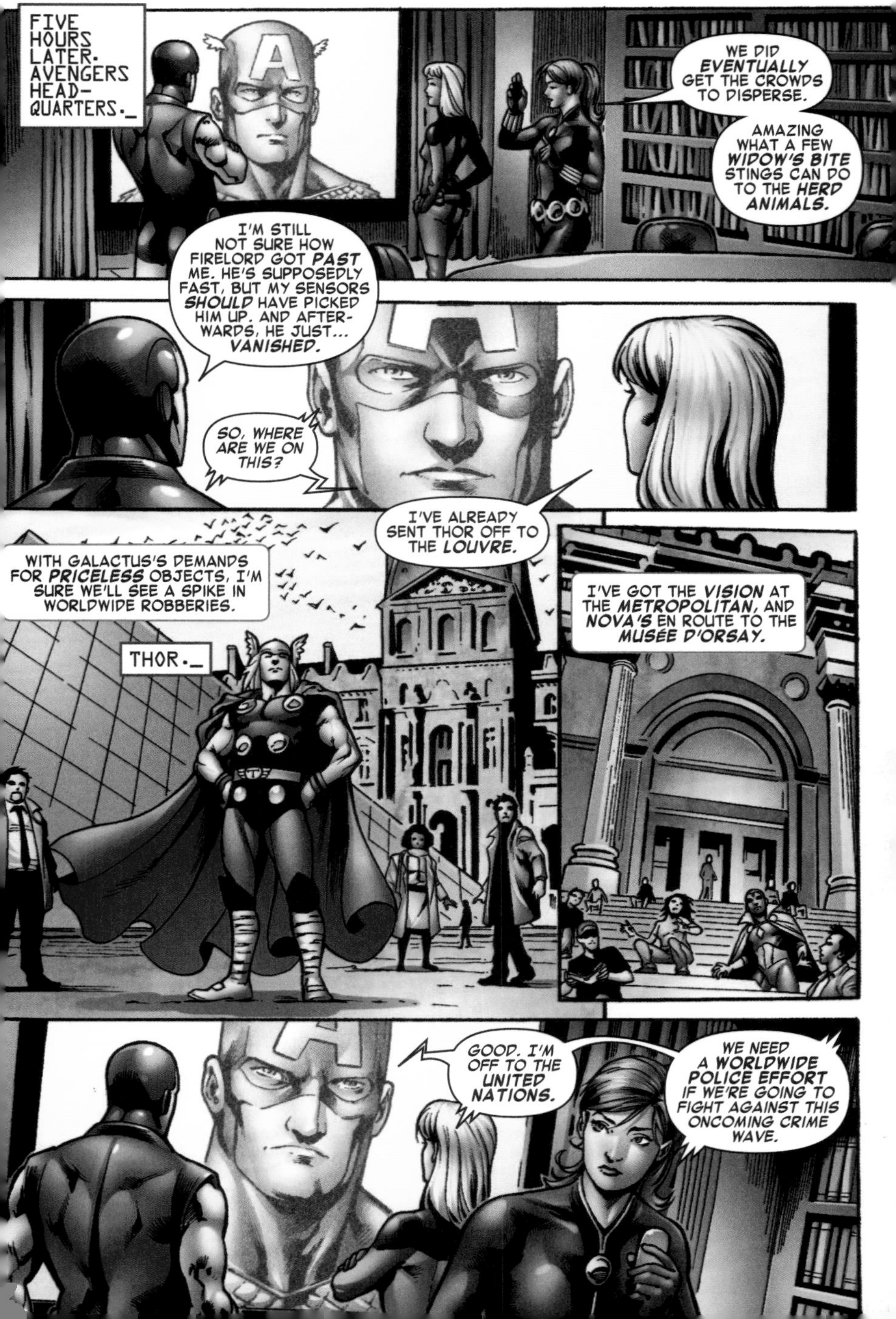
FIVE HOURS LATER. AVENGERS HEAD-QUARTERS._
WE DID EVENTUALLY GET THE CROWDS TO DISPERSE.
AMAZING WHAT A FEW WIDOW'S BITE STINGS CAN DO TO THE HERD ANIMALS.
I'M STILL NOT SURE HOW FIRELORD GOT PAST ME. HE'S SUPPOSEDLY FAST, BUT MY SENSORS SHOULD HAVE PICKED HIM UP. AND AFTER-WARDS, HE JUST... VANISHED.
SO, WHERE ARE WE ON THIS?
I'VE ALREADY SENT THOR OFF TO THE LOUVRE.
WITH GALACTUS'S DEMANDS FOR PRICELESS OBJECTS, I'M SURE WE'LL SEE A SPIKE IN WORLDWIDE ROBBERIES.
THOR._
I'VE GOT THE VISION AT THE METROPOLITAN, AND NOVA'S EN ROUTE TO THE MUSÉE D'ORSAY.
GOOD. I'M OFF TO THE UNITED NATIONS.
WE NEED A WORLDWIDE POLICE EFFORT IF WE'RE GOING TO FIGHT AGAINST THIS ONCOMING CRIME WAVE.

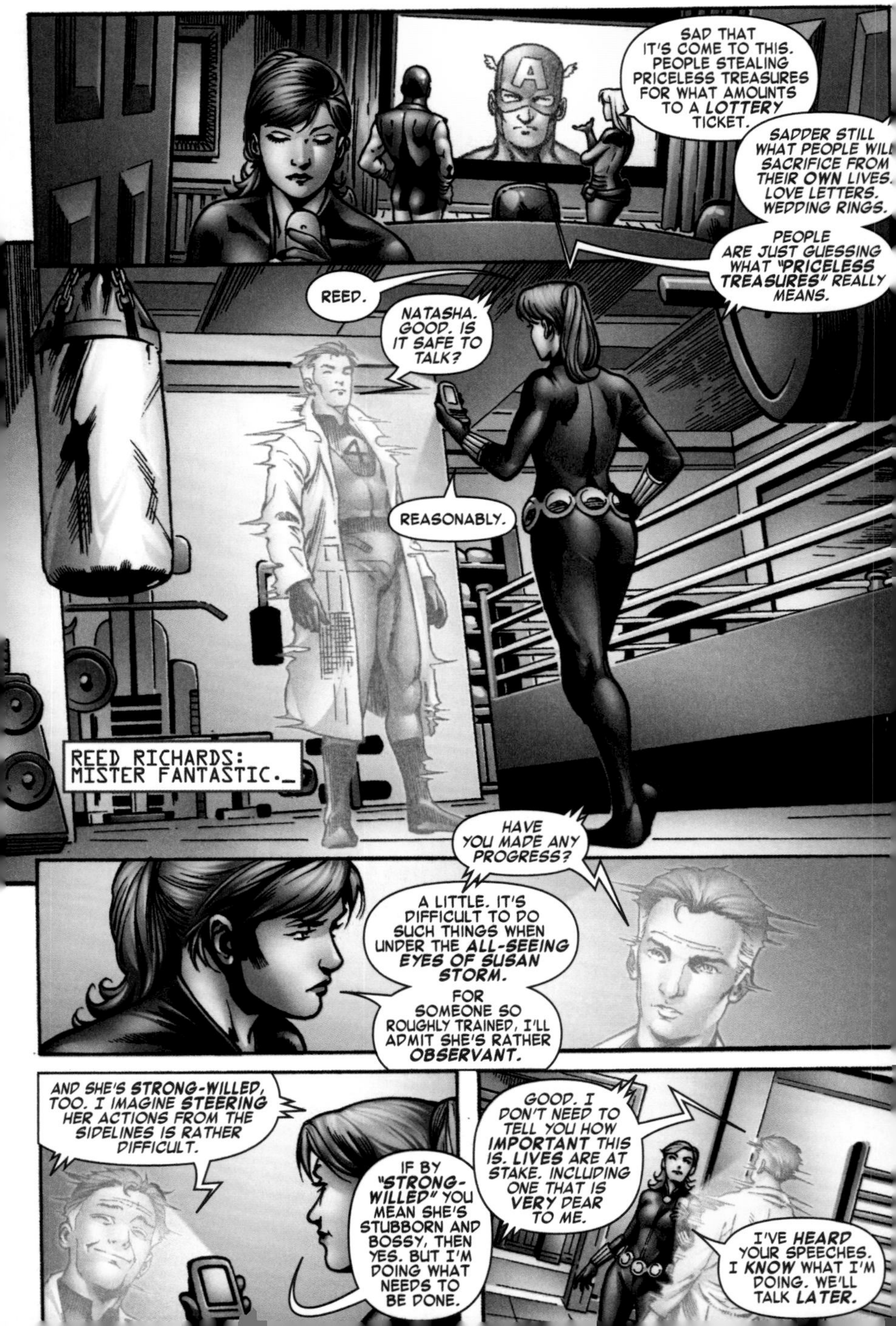
SAD THAT IT'S COME TO THIS. PEOPLE STEALING PRICELESS TREASURES FOR WHAT AMOUNTS TO A LOTTERY TICKET.
SADDER STILL WHAT PEOPLE WILL SACRIFICE FROM THEIR OWN LIVES. LOVE LETTERS. WEDDING RINGS.
PEOPLE ARE JUST GUESSING WHAT "PRICELESS TREASURES" REALLY MEANS.
REED.
NATASHA. GOOD. IS IT SAFE TO TALK?
REASONABLY.
REED RICHARDS: MISTER FANTASTIC._
HAVE YOU MADE ANY PROGRESS?
A LITTLE. IT'S DIFFICULT TO DO SUCH THINGS WHEN UNDER THE ALL-SEEING EYES OF SUSAN STORM.
FOR SOMEONE SO ROUGHLY TRAINED, I'LL ADMIT SHE'S RATHER OBSERVANT.
AND SHE'S STRONG-WILLED, TOO. I IMAGINE STEERING HER ACTIONS FROM THE SIDELINES IS RATHER DIFFICULT.
IF BY "STRONG-WILLED" YOU MEAN SHE'S STUBBORN AND BOSSY, THEN YES. BUT I'M DOING WHAT NEEDS TO BE DONE.
GOOD. I DON'T NEED TO TELL YOU HOW IMPORTANT THIS IS. LIVES ARE AT STAKE. INCLUDING ONE THAT IS VERY DEAR TO ME.
I'VE HEARD YOUR SPEECHES. I KNOW WHAT I'M DOING. WE'LL TALK LATER.

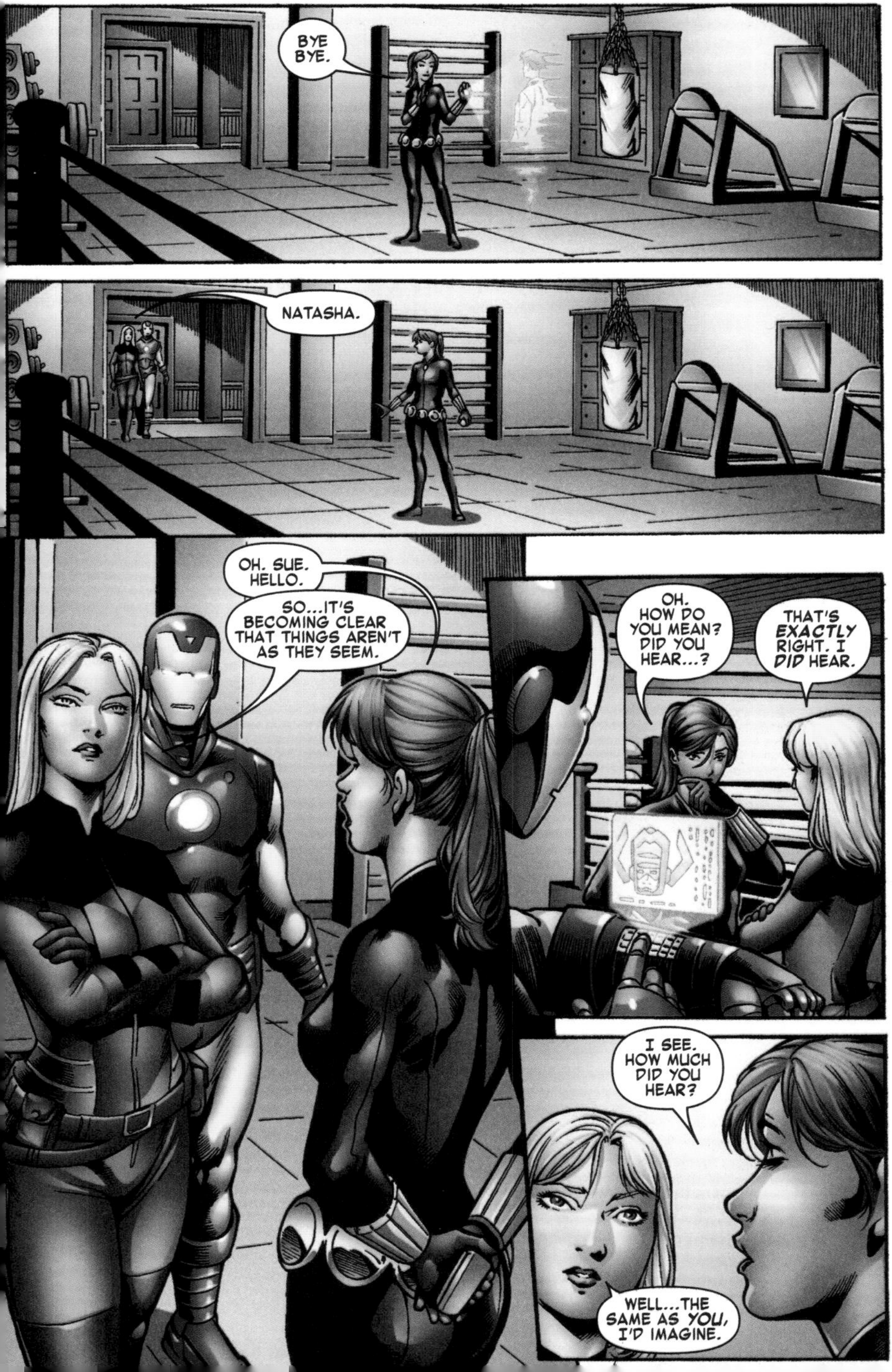
BYE BYE.
NATASHA.
OH. SUE. HELLO.
SO...IT'S BECOMING CLEAR THAT THINGS AREN'T AS THEY SEEM.
OH. HOW DO YOU MEAN? DID YOU HEAR...?
THAT'S EXACTLY RIGHT. I DID HEAR.
I SEE. HOW MUCH DID YOU HEAR?
WELL...THE SAME AS YOU, I'D IMAGINE.

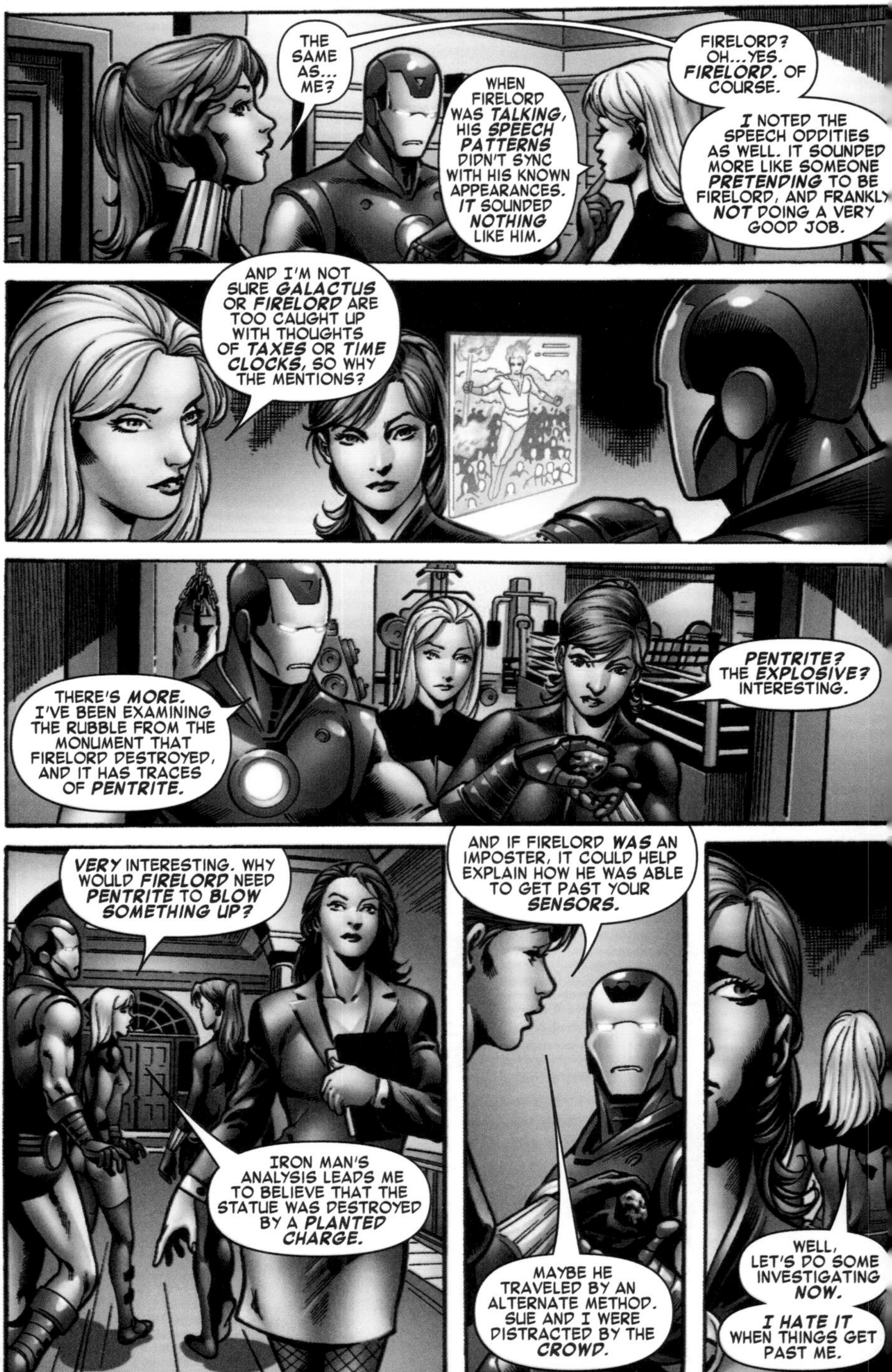

THE SAME AS... ME?
WHEN FIRELORD WAS TALKING, HIS SPEECH PATTERNS DIDN'T SYNC WITH HIS KNOWN APPEARANCES. IT SOUNDED NOTHING LIKE HIM.
FIRELORD? OH...YES. FIRELORD. OF COURSE.
I NOTED THE SPEECH ODDITIES AS WELL. IT SOUNDED MORE LIKE SOMEONE PRETENDING TO BE FIRELORD, AND FRANKLY NOT DOING A VERY GOOD JOB.
AND I'M NOT SURE GALACTUS OR FIRELORD ARE TOO CAUGHT UP WITH THOUGHTS OF TAXES OR TIME CLOCKS, SO WHY THE MENTIONS?
THERE'S MORE. I'VE BEEN EXAMINING THE RUBBLE FROM THE MONUMENT THAT FIRELORD DESTROYED, AND IT HAS TRACES OF PENTRITE.
PENTRITE? THE EXPLOSIVE? INTERESTING.
VERY INTERESTING. WHY WOULD FIRELORD NEED PENTRITE TO BLOW SOMETHING UP?
IRON MAN'S ANALYSIS LEADS ME TO BELIEVE THAT THE STATUE WAS DESTROYED BY A PLANTED CHARGE.
AND IF FIRELORD WAS AN IMPOSTER, IT COULD HELP EXPLAIN HOW HE WAS ABLE TO GET PAST YOUR SENSORS.
MAYBE HE TRAVELED BY AN ALTERNATE METHOD. SUE AND I WERE DISTRACTED BY THE CROWD.
WELL, LET'S DO SOME INVESTIGATING NOW.
I HATE IT WHEN THINGS GET PAST ME.

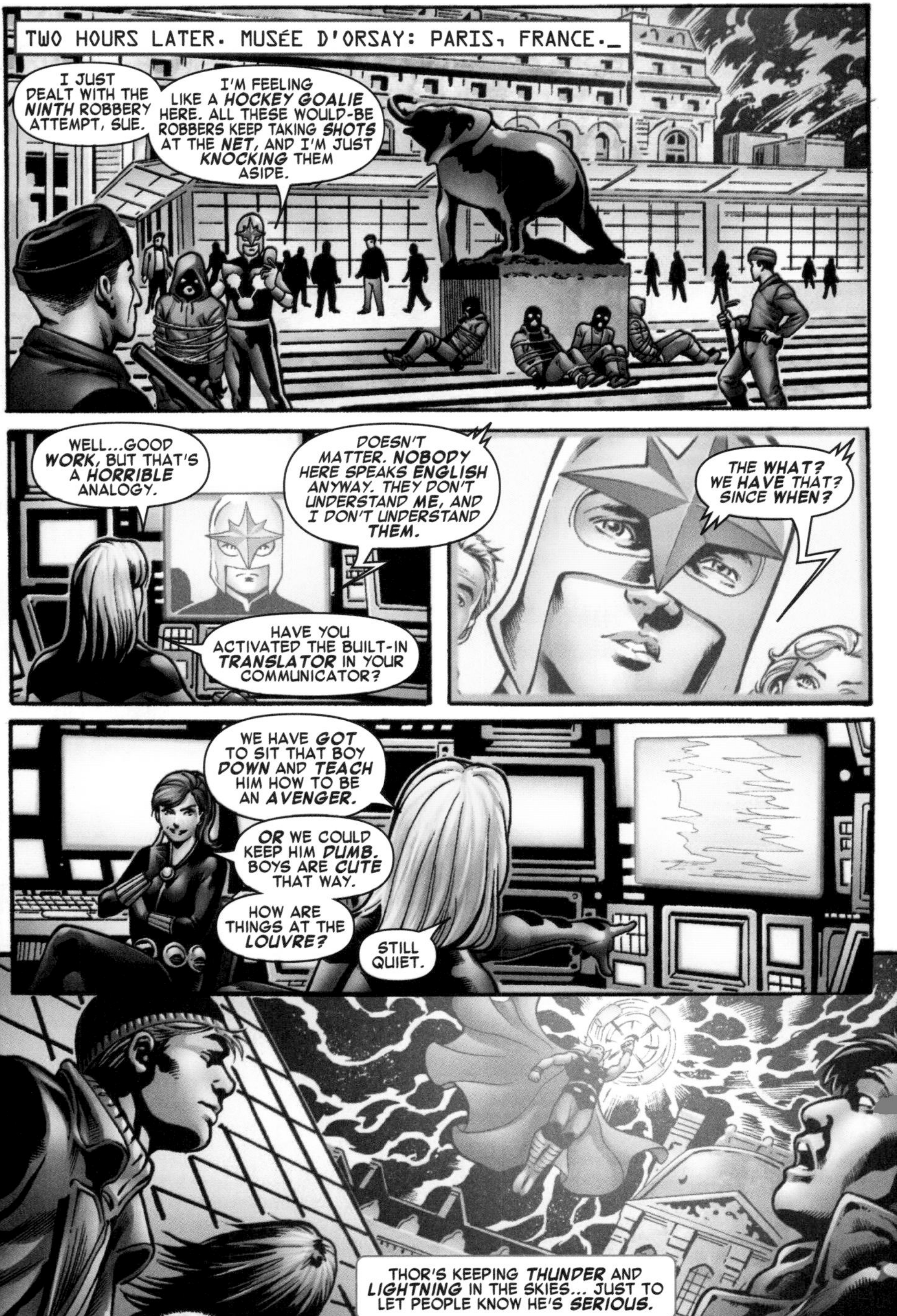
TWO HOURS LATER. MUSÉE D'ORSAY: PARIS, FRANCE._
I JUST DEALT WITH THE NINTH ROBBERY ATTEMPT, SUE.
I'M FEELING LIKE A HOCKEY GOALIE HERE. ALL THESE WOULD-BE ROBBERS KEEP TAKING SHOTS AT THE NET, AND I'M JUST KNOCKING THEM ASIDE.
WELL...GOOD WORK, BUT THAT'S A HORRIBLE ANALOGY.
DOESN'T MATTER. NOBODY HERE SPEAKS ENGLISH ANYWAY. THEY DON'T UNDERSTAND ME, AND I DON'T UNDERSTAND THEM.
HAVE YOU ACTIVATED THE BUILT-IN TRANSLATOR IN YOUR COMMUNICATOR?
THE WHAT? WE HAVE THAT? SINCE WHEN?
WE HAVE GOT TO SIT THAT BOY DOWN AND TEACH HIM HOW TO BE AN AVENGER.
OR WE COULD KEEP HIM DUMB. BOYS ARE CUTE THAT WAY.
HOW ARE THINGS AT THE LOUVRE?
STILL QUIET.
THOR'S KEEPING THUNDER AND LIGHTNING IN THE SKIES... JUST TO LET PEOPLE KNOW HE'S SERIOUS.

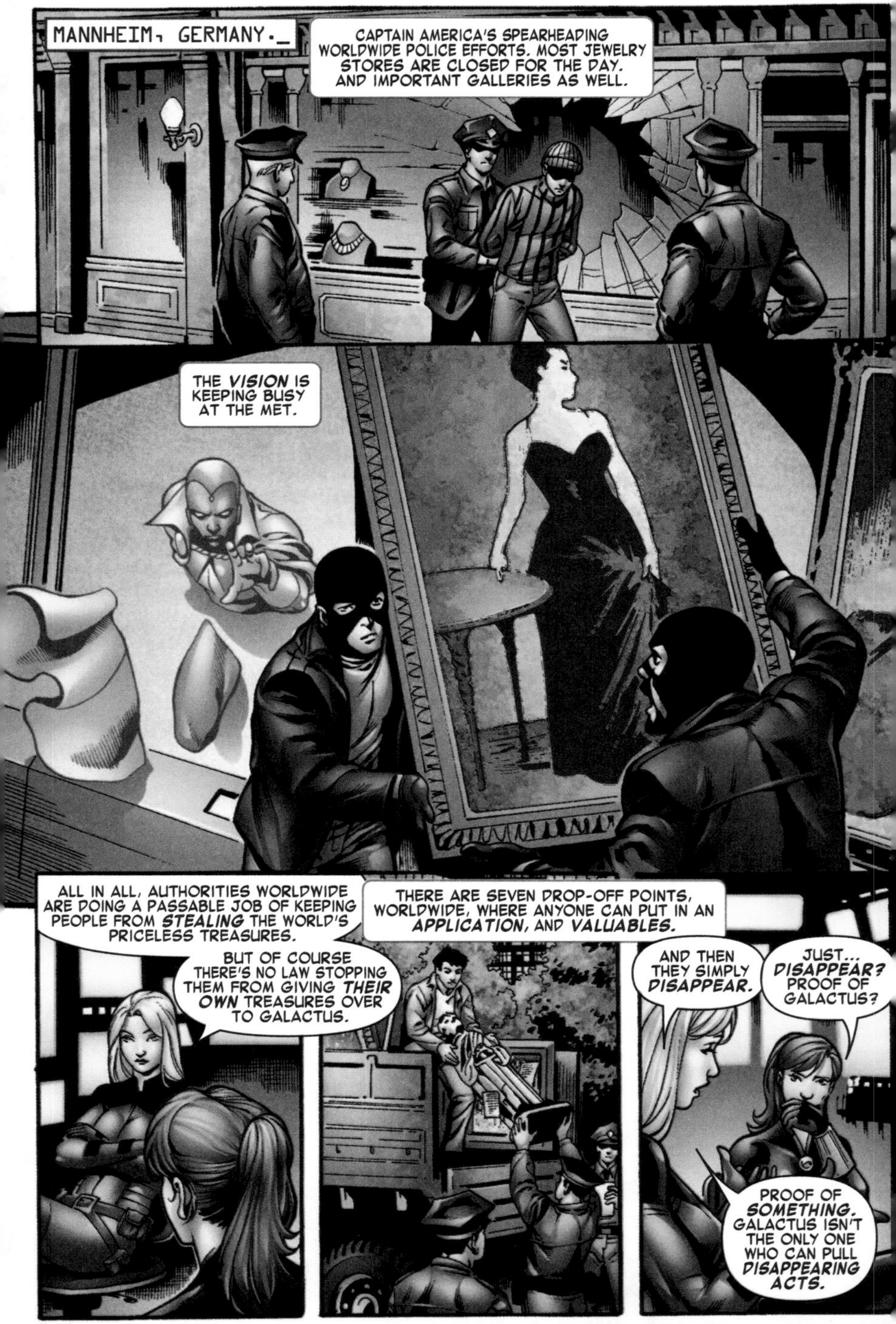
MANNHEIM, GERMANY._
CAPTAIN AMERICA'S SPEARHEADING WORLDWIDE POLICE EFFORTS. MOST JEWELRY STORES ARE CLOSED FOR THE DAY. AND IMPORTANT GALLERIES AS WELL.
THE *VISION* IS KEEPING BUSY AT THE MET.
ALL IN ALL, AUTHORITIES WORLDWIDE ARE DOING A PASSABLE JOB OF KEEPING PEOPLE FROM *STEALING* THE WORLD'S PRICELESS TREASURES.
BUT OF COURSE THERE'S NO LAW STOPPING THEM FROM GIVING *THEIR OWN* TREASURES OVER TO GALACTUS.
THERE ARE SEVEN DROP-OFF POINTS, WORLDWIDE, WHERE ANYONE CAN PUT IN AN *APPLICATION*, AND *VALUABLES.*
AND THEN THEY SIMPLY *DISAPPEAR.*
JUST... *DISAPPEAR?* PROOF OF GALACTUS?
PROOF OF *SOMETHING.* GALACTUS ISN'T THE ONLY ONE WHO CAN PULL *DISAPPEARING ACTS.*

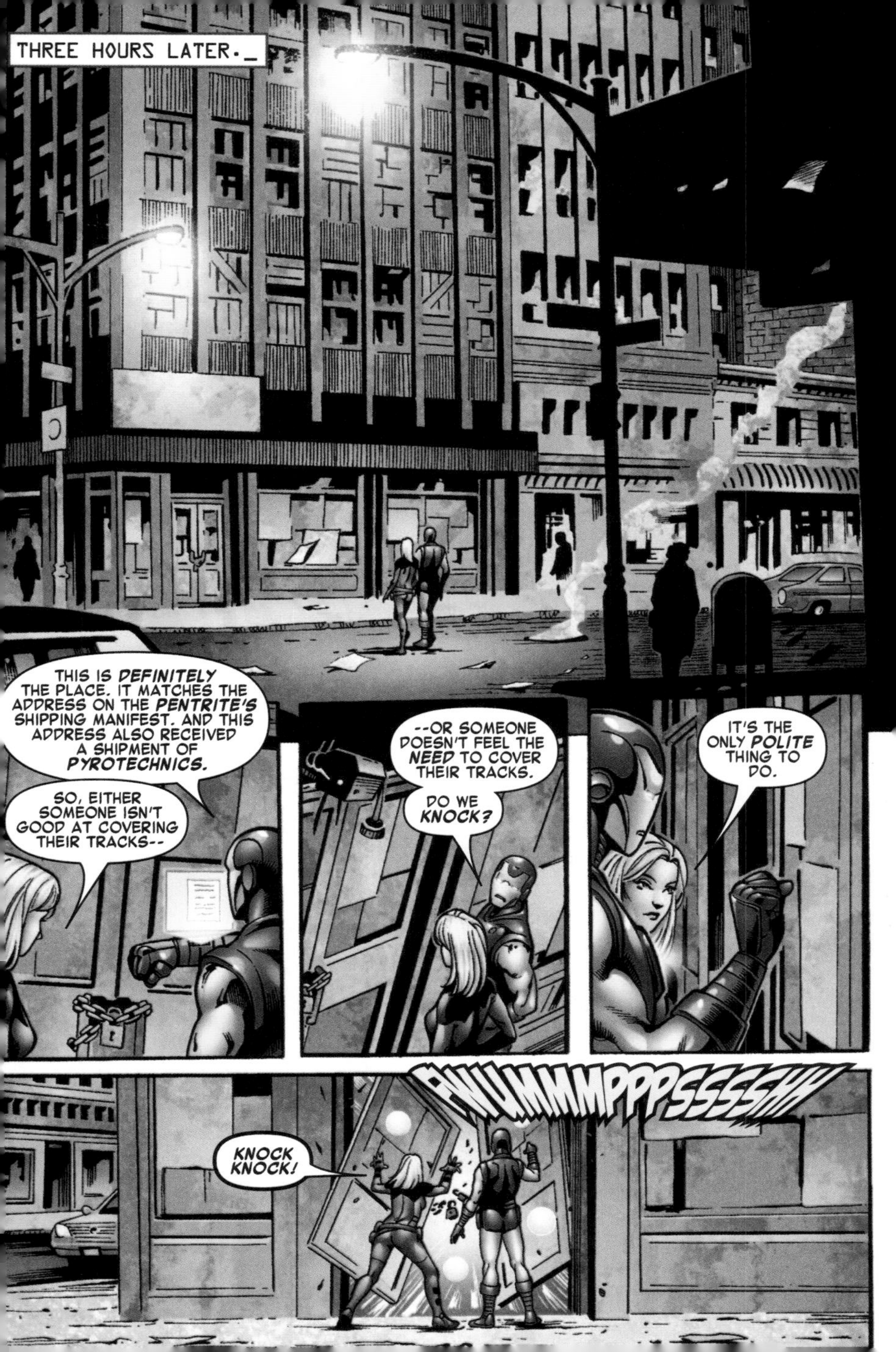
THREE HOURS LATER._
THIS IS DEFINITELY THE PLACE. IT MATCHES THE ADDRESS ON THE PENTRITE'S SHIPPING MANIFEST. AND THIS ADDRESS ALSO RECEIVED A SHIPMENT OF PYROTECHNICS.
SO, EITHER SOMEONE ISN'T GOOD AT COVERING THEIR TRACKS--
--OR SOMEONE DOESN'T FEEL THE NEED TO COVER THEIR TRACKS.
DO WE KNOCK?
IT'S THE ONLY POLITE THING TO DO.
KNOCK KNOCK!

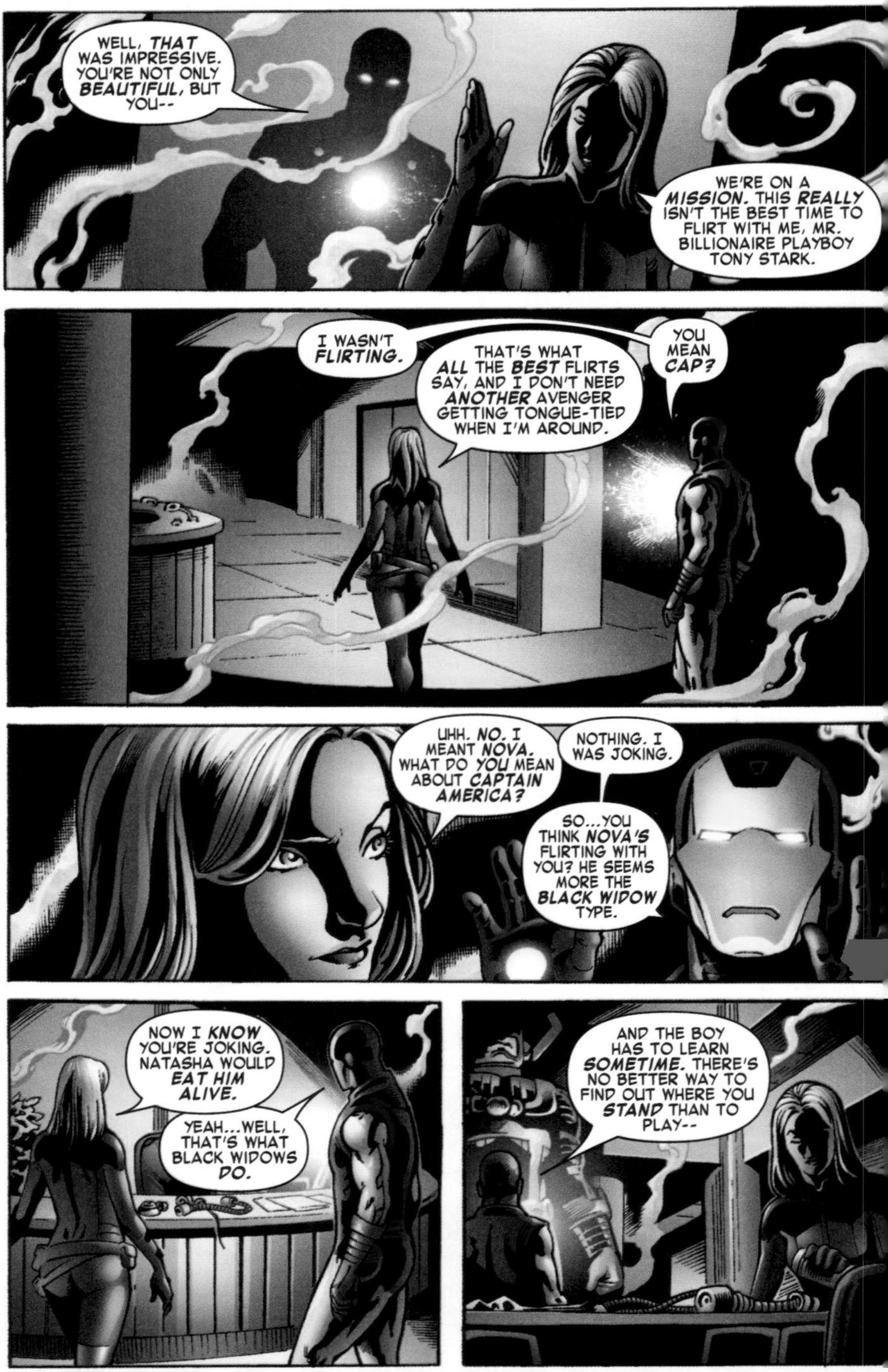
WELL, THAT WAS IMPRESSIVE. YOU'RE NOT ONLY BEAUTIFUL, BUT YOU--
WE'RE ON A MISSION. THIS REALLY ISN'T THE BEST TIME TO FLIRT WITH ME, MR. BILLIONAIRE PLAYBOY TONY STARK.
I WASN'T FLIRTING.
THAT'S WHAT ALL THE BEST FLIRTS SAY, AND I DON'T NEED ANOTHER AVENGER GETTING TONGUE-TIED WHEN I'M AROUND.
YOU MEAN CAP?
UHH. NO. I MEANT NOVA. WHAT DO YOU MEAN ABOUT CAPTAIN AMERICA?
NOTHING. I WAS JOKING.
SO...YOU THINK NOVA'S FLIRTING WITH YOU? HE SEEMS MORE THE BLACK WIDOW TYPE.
NOW I KNOW YOU'RE JOKING. NATASHA WOULD EAT HIM ALIVE.
YEAH...WELL, THAT'S WHAT BLACK WIDOWS DO.
AND THE BOY HAS TO LEARN SOMETIME. THERE'S NO BETTER WAY TO FIND OUT WHERE YOU STAND THAN TO PLAY--

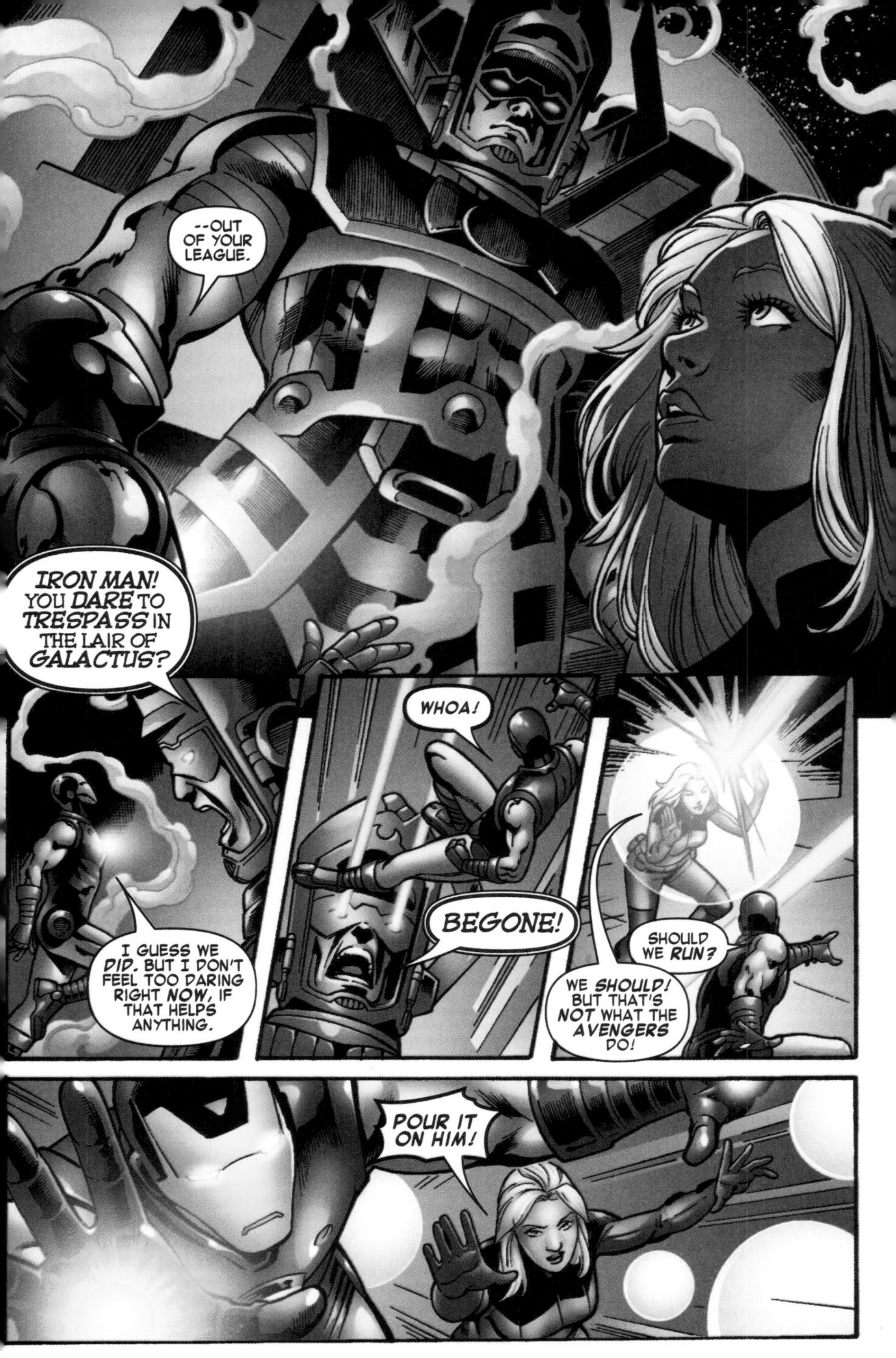

--OUT OF YOUR LEAGUE.
IRON MAN! YOU DARE TO TRESPASS IN THE LAIR OF GALACTUS?
I GUESS WE DID. BUT I DON'T FEEL TOO DARING RIGHT NOW, IF THAT HELPS ANYTHING.
WHOA!
BEGONE!
SHOULD WE RUN?
WE SHOULD! BUT THAT'S NOT WHAT THE AVENGERS DO!
POUR IT ON HIM!

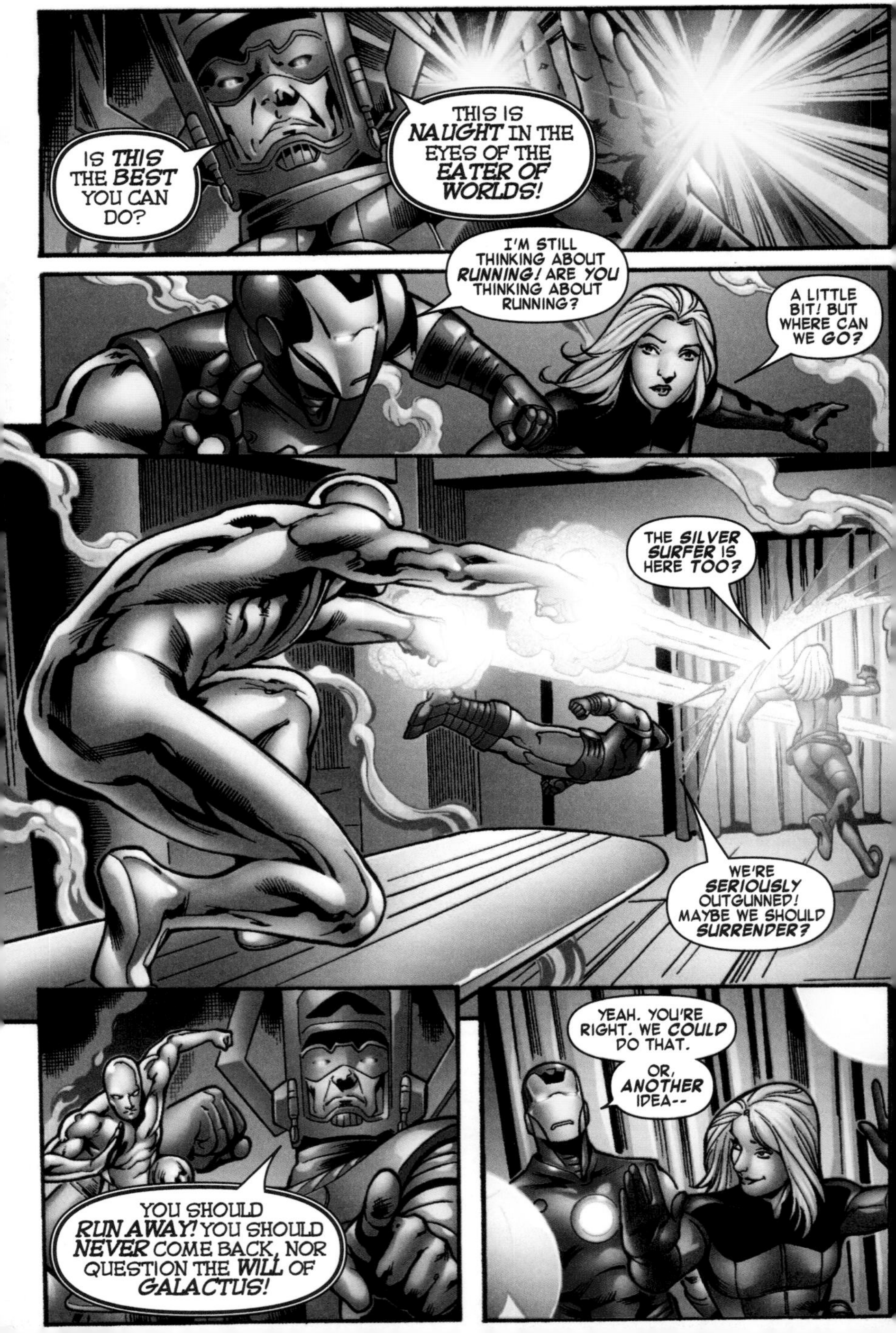
IS THIS THE BEST YOU CAN DO?
THIS IS NAUGHT IN THE EYES OF THE EATER OF WORLDS!
I'M STILL THINKING ABOUT RUNNING! ARE YOU THINKING ABOUT RUNNING?
A LITTLE BIT! BUT WHERE CAN WE GO?
THE SILVER SURFER IS HERE TOO?
WE'RE SERIOUSLY OUTGUNNED! MAYBE WE SHOULD SURRENDER?
YOU SHOULD RUN AWAY! YOU SHOULD NEVER COME BACK, NOR QUESTION THE WILL OF GALACTUS!
YEAH. YOU'RE RIGHT. WE COULD DO THAT.
OR, ANOTHER IDEA--

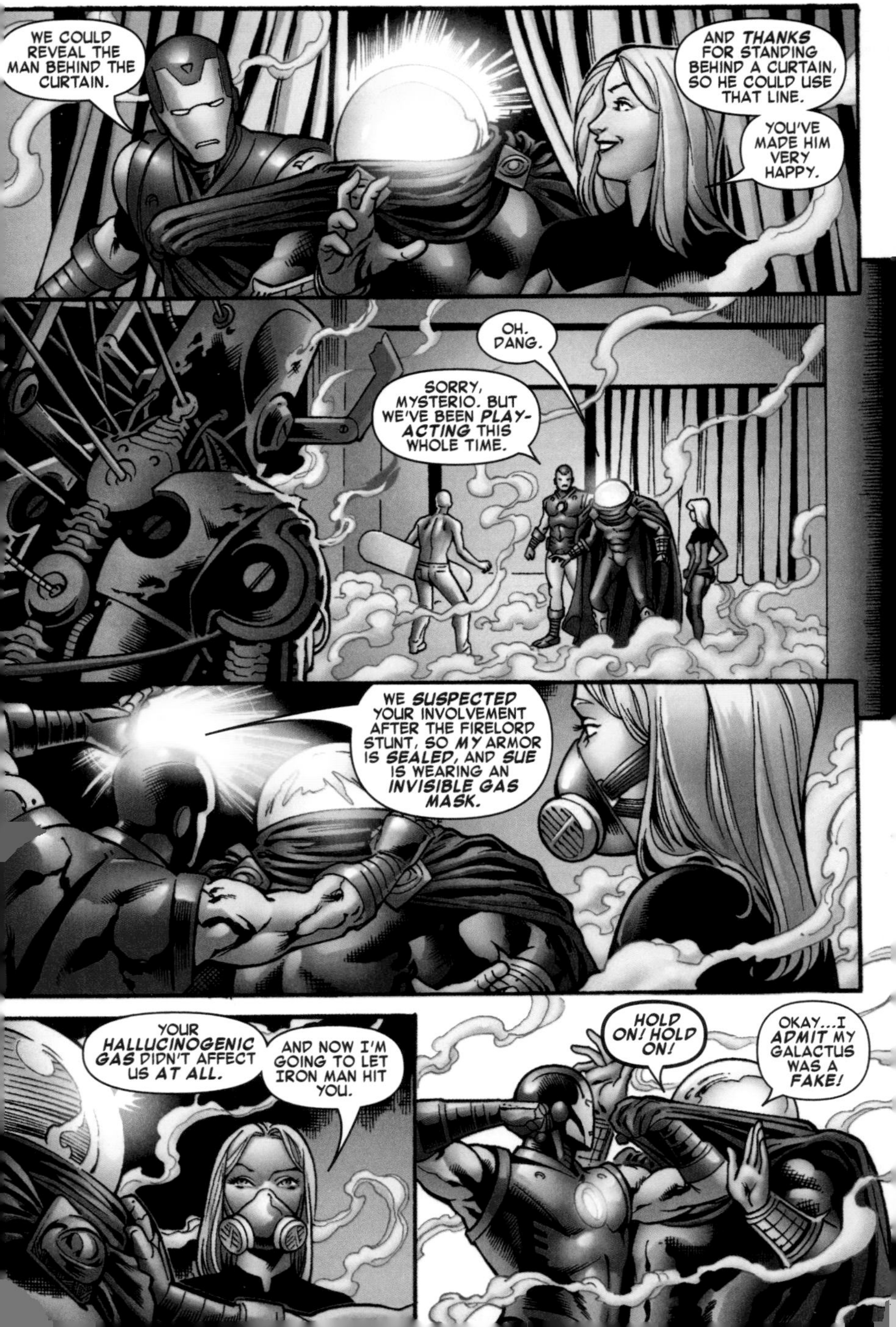
WE COULD REVEAL THE MAN BEHIND THE CURTAIN.
AND THANKS FOR STANDING BEHIND A CURTAIN, SO HE COULD USE THAT LINE.
YOU'VE MADE HIM VERY HAPPY.
OH. DANG.
SORRY, MYSTERIO. BUT WE'VE BEEN PLAY-ACTING THIS WHOLE TIME.
WE SUSPECTED YOUR INVOLVEMENT AFTER THE FIRELORD STUNT, SO MY ARMOR IS SEALED, AND SUE IS WEARING AN INVISIBLE GAS MASK.
YOUR HALLUCINOGENIC GAS DIDN'T AFFECT US AT ALL.
AND NOW I'M GOING TO LET IRON MAN HIT YOU.
HOLD ON! HOLD ON!
OKAY...I ADMIT MY GALACTUS WAS A FAKE!

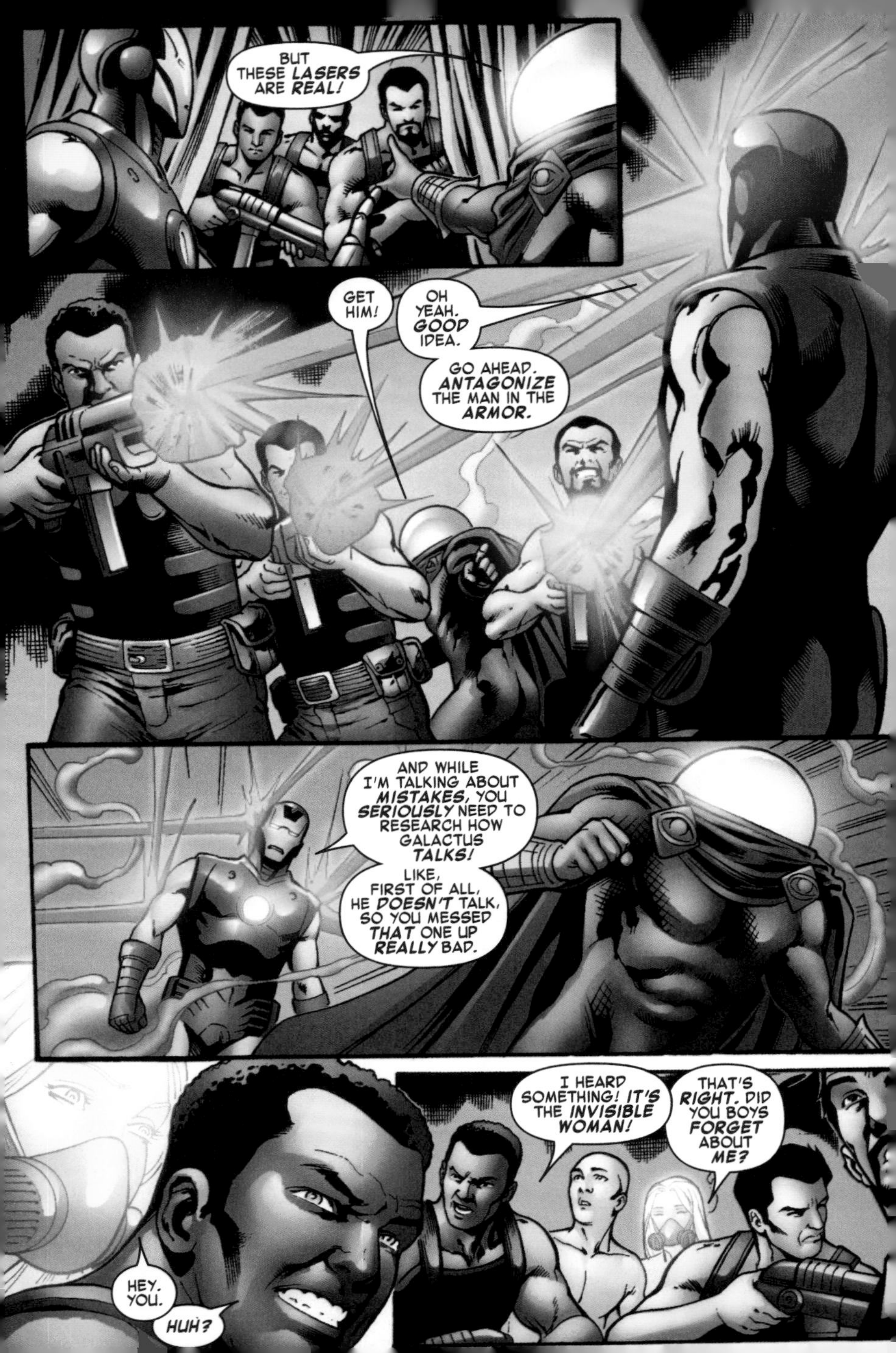

BUT THESE LASERS ARE REAL!
GET HIM!
OH YEAH. GOOD IDEA.
GO AHEAD. ANTAGONIZE THE MAN IN THE ARMOR.
AND WHILE I'M TALKING ABOUT MISTAKES, YOU SERIOUSLY NEED TO RESEARCH HOW GALACTUS TALKS!
LIKE, FIRST OF ALL, HE DOESN'T TALK, SO YOU MESSED THAT ONE UP REALLY BAD.
I HEARD SOMETHING! IT'S THE INVISIBLE WOMAN!
THAT'S RIGHT. DID YOU BOYS FORGET ABOUT ME?
HEY. YOU.
HUH?

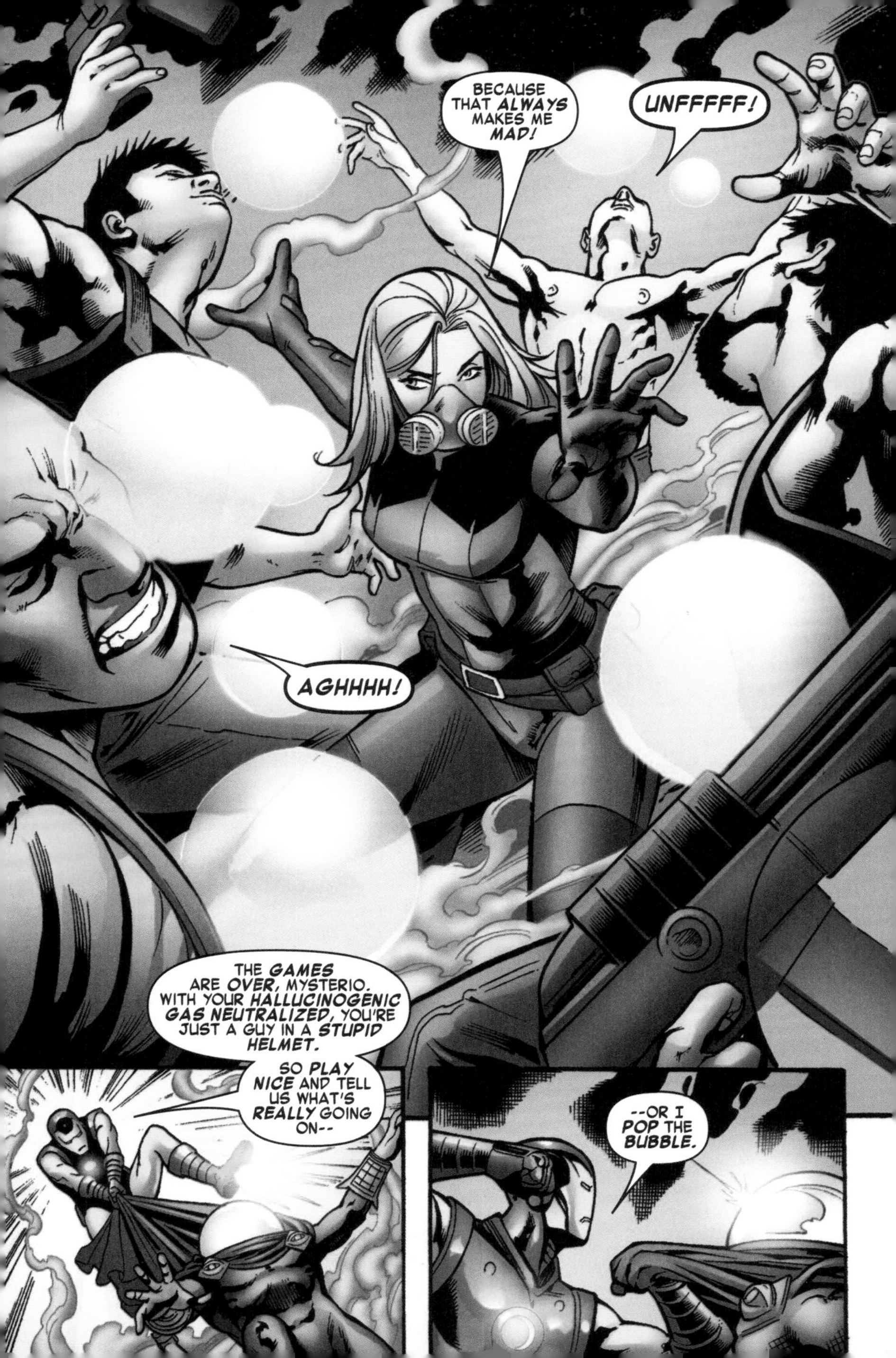
BECAUSE THAT ALWAYS MAKES ME MAD!
UNFFFFF!
AGHHHH!
THE GAMES ARE OVER, MYSTERIO. WITH YOUR HALLUCINOGENIC GAS NEUTRALIZED, YOU'RE JUST A GUY IN A STUPID HELMET.
SO PLAY NICE AND TELL US WHAT'S REALLY GOING ON--
--OR I POP THE BUBBLE.

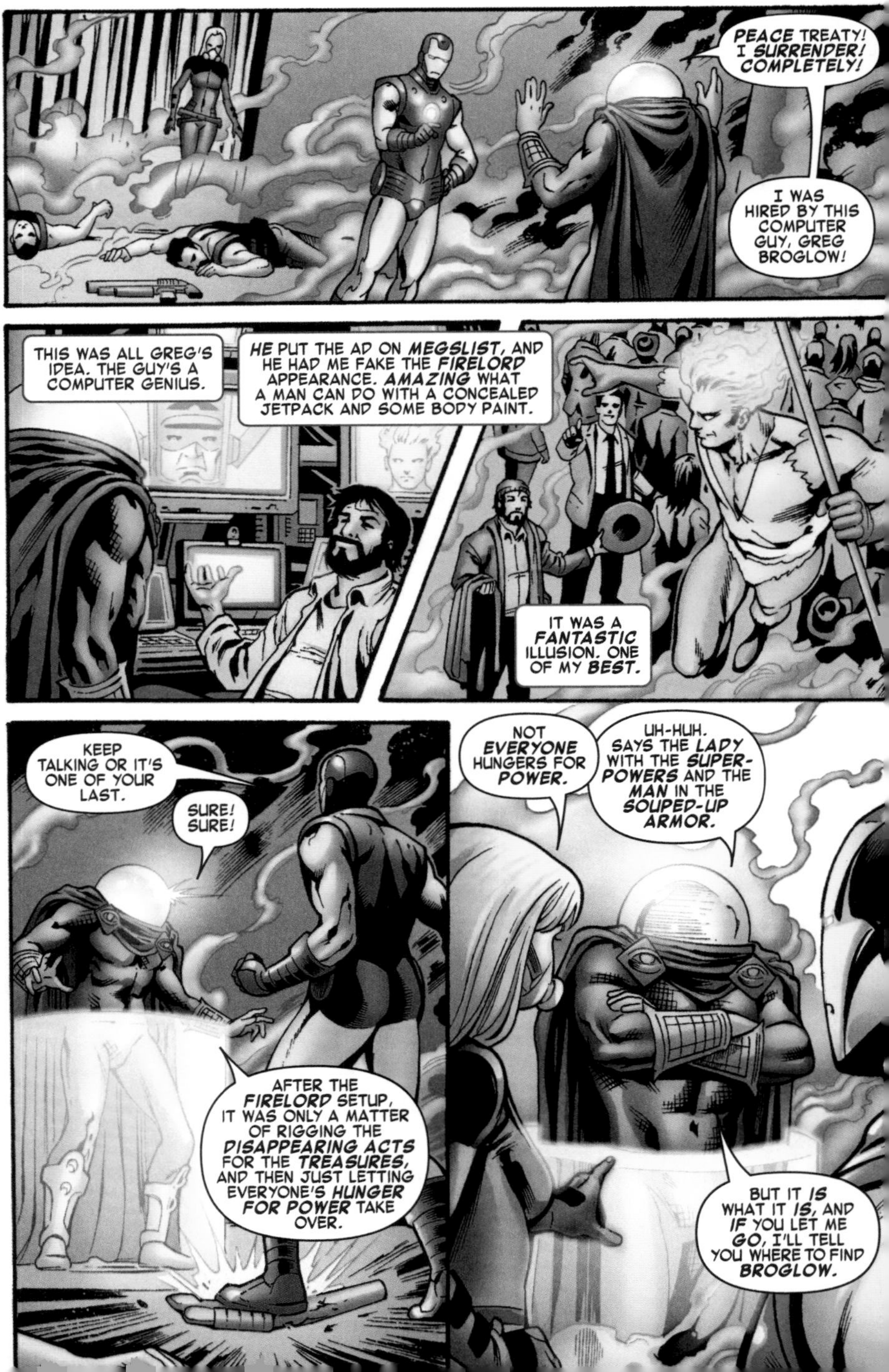
PEACE TREATY! I SURRENDER! COMPLETELY!
I WAS HIRED BY THIS COMPUTER GUY, GREG BROGLOW!
THIS WAS ALL GREG'S IDEA. THE GUY'S A COMPUTER GENIUS.
HE PUT THE AD ON MEGSLIST, AND HE HAD ME FAKE THE FIRELORD APPEARANCE. AMAZING WHAT A MAN CAN DO WITH A CONCEALED JETPACK AND SOME BODY PAINT.
IT WAS A FANTASTIC ILLUSION. ONE OF MY BEST.
KEEP TALKING OR IT'S ONE OF YOUR LAST.
SURE! SURE!
AFTER THE FIRELORD SETUP, IT WAS ONLY A MATTER OF RIGGING THE DISAPPEARING ACTS FOR THE TREASURES, AND THEN JUST LETTING EVERYONE'S HUNGER FOR POWER TAKE OVER.
NOT EVERYONE HUNGERS FOR POWER.
UH-HUH. SAYS THE LADY WITH THE SUPER-POWERS AND THE MAN IN THE SOUPED-UP ARMOR.
BUT IT IS WHAT IT IS, AND IF YOU LET ME GO, I'LL TELL YOU WHERE TO FIND BROGLOW.

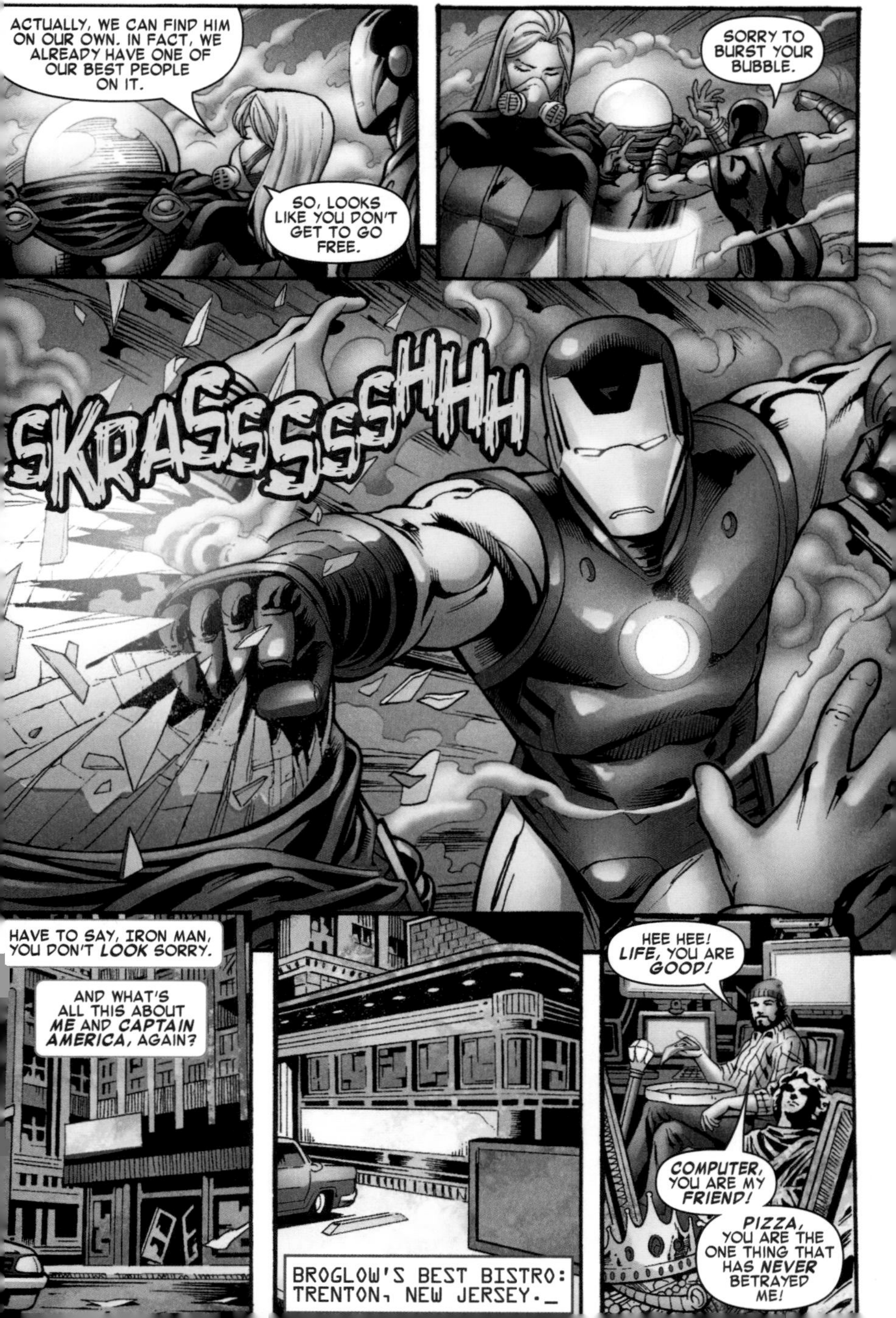
ACTUALLY, WE CAN FIND HIM ON OUR OWN. IN FACT, WE ALREADY HAVE ONE OF OUR BEST PEOPLE ON IT.
SO, LOOKS LIKE YOU DON'T GET TO GO FREE.
SORRY TO BURST YOUR BUBBLE.
SKRASSSSSSHHH
HAVE TO SAY, IRON MAN, YOU DON'T LOOK SORRY.
AND WHAT'S ALL THIS ABOUT ME AND CAPTAIN AMERICA, AGAIN?
BROGLOW'S BEST BISTRO: TRENTON, NEW JERSEY._
HEE HEE! LIFE, YOU ARE GOOD!
COMPUTER, YOU ARE MY FRIEND!
PIZZA, YOU ARE THE ONE THING THAT HAS NEVER BETRAYED ME!

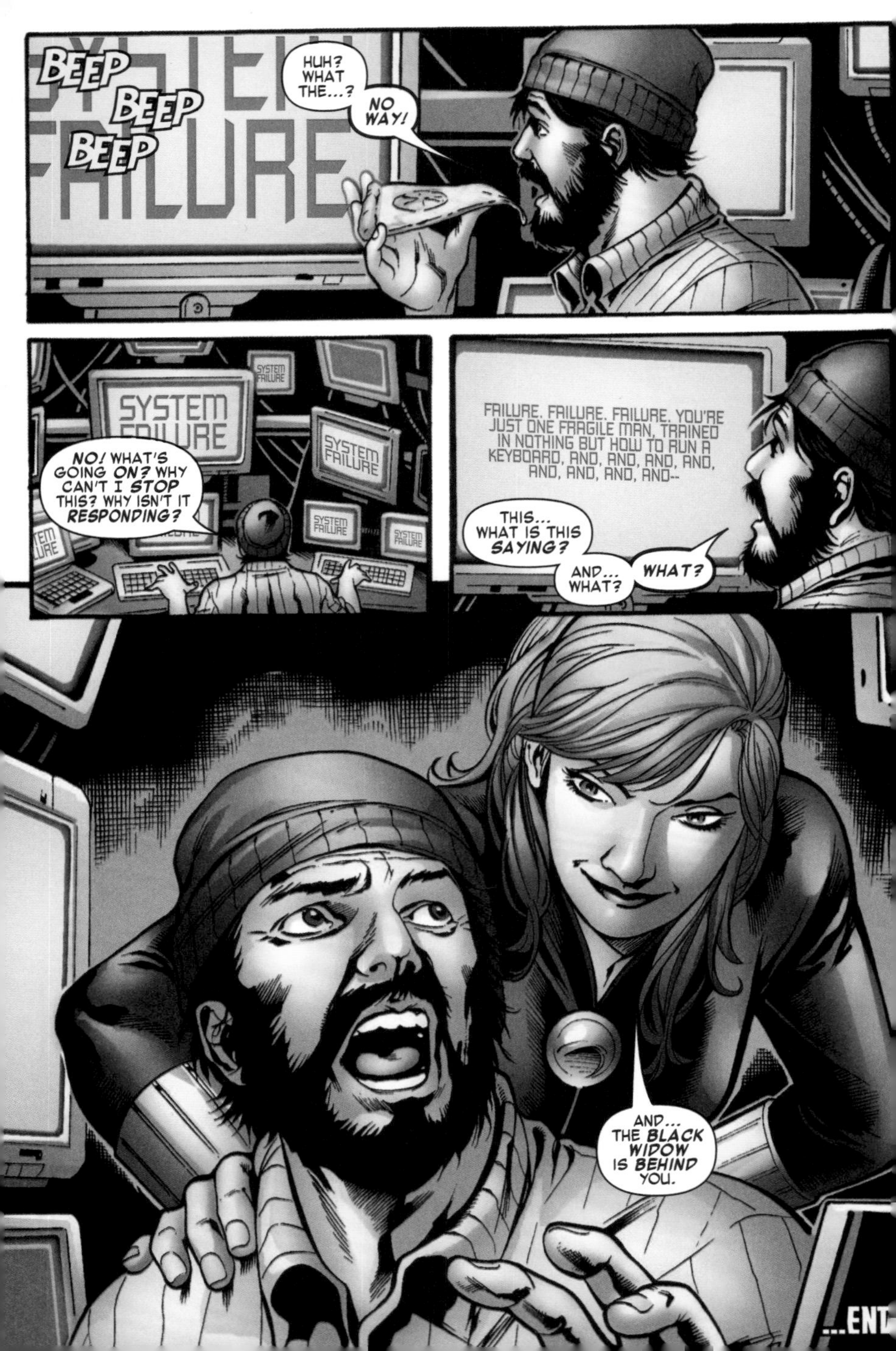
BEEP
BEEP
BEEP
HUH? WHAT THE...?
NO WAY!
SYSTEM FAILURE
SYSTEM FAILURE
SYSTEM FAILURE
NO! WHAT'S GOING ON? WHY CAN'T I STOP THIS? WHY ISN'T IT RESPONDING?
SYSTEM FAILURE
SYSTEM FAILURE
FAILURE. FAILURE. FAILURE. YOU'RE JUST ONE FRAGILE MAN, TRAINED IN NOTHING BUT HOW TO RUN A KEYBOARD, AND, AND, AND, AND, AND, AND, AND, AND--
THIS... WHAT IS THIS SAYING?
AND... WHAT?
WHAT?
AND... THE BLACK WIDOW IS BEHIND YOU.
...EN

#3

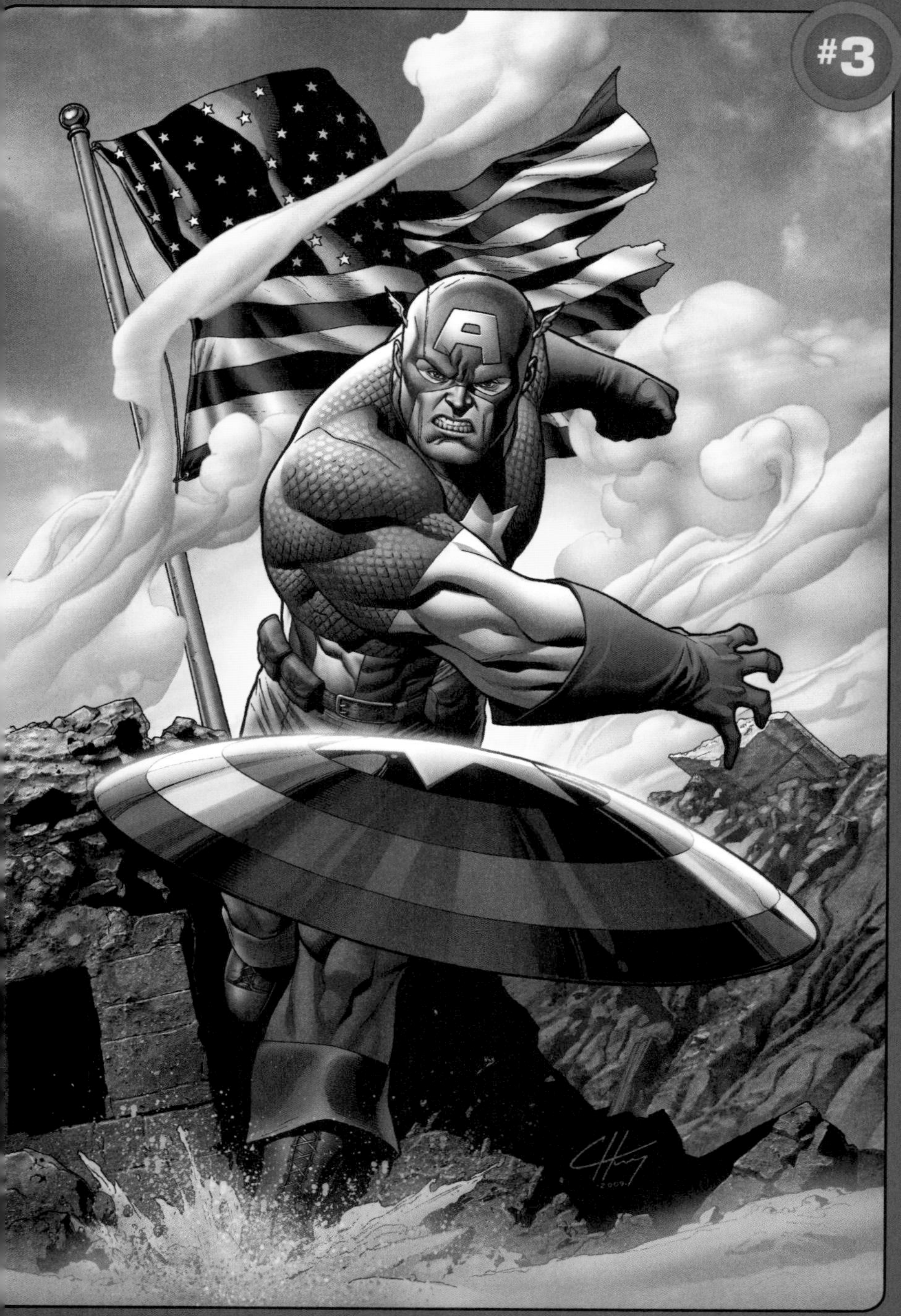

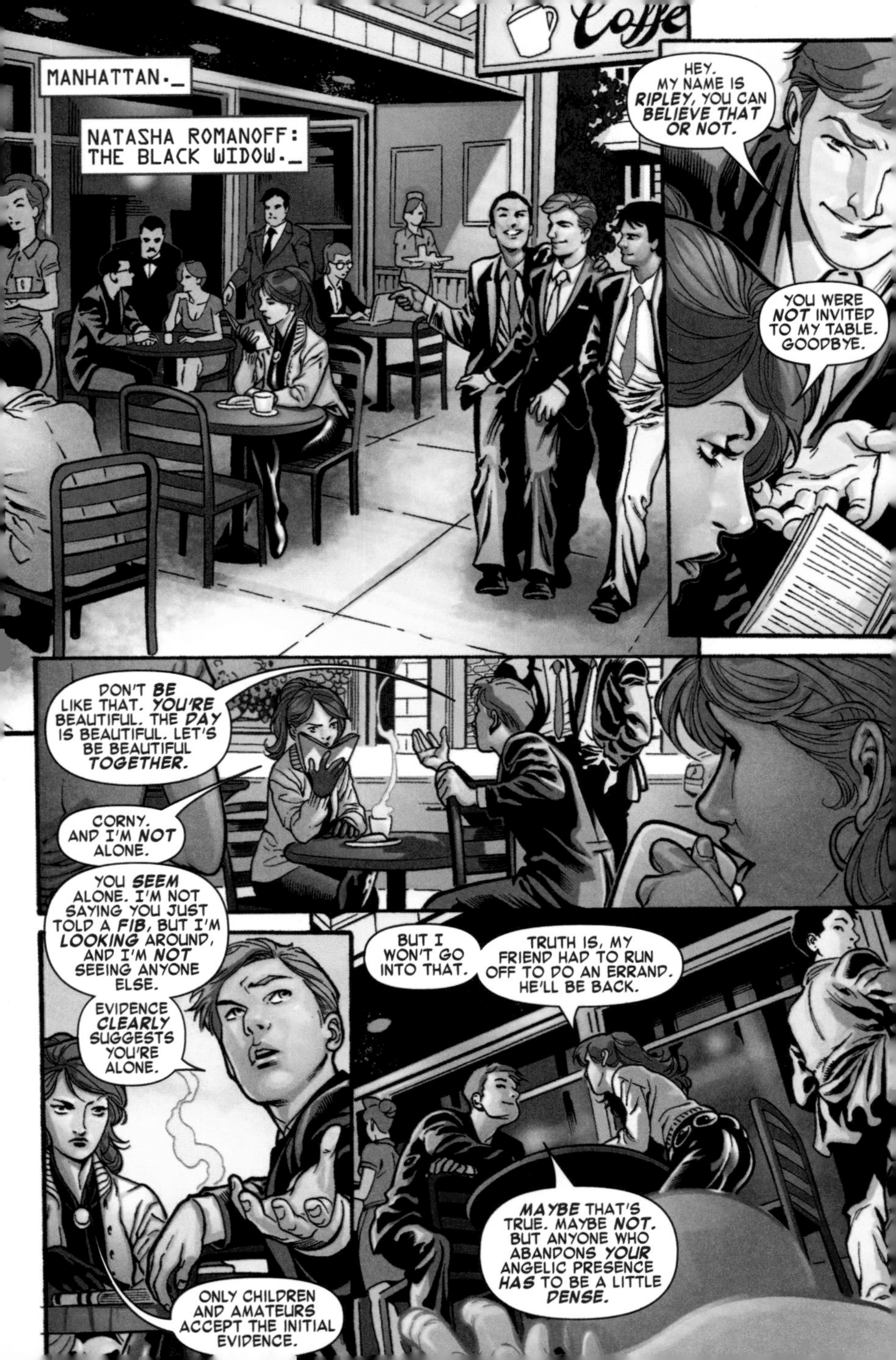

Coffe
MANHATTAN._
NATASHA ROMANOFF: THE BLACK WIDOW._
HEY. MY NAME IS RIPLEY, YOU CAN BELIEVE THAT OR NOT.
YOU WERE NOT INVITED TO MY TABLE. GOODBYE.
DON'T BE LIKE THAT. YOU'RE BEAUTIFUL. THE DAY IS BEAUTIFUL. LET'S BE BEAUTIFUL TOGETHER.
CORNY. AND I'M NOT ALONE.
YOU SEEM ALONE. I'M NOT SAYING YOU JUST TOLD A FIB, BUT I'M LOOKING AROUND, AND I'M NOT SEEING ANYONE ELSE.
EVIDENCE CLEARLY SUGGESTS YOU'RE ALONE.
ONLY CHILDREN AND AMATEURS ACCEPT THE INITIAL EVIDENCE.
BUT I WON'T GO INTO THAT.
TRUTH IS, MY FRIEND HAD TO RUN OFF TO DO AN ERRAND. HE'LL BE BACK.
MAYBE THAT'S TRUE. MAYBE NOT. BUT ANYONE WHO ABANDONS YOUR ANGELIC PRESENCE HAS TO BE A LITTLE DENSE.

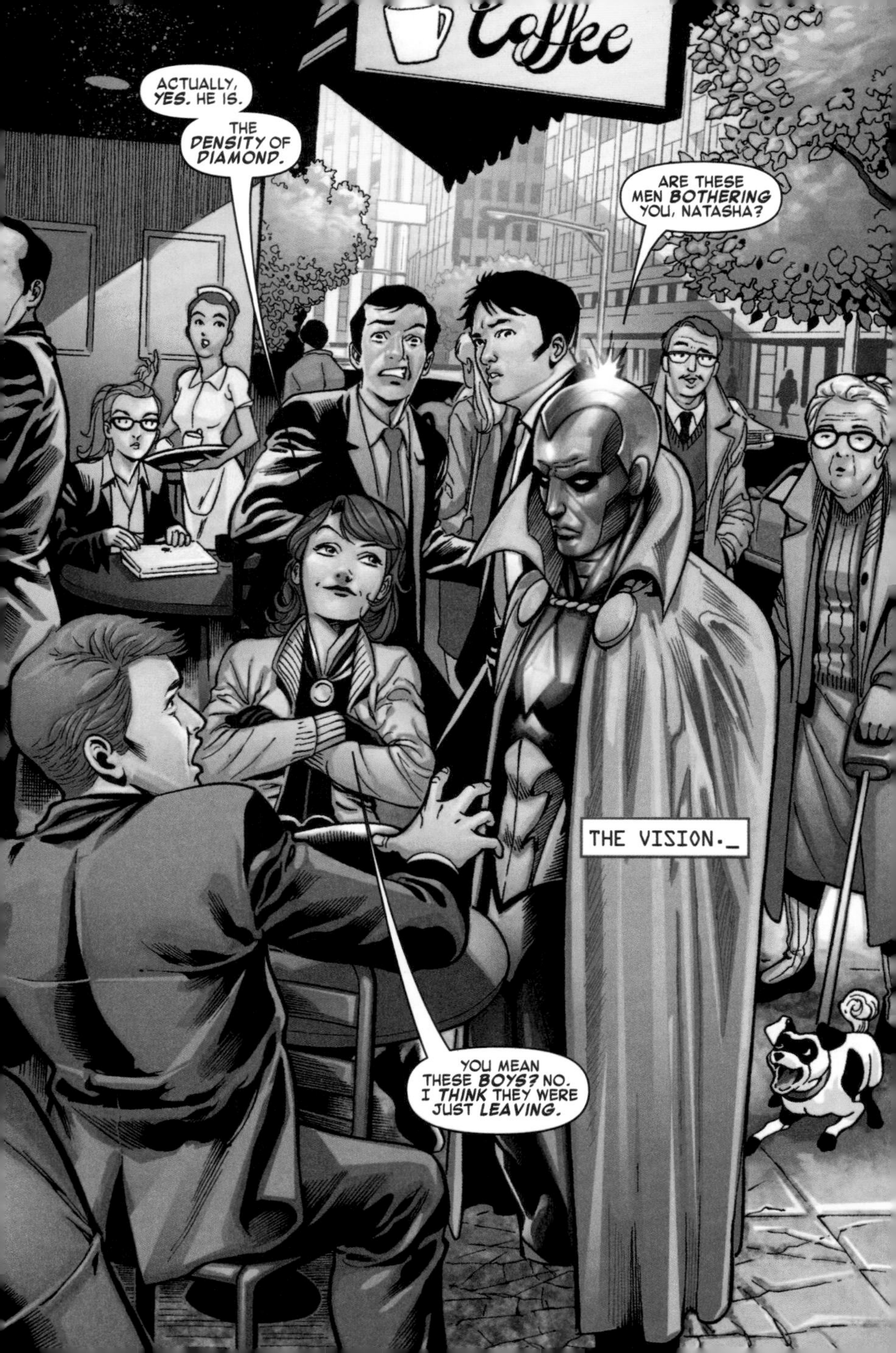
Coffee
ACTUALLY, YES. HE IS.
THE DENSITY OF DIAMOND.
ARE THESE MEN BOTHERING YOU, NATASHA?
THE VISION._
YOU MEAN THESE BOYS? NO. I THINK THEY WERE JUST LEAVING.

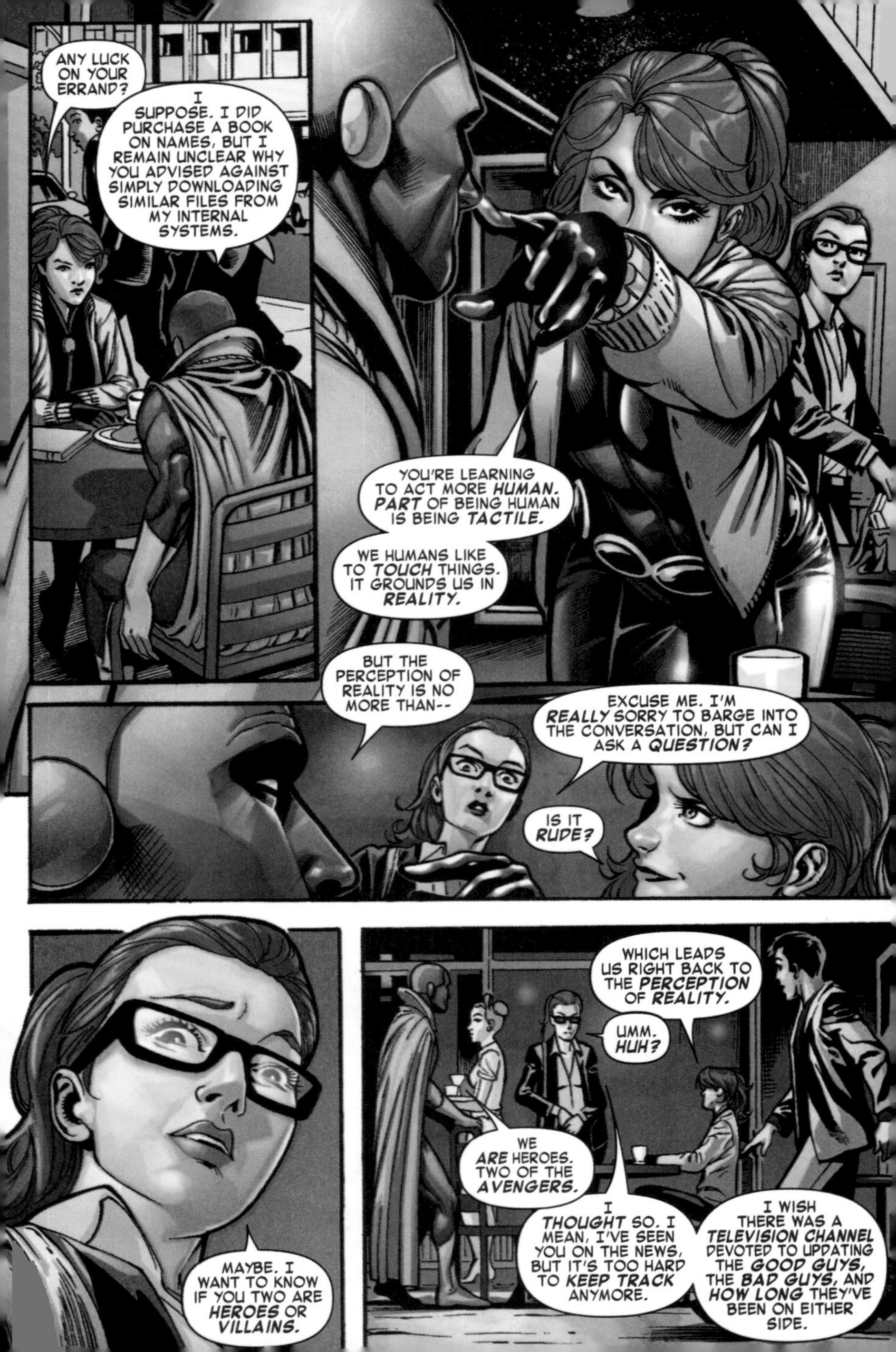
ANY LUCK ON YOUR ERRAND?
I SUPPOSE. I DID PURCHASE A BOOK ON NAMES, BUT I REMAIN UNCLEAR WHY YOU ADVISED AGAINST SIMPLY DOWNLOADING SIMILAR FILES FROM MY INTERNAL SYSTEMS.
YOU'RE LEARNING TO ACT MORE HUMAN. PART OF BEING HUMAN IS BEING TACTILE.
WE HUMANS LIKE TO TOUCH THINGS. IT GROUNDS US IN REALITY.
BUT THE PERCEPTION OF REALITY IS NO MORE THAN--
EXCUSE ME. I'M REALLY SORRY TO BARGE INTO THE CONVERSATION, BUT CAN I ASK A QUESTION?
IS IT RUDE?
MAYBE. I WANT TO KNOW IF YOU TWO ARE HEROES OR VILLAINS.
WHICH LEADS US RIGHT BACK TO THE PERCEPTION OF REALITY.
UMM. HUH?
WE ARE HEROES. TWO OF THE AVENGERS.
I THOUGHT SO. I MEAN, I'VE SEEN YOU ON THE NEWS, BUT IT'S TOO HARD TO KEEP TRACK ANYMORE.
I WISH THERE WAS A TELEVISION CHANNEL DEVOTED TO UPDATING THE GOOD GUYS, THE BAD GUYS, AND HOW LONG THEY'VE BEEN ON EITHER SIDE.

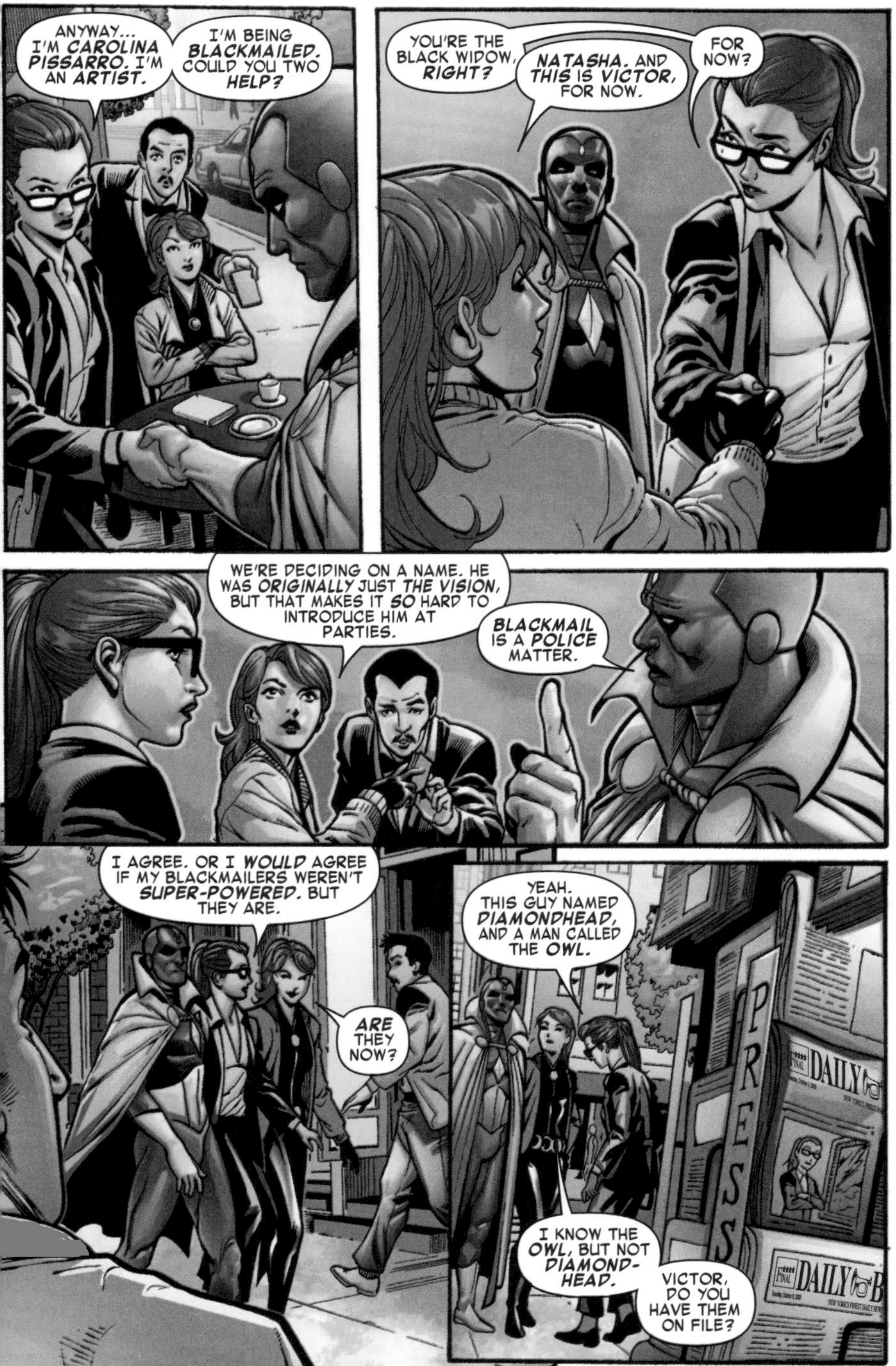
ANYWAY... I'M CAROLINA PISSARRO. I'M AN ARTIST.
I'M BEING BLACKMAILED. COULD YOU TWO HELP?
YOU'RE THE BLACK WIDOW, RIGHT?
NATASHA. AND THIS IS VICTOR, FOR NOW.
FOR NOW?
WE'RE DECIDING ON A NAME. HE WAS ORIGINALLY JUST THE VISION, BUT THAT MAKES IT SO HARD TO INTRODUCE HIM AT PARTIES.
BLACKMAIL IS A POLICE MATTER.
I AGREE. OR I WOULD AGREE IF MY BLACKMAILERS WEREN'T SUPER-POWERED. BUT THEY ARE.
ARE THEY NOW?
YEAH. THIS GUY NAMED DIAMONDHEAD, AND A MAN CALLED THE OWL.
PRESS
DAILY
I KNOW THE OWL, BUT NOT DIAMOND-HEAD.
VICTOR, DO YOU HAVE THEM ON FILE?

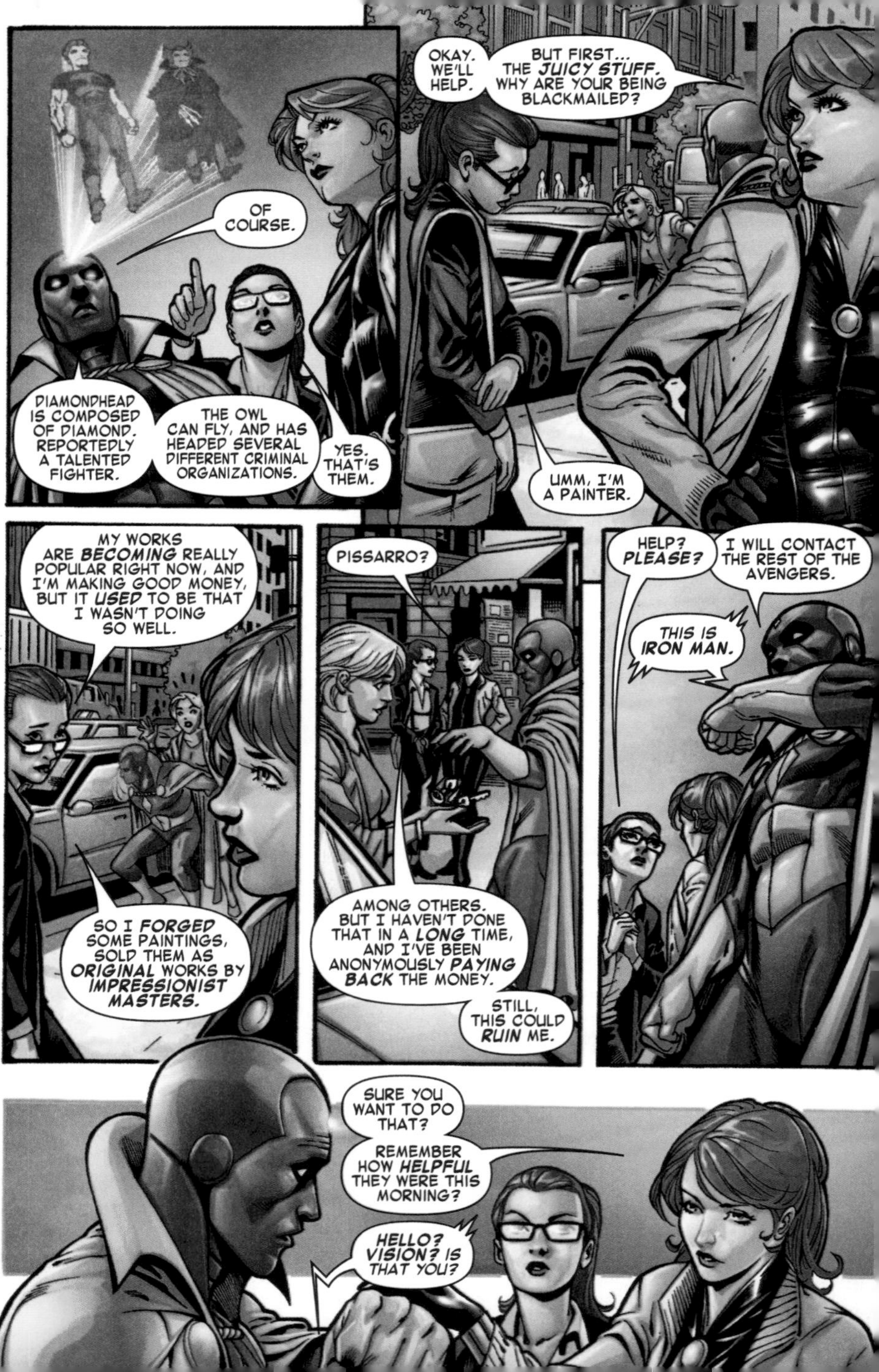
OF COURSE.
DIAMONDHEAD IS COMPOSED OF DIAMOND. REPORTEDLY A TALENTED FIGHTER.
THE OWL CAN FLY, AND HAS HEADED SEVERAL DIFFERENT CRIMINAL ORGANIZATIONS.
YES. THAT'S THEM.
OKAY. WE'LL HELP.
BUT FIRST... THE JUICY STUFF. WHY ARE YOUR BEING BLACKMAILED?
UMM, I'M A PAINTER.
MY WORKS ARE BECOMING REALLY POPULAR RIGHT NOW, AND I'M MAKING GOOD MONEY, BUT IT USED TO BE THAT I WASN'T DOING SO WELL.
SO I FORGED SOME PAINTINGS, SOLD THEM AS ORIGINAL WORKS BY IMPRESSIONIST MASTERS.
PISSARRO?
AMONG OTHERS. BUT I HAVEN'T DONE THAT IN A LONG TIME, AND I'VE BEEN ANONYMOUSLY PAYING BACK THE MONEY.
STILL, THIS COULD RUIN ME.
HELP? PLEASE?
I WILL CONTACT THE REST OF THE AVENGERS.
THIS IS IRON MAN.
SURE YOU WANT TO DO THAT?
REMEMBER HOW HELPFUL THEY WERE THIS MORNING?
HELLO? VISION? IS THAT YOU?

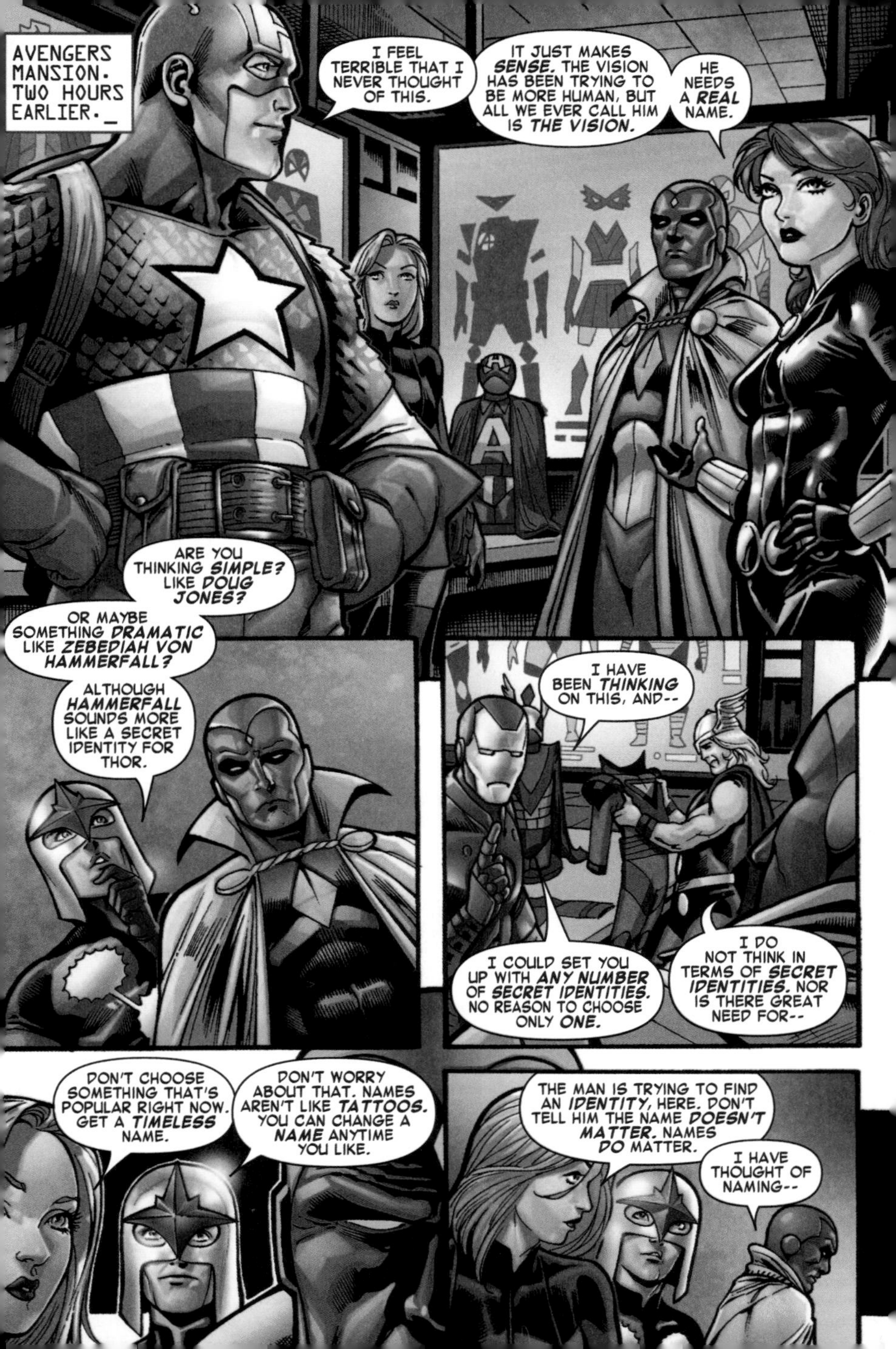

AVENGERS MANSION. TWO HOURS EARLIER._
I FEEL TERRIBLE THAT I NEVER THOUGHT OF THIS.
IT JUST MAKES SENSE. THE VISION HAS BEEN TRYING TO BE MORE HUMAN, BUT ALL WE EVER CALL HIM IS THE VISION.
HE NEEDS A REAL NAME.
ARE YOU THINKING SIMPLE? LIKE DOUG JONES?
OR MAYBE SOMETHING DRAMATIC LIKE ZEBEDIAH VON HAMMERFALL?
ALTHOUGH HAMMERFALL SOUNDS MORE LIKE A SECRET IDENTITY FOR THOR.
I HAVE BEEN THINKING ON THIS, AND--
I COULD SET YOU UP WITH ANY NUMBER OF SECRET IDENTITIES. NO REASON TO CHOOSE ONLY ONE.
I DO NOT THINK IN TERMS OF SECRET IDENTITIES. NOR IS THERE GREAT NEED FOR--
DON'T CHOOSE SOMETHING THAT'S POPULAR RIGHT NOW. GET A TIMELESS NAME.
DON'T WORRY ABOUT THAT. NAMES AREN'T LIKE TATTOOS. YOU CAN CHANGE A NAME ANYTIME YOU LIKE.
THE MAN IS TRYING TO FIND AN IDENTITY, HERE. DON'T TELL HIM THE NAME DOESN'T MATTER. NAMES DO MATTER.
I HAVE THOUGHT OF NAMING--

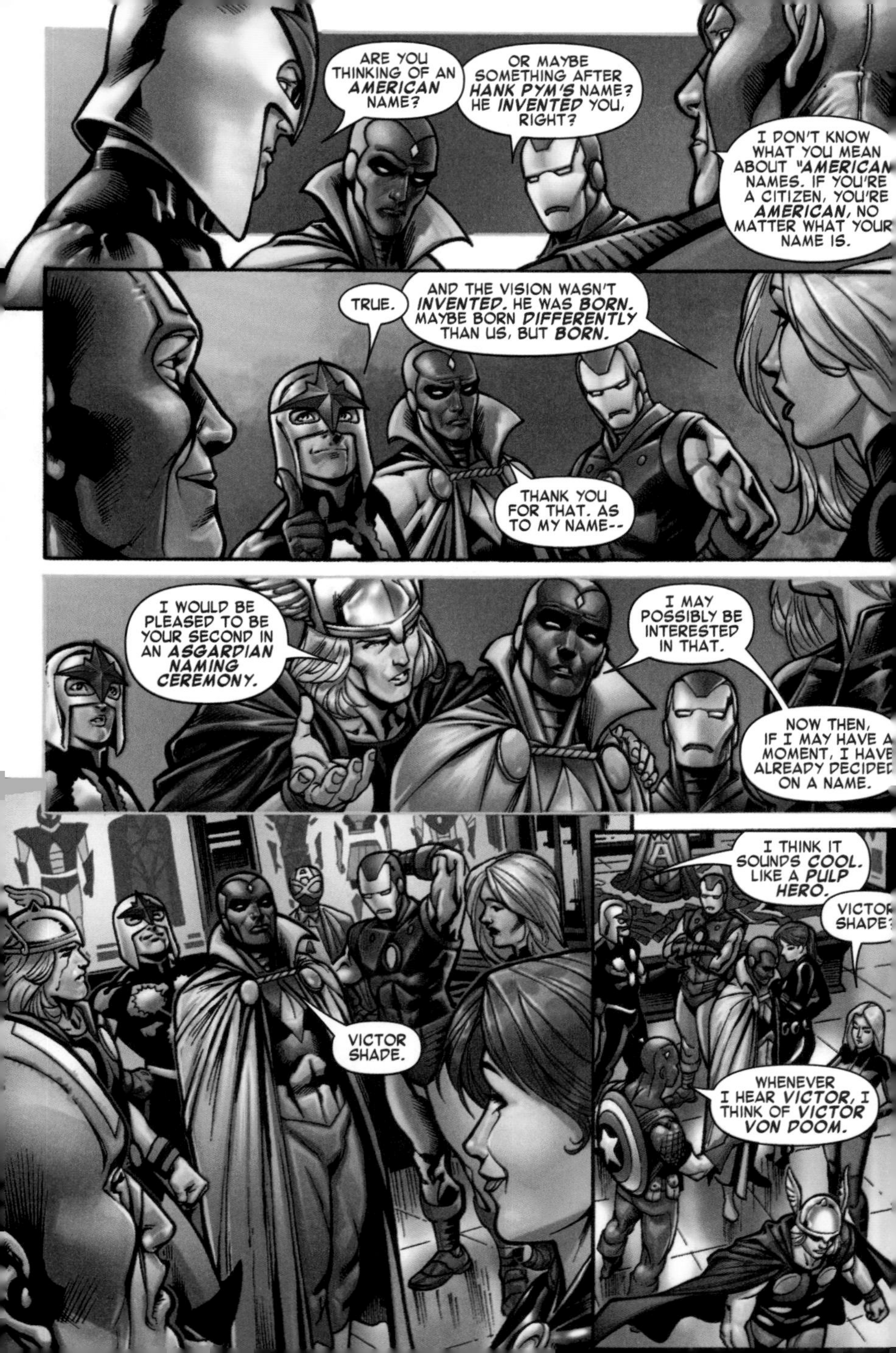
ARE YOU THINKING OF AN AMERICAN NAME?
OR MAYBE SOMETHING AFTER HANK PYM'S NAME? HE INVENTED YOU, RIGHT?
I DON'T KNOW WHAT YOU MEAN ABOUT "AMERICAN NAMES. IF YOU'RE A CITIZEN, YOU'RE AMERICAN, NO MATTER WHAT YOUR NAME IS.
TRUE.
AND THE VISION WASN'T INVENTED. HE WAS BORN. MAYBE BORN DIFFERENTLY THAN US, BUT BORN.
THANK YOU FOR THAT. AS TO MY NAME--
I WOULD BE PLEASED TO BE YOUR SECOND IN AN ASGARDIAN NAMING CEREMONY.
I MAY POSSIBLY BE INTERESTED IN THAT.
NOW THEN, IF I MAY HAVE A MOMENT, I HAVE ALREADY DECIDED ON A NAME.
VICTOR SHADE.
I THINK IT SOUNDS COOL. LIKE A PULP HERO.
VICTOR SHADE?
WHENEVER I HEAR VICTOR, I THINK OF VICTOR VON DOOM.

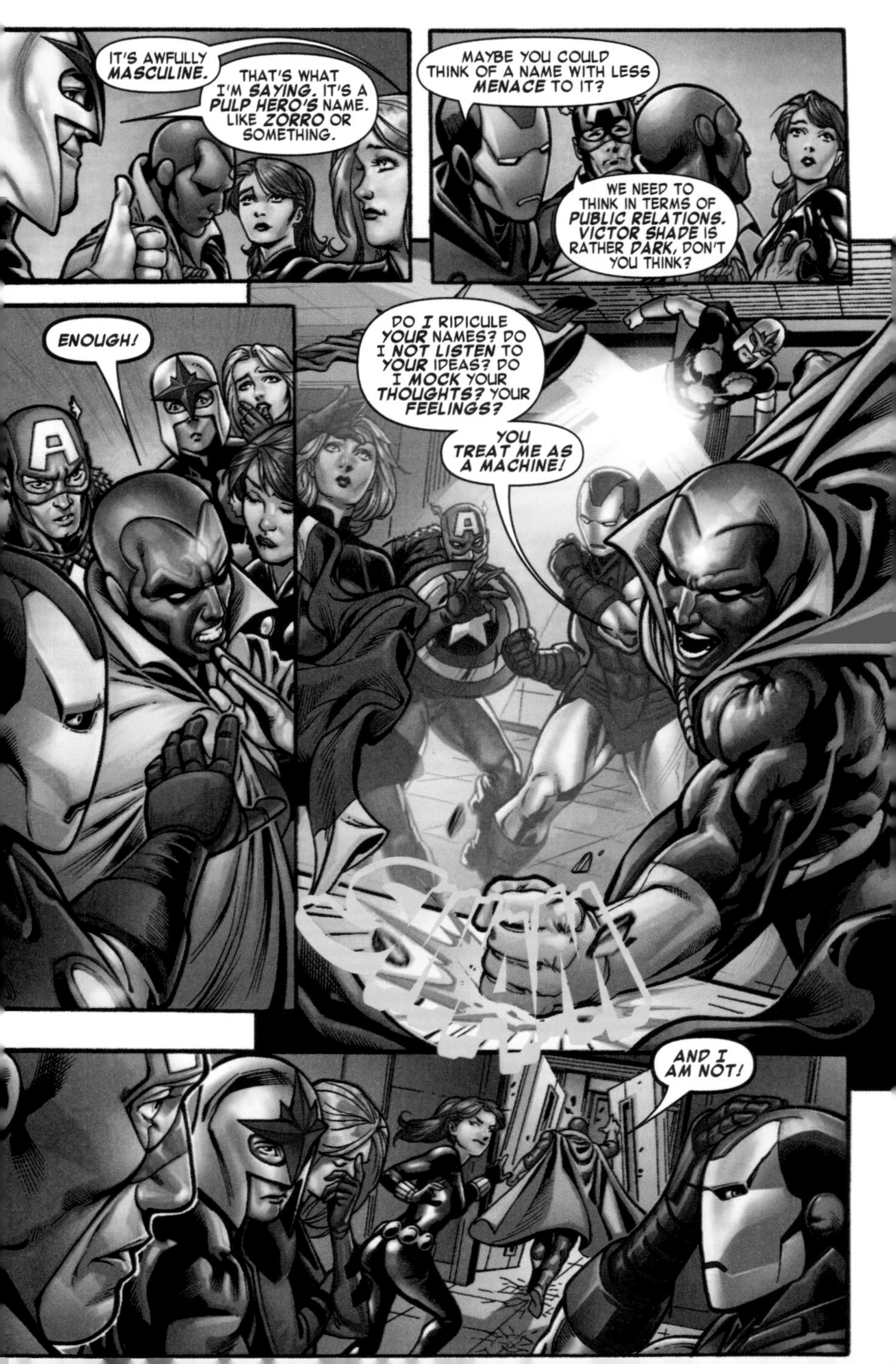
IT'S AWFULLY MASCULINE.
THAT'S WHAT I'M SAYING. IT'S A PULP HERO'S NAME. LIKE ZORRO OR SOMETHING.
MAYBE YOU COULD THINK OF A NAME WITH LESS MENACE TO IT?
WE NEED TO THINK IN TERMS OF PUBLIC RELATIONS. VICTOR SHADE IS RATHER DARK, DON'T YOU THINK?
ENOUGH!
DO I RIDICULE YOUR NAMES? DO I NOT LISTEN TO YOUR IDEAS? DO I MOCK YOUR THOUGHTS? YOUR FEELINGS?
YOU TREAT ME AS A MACHINE!
AND I AM NOT!

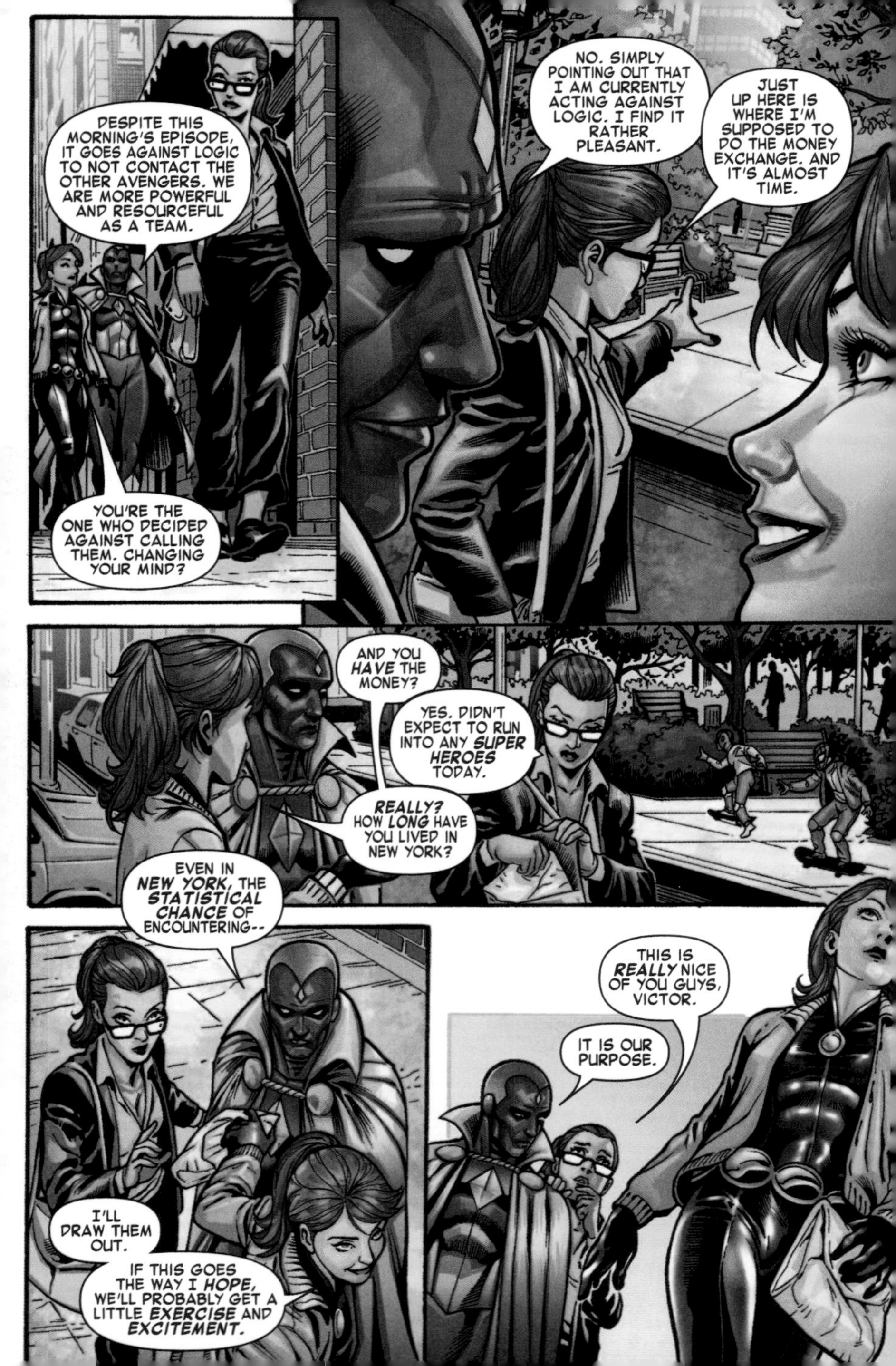
DESPITE THIS MORNING'S EPISODE, IT GOES AGAINST LOGIC TO NOT CONTACT THE OTHER AVENGERS. WE ARE MORE POWERFUL AND RESOURCEFUL AS A TEAM.
YOU'RE THE ONE WHO DECIDED AGAINST CALLING THEM. CHANGING YOUR MIND?
NO. SIMPLY POINTING OUT THAT I AM CURRENTLY ACTING AGAINST LOGIC. I FIND IT RATHER PLEASANT.
JUST UP HERE IS WHERE I'M SUPPOSED TO DO THE MONEY EXCHANGE. AND IT'S ALMOST TIME.
AND YOU HAVE THE MONEY?
YES. DIDN'T EXPECT TO RUN INTO ANY SUPER HEROES TODAY.
REALLY? HOW LONG HAVE YOU LIVED IN NEW YORK?
EVEN IN NEW YORK, THE STATISTICAL CHANCE OF ENCOUNTERING--
I'LL DRAW THEM OUT.
IF THIS GOES THE WAY I HOPE, WE'LL PROBABLY GET A LITTLE EXERCISE AND EXCITEMENT.
THIS IS REALLY NICE OF YOU GUYS, VICTOR.
IT IS OUR PURPOSE.

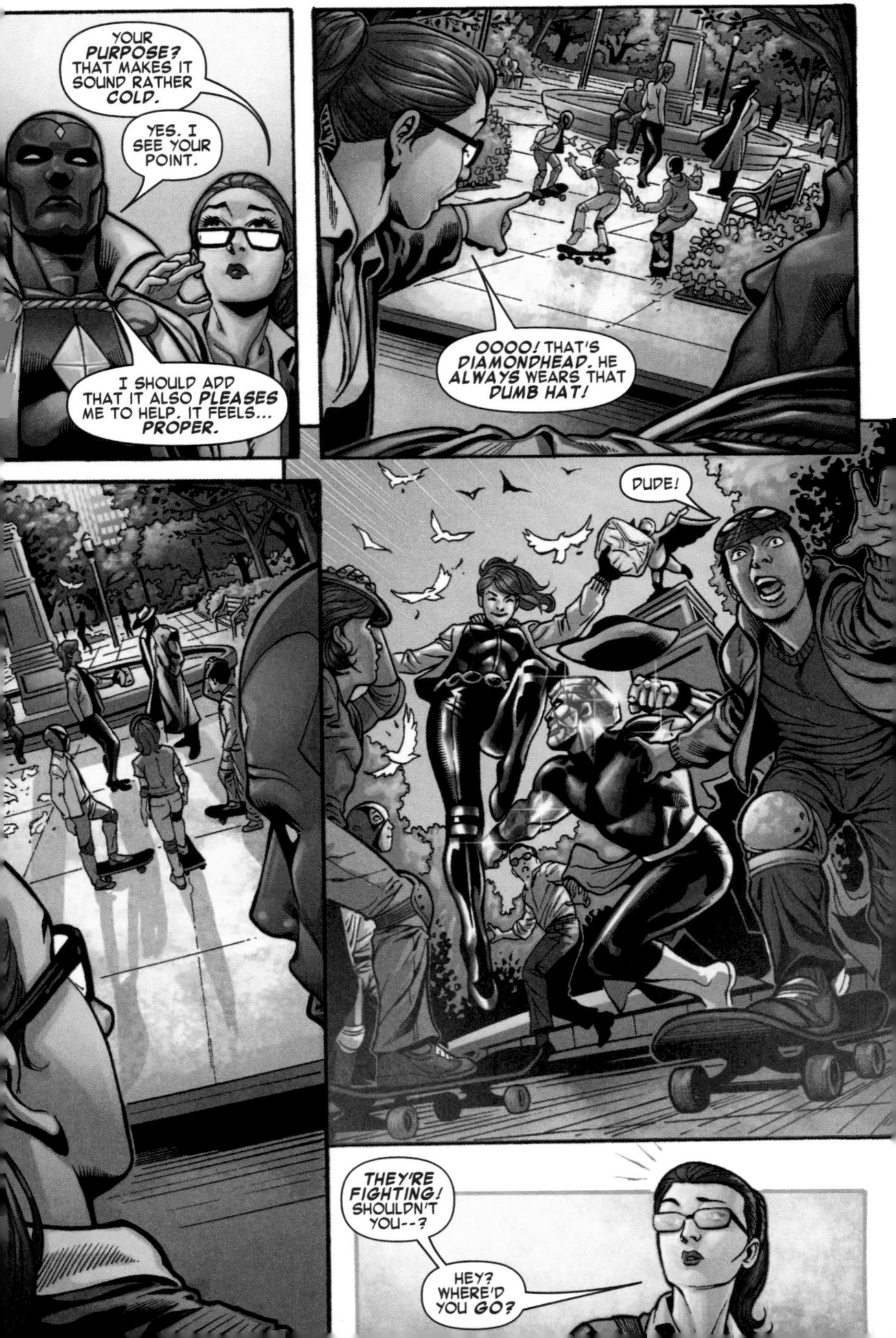

YOUR PURPOSE? THAT MAKES IT SOUND RATHER COLD.
YES. I SEE YOUR POINT.
I SHOULD ADD THAT IT ALSO PLEASES ME TO HELP. IT FEELS... PROPER.
OOOO! THAT'S DIAMONDHEAD. HE ALWAYS WEARS THAT DUMB HAT!
DUDE!
THEY'RE FIGHTING! SHOULDN'T YOU--?
HEY? WHERE'D YOU GO?

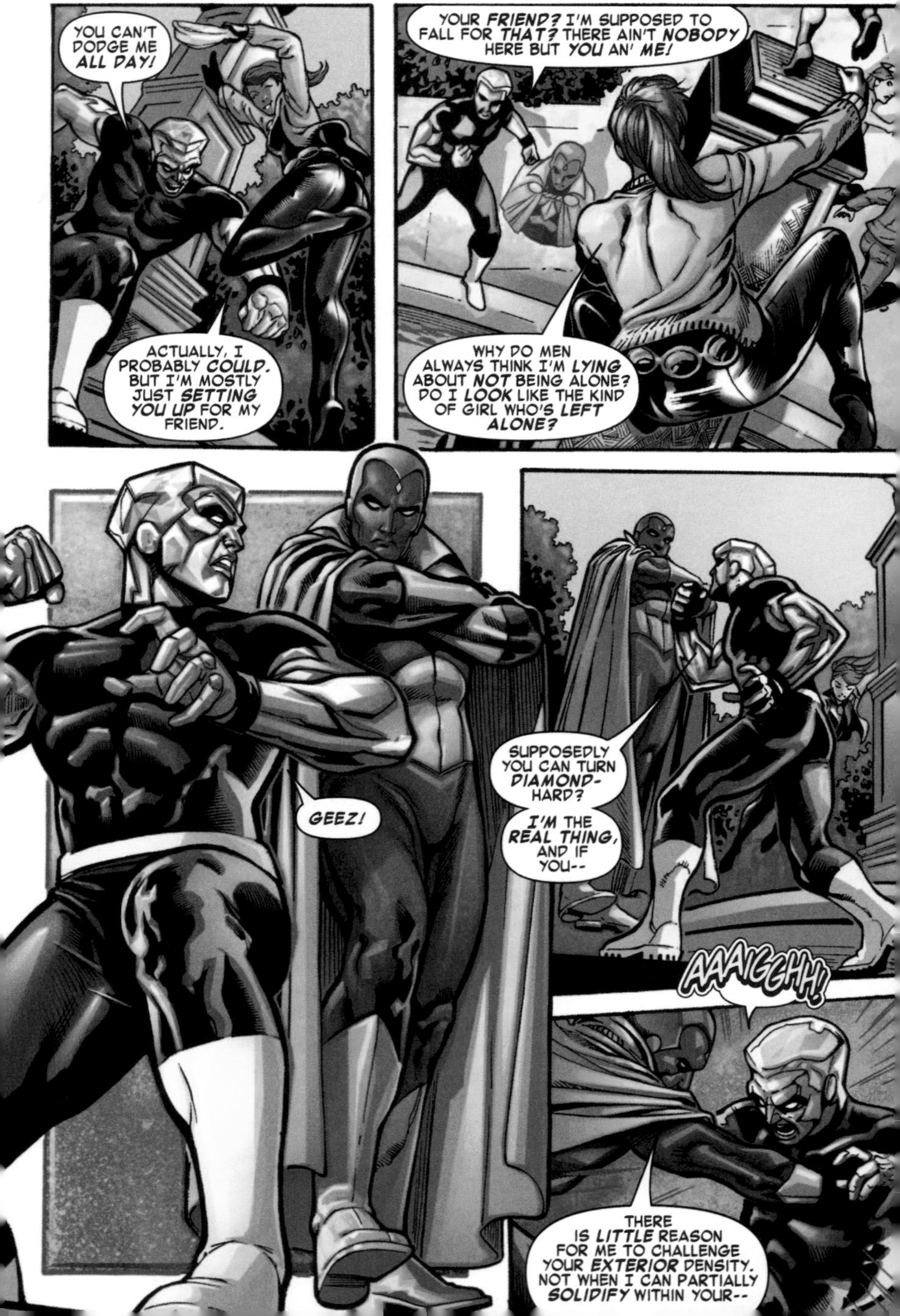
YOU CAN'T DODGE ME ALL DAY!
ACTUALLY, I PROBABLY COULD. BUT I'M MOSTLY JUST SETTING YOU UP FOR MY FRIEND.
YOUR FRIEND? I'M SUPPOSED TO FALL FOR THAT? THERE AIN'T NOBODY HERE BUT YOU AN' ME!
WHY DO MEN ALWAYS THINK I'M LYING ABOUT NOT BEING ALONE? DO I LOOK LIKE THE KIND OF GIRL WHO'S LEFT ALONE?
GEEZ!
SUPPOSEDLY YOU CAN TURN DIAMOND-HARD?
I'M THE REAL THING, AND IF YOU--
AAAIGGHH!
THERE IS LITTLE REASON FOR ME TO CHALLENGE YOUR EXTERIOR DENSITY. NOT WHEN I CAN PARTIALLY SOLIDIFY WITHIN YOUR--

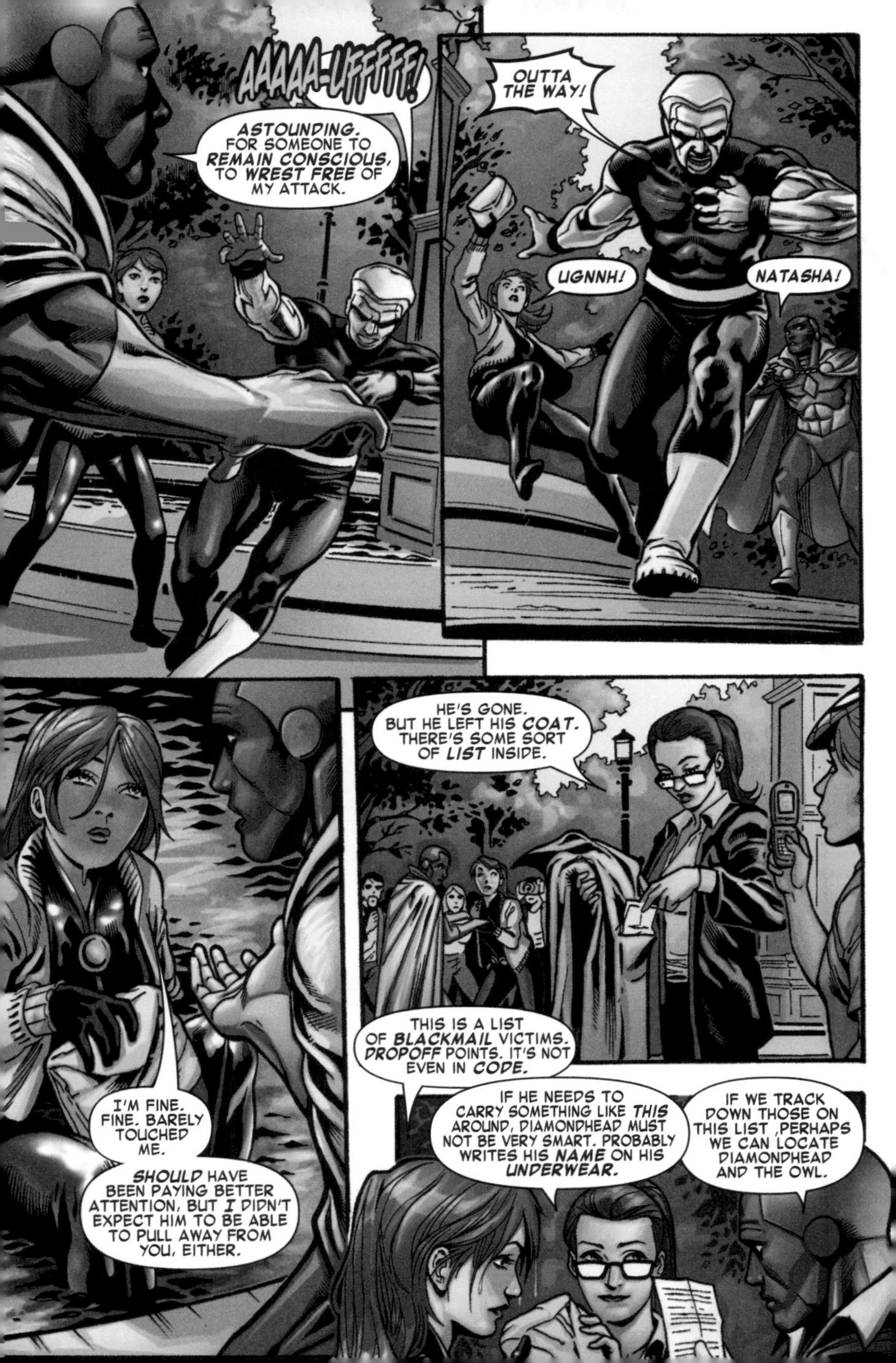
AAAAA-UFFFFF!
ASTOUNDING. FOR SOMEONE TO REMAIN CONSCIOUS, TO WREST FREE OF MY ATTACK.
OUTTA THE WAY!
UGNNH!
NATASHA!
I'M FINE. FINE. BARELY TOUCHED ME.
SHOULD HAVE BEEN PAYING BETTER ATTENTION, BUT I DIDN'T EXPECT HIM TO BE ABLE TO PULL AWAY FROM YOU, EITHER.
HE'S GONE. BUT HE LEFT HIS COAT. THERE'S SOME SORT OF LIST INSIDE.
THIS IS A LIST OF BLACKMAIL VICTIMS. DROPOFF POINTS. IT'S NOT EVEN IN CODE.
IF HE NEEDS TO CARRY SOMETHING LIKE THIS AROUND, DIAMONDHEAD MUST NOT BE VERY SMART. PROBABLY WRITES HIS NAME ON HIS UNDERWEAR.
IF WE TRACK DOWN THOSE ON THIS LIST ,PERHAPS WE CAN LOCATE DIAMONDHEAD AND THE OWL.

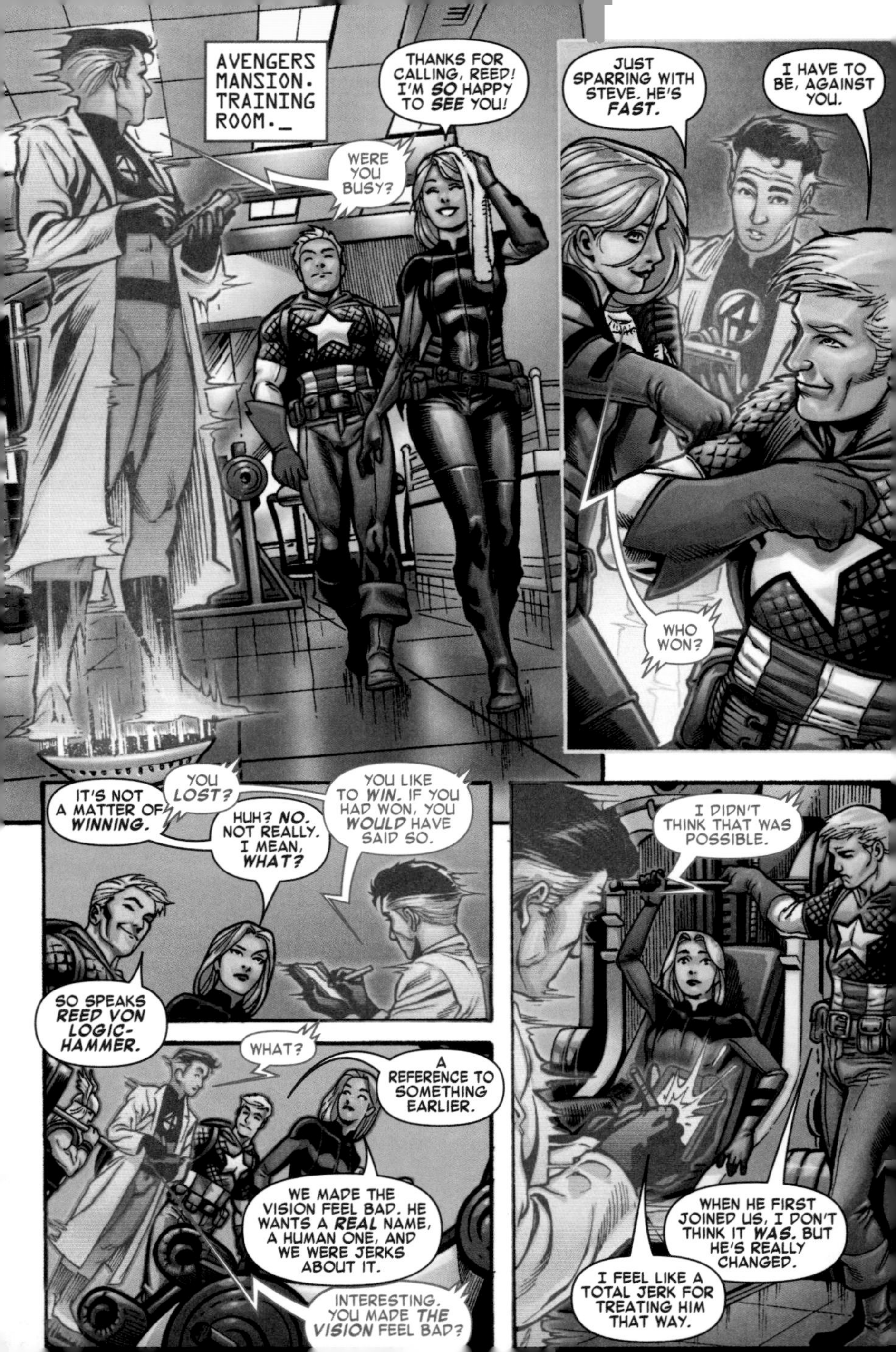
AVENGERS MANSION. TRAINING ROOM._
THANKS FOR CALLING, REED! I'M SO HAPPY TO SEE YOU!
WERE YOU BUSY?
JUST SPARRING WITH STEVE. HE'S FAST.
I HAVE TO BE, AGAINST YOU.
WHO WON?
YOU LOST?
IT'S NOT A MATTER OF WINNING.
HUH? NO. NOT REALLY. I MEAN, WHAT?
YOU LIKE TO WIN. IF YOU HAD WON, YOU WOULD HAVE SAID SO.
SO SPEAKS REED VON LOGIC-HAMMER.
WHAT?
A REFERENCE TO SOMETHING EARLIER.
WE MADE THE VISION FEEL BAD. HE WANTS A REAL NAME, A HUMAN ONE, AND WE WERE JERKS ABOUT IT.
INTERESTING. YOU MADE THE VISION FEEL BAD?
I DIDN'T THINK THAT WAS POSSIBLE.
WHEN HE FIRST JOINED US, I DON'T THINK IT WAS. BUT HE'S REALLY CHANGED.
I FEEL LIKE A TOTAL JERK FOR TREATING HIM THAT WAY.

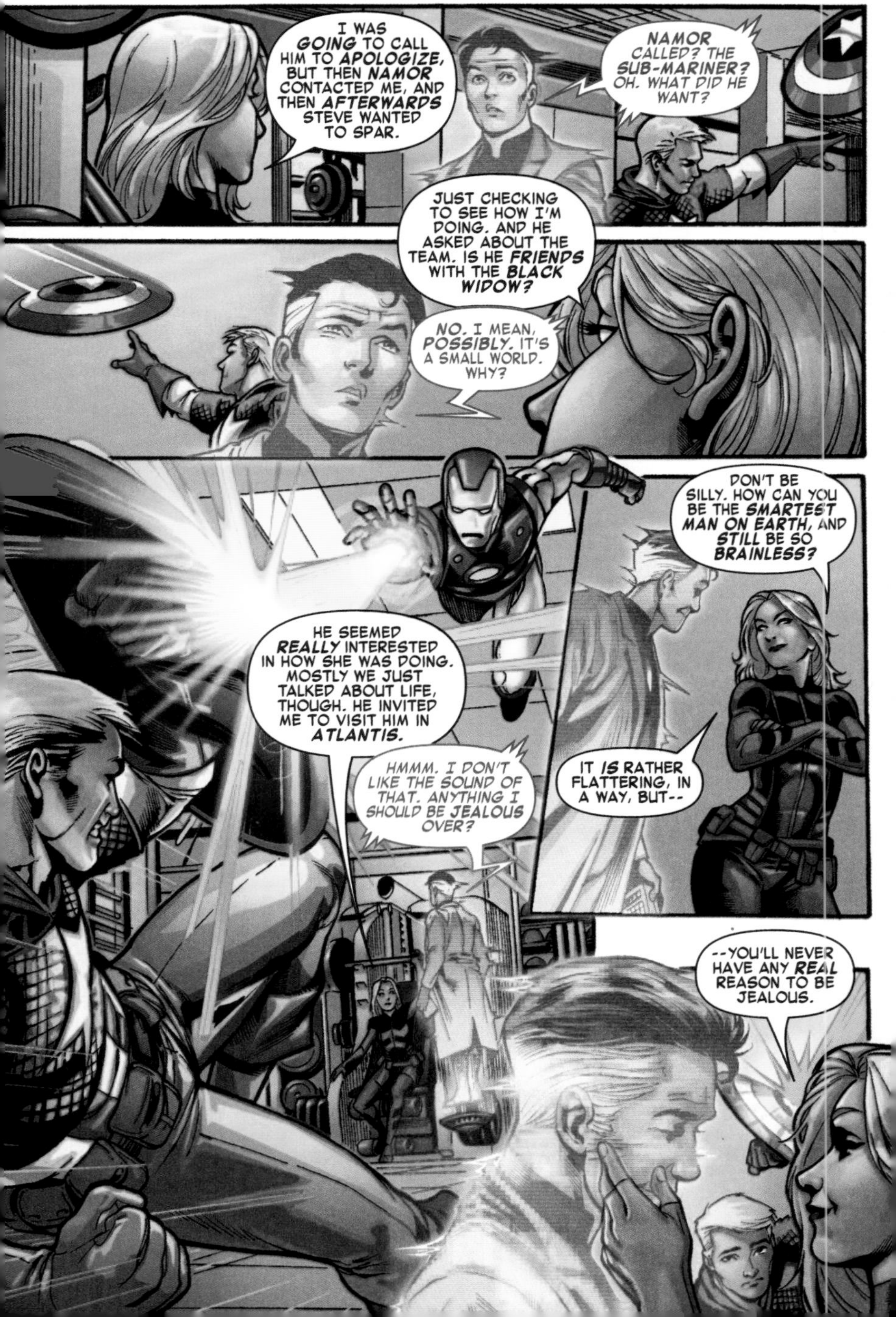
I WAS GOING TO CALL HIM TO APOLOGIZE, BUT THEN NAMOR CONTACTED ME, AND THEN AFTERWARDS STEVE WANTED TO SPAR.
NAMOR CALLED? THE SUB-MARINER? OH. WHAT DID HE WANT?
JUST CHECKING TO SEE HOW I'M DOING. AND HE ASKED ABOUT THE TEAM. IS HE FRIENDS WITH THE BLACK WIDOW?
NO. I MEAN, POSSIBLY. IT'S A SMALL WORLD. WHY?
HE SEEMED REALLY INTERESTED IN HOW SHE WAS DOING. MOSTLY WE JUST TALKED ABOUT LIFE, THOUGH. HE INVITED ME TO VISIT HIM IN ATLANTIS.
HMMM. I DON'T LIKE THE SOUND OF THAT. ANYTHING I SHOULD BE JEALOUS OVER?
DON'T BE SILLY. HOW CAN YOU BE THE SMARTEST MAN ON EARTH, AND STILL BE SO BRAINLESS?
IT IS RATHER FLATTERING, IN A WAY, BUT--
--YOU'LL NEVER HAVE ANY REAL REASON TO BE JEALOUS.

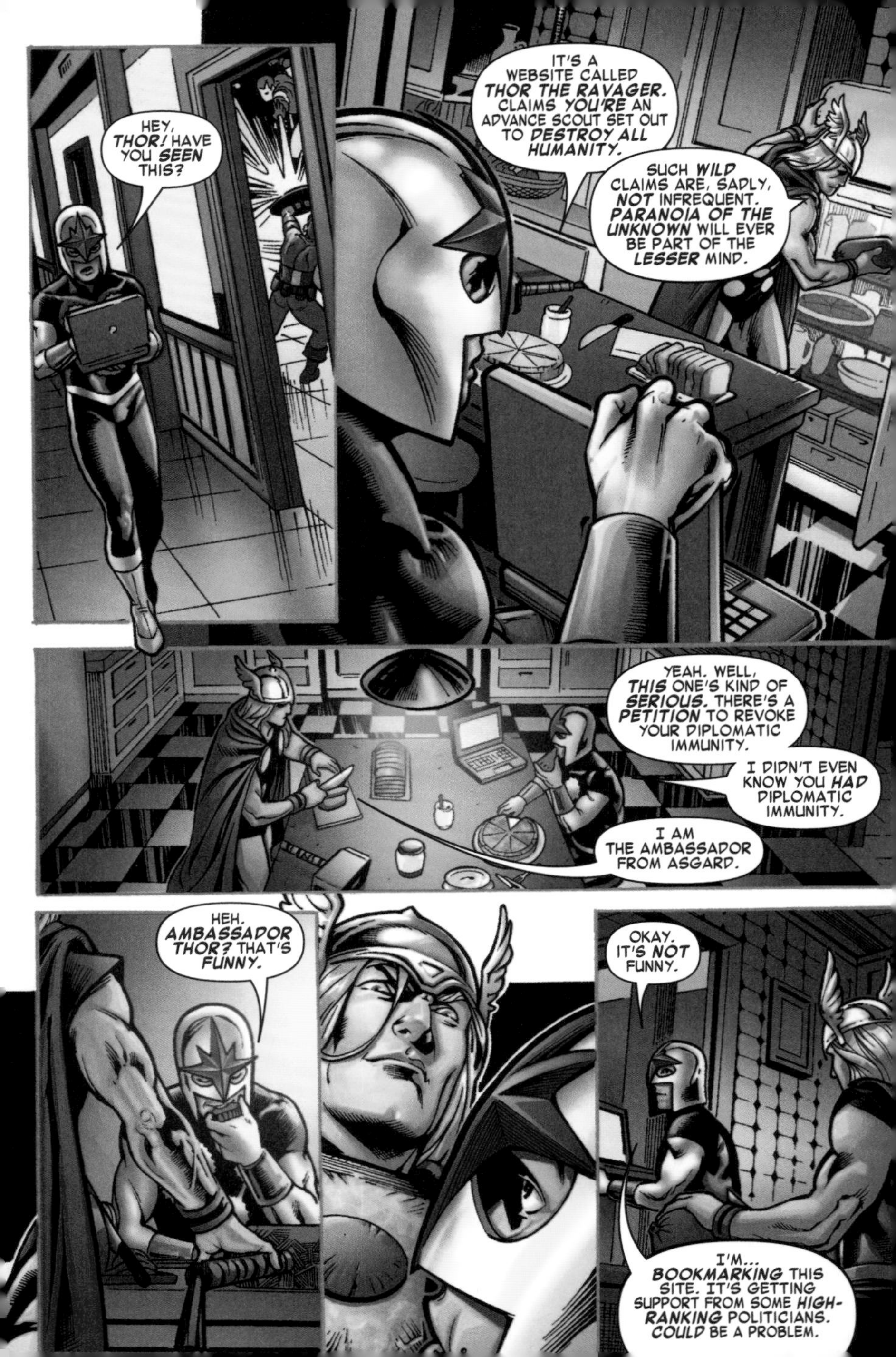
HEY, THOR! HAVE YOU SEEN THIS?
IT'S A WEBSITE CALLED THOR THE RAVAGER. CLAIMS YOU'RE AN ADVANCE SCOUT SET OUT TO DESTROY ALL HUMANITY.
SUCH WILD CLAIMS ARE, SADLY, NOT INFREQUENT. PARANOIA OF THE UNKNOWN WILL EVER BE PART OF THE LESSER MIND.
YEAH. WELL, THIS ONE'S KIND OF SERIOUS. THERE'S A PETITION TO REVOKE YOUR DIPLOMATIC IMMUNITY.
I DIDN'T EVEN KNOW YOU HAD DIPLOMATIC IMMUNITY.
I AM THE AMBASSADOR FROM ASGARD.
HEH. AMBASSADOR THOR? THAT'S FUNNY.
OKAY. IT'S NOT FUNNY.
I'M... BOOKMARKING THIS SITE. IT'S GETTING SUPPORT FROM SOME HIGH-RANKING POLITICIANS. COULD BE A PROBLEM.

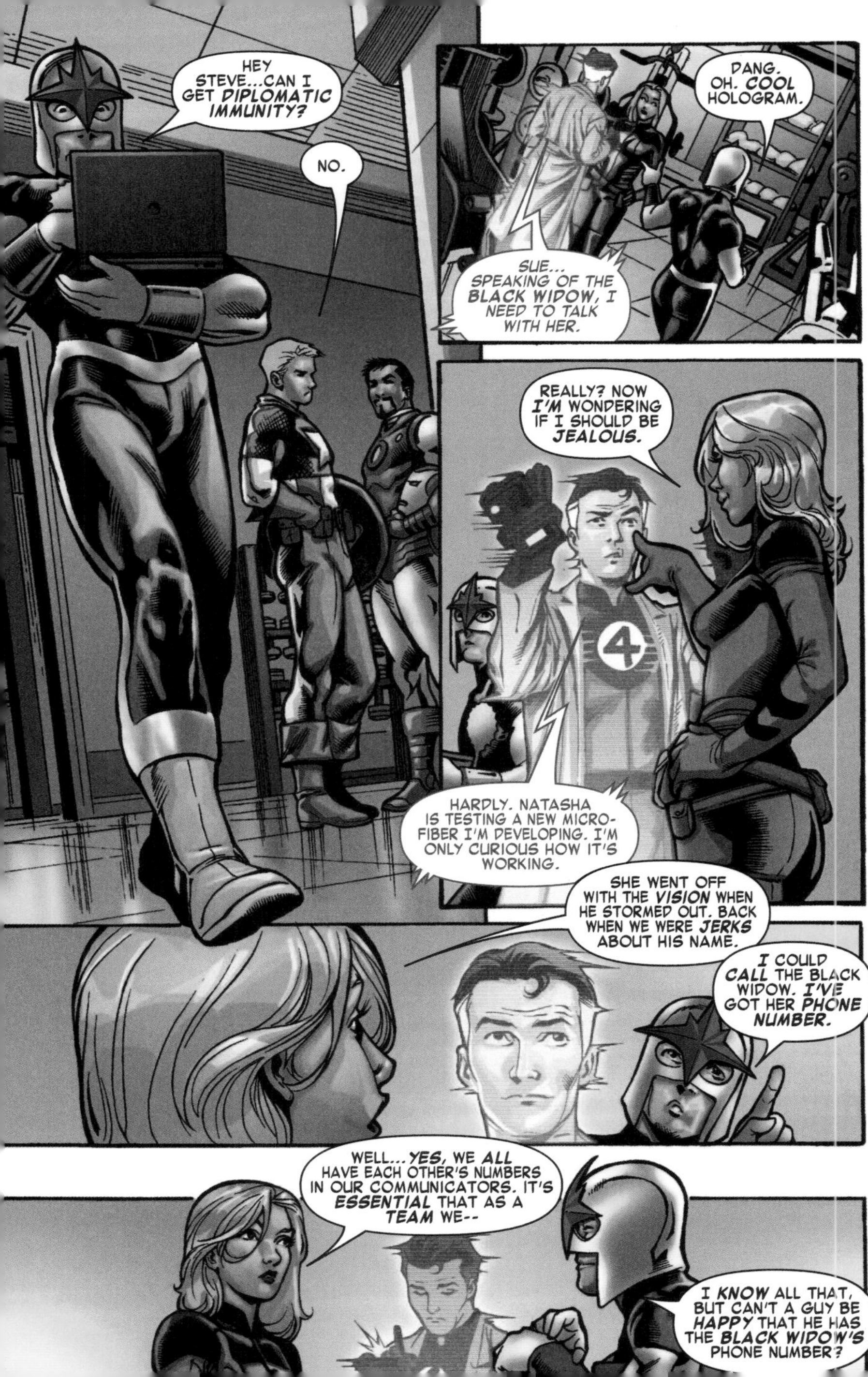
HEY STEVE...CAN I GET DIPLOMATIC IMMUNITY?
NO.
DANG. OH. COOL HOLOGRAM.
SUE... SPEAKING OF THE BLACK WIDOW, I NEED TO TALK WITH HER.
REALLY? NOW I'M WONDERING IF I SHOULD BE JEALOUS.
HARDLY. NATASHA IS TESTING A NEW MICRO-FIBER I'M DEVELOPING. I'M ONLY CURIOUS HOW IT'S WORKING.
SHE WENT OFF WITH THE VISION WHEN HE STORMED OUT. BACK WHEN WE WERE JERKS ABOUT HIS NAME.
I COULD CALL THE BLACK WIDOW. I'VE GOT HER PHONE NUMBER.
WELL... YES, WE ALL HAVE EACH OTHER'S NUMBERS IN OUR COMMUNICATORS. IT'S ESSENTIAL THAT AS A TEAM WE--
I KNOW ALL THAT, BUT CAN'T A GUY BE HAPPY THAT HE HAS THE BLACK WIDOW'S PHONE NUMBER?

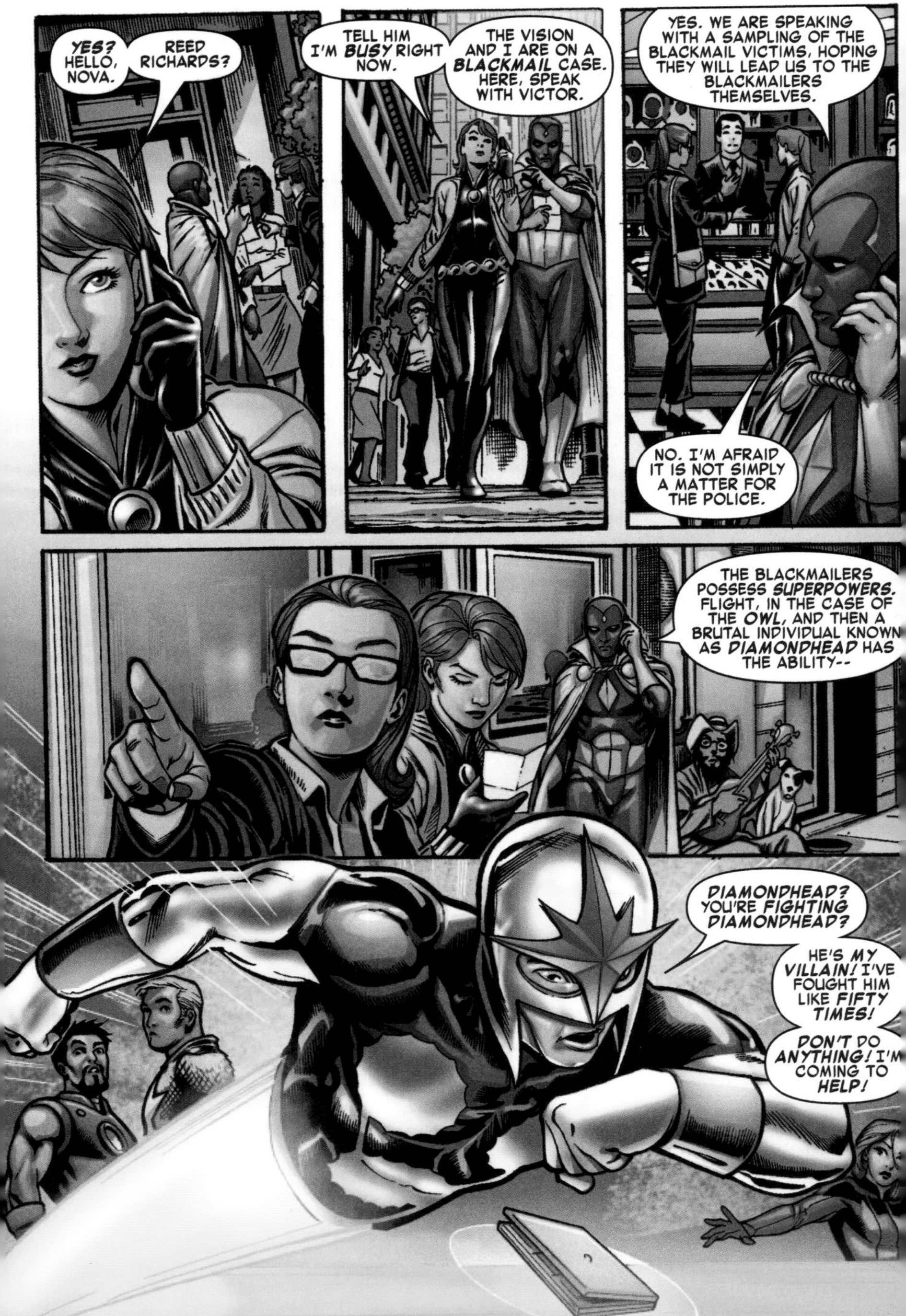
YES? HELLO, NOVA.
REED RICHARDS?
TELL HIM I'M BUSY RIGHT NOW.
THE VISION AND I ARE ON A BLACKMAIL CASE. HERE, SPEAK WITH VICTOR.
YES. WE ARE SPEAKING WITH A SAMPLING OF THE BLACKMAIL VICTIMS, HOPING THEY WILL LEAD US TO THE BLACKMAILERS THEMSELVES.
NO. I'M AFRAID IT IS NOT SIMPLY A MATTER FOR THE POLICE.
THE BLACKMAILERS POSSESS SUPERPOWERS. FLIGHT, IN THE CASE OF THE OWL, AND THEN A BRUTAL INDIVIDUAL KNOWN AS DIAMONDHEAD HAS THE ABILITY--
DIAMONDHEAD? YOU'RE FIGHTING DIAMONDHEAD?
HE'S MY VILLAIN! I'VE FOUGHT HIM LIKE FIFTY TIMES!
DON'T DO ANYTHING! I'M COMING TO HELP!

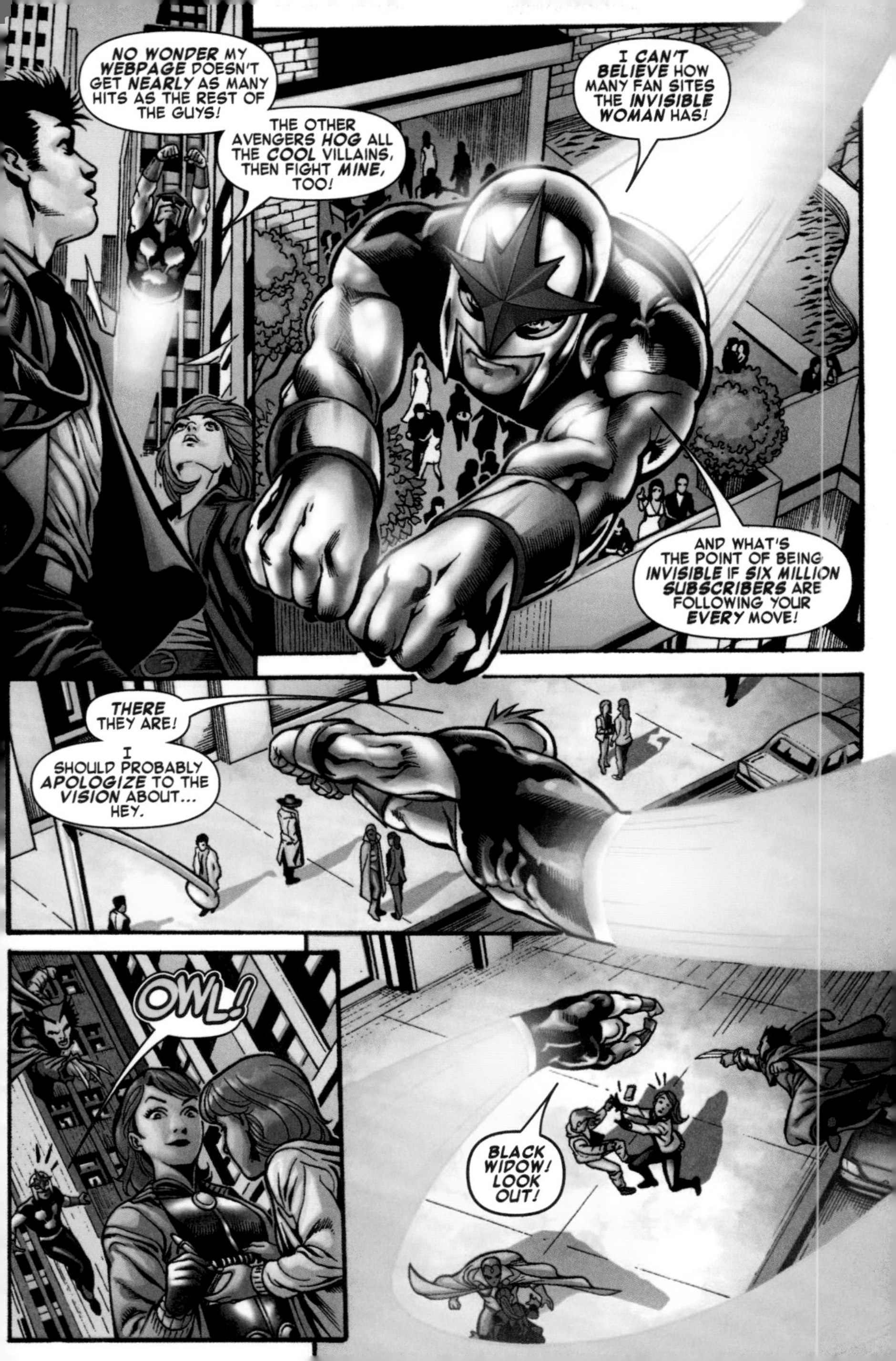
NO WONDER MY WEBPAGE DOESN'T GET NEARLY AS MANY HITS AS THE REST OF THE GUYS!
THE OTHER AVENGERS HOG ALL THE COOL VILLAINS, THEN FIGHT MINE, TOO!
I CAN'T BELIEVE HOW MANY FAN SITES THE INVISIBLE WOMAN HAS!
AND WHAT'S THE POINT OF BEING INVISIBLE IF SIX MILLION SUBSCRIBERS ARE FOLLOWING YOUR EVERY MOVE!
THERE THEY ARE!
I SHOULD PROBABLY APOLOGIZE TO THE VISION ABOUT... HEY.
OWL!
BLACK WIDOW! LOOK OUT!

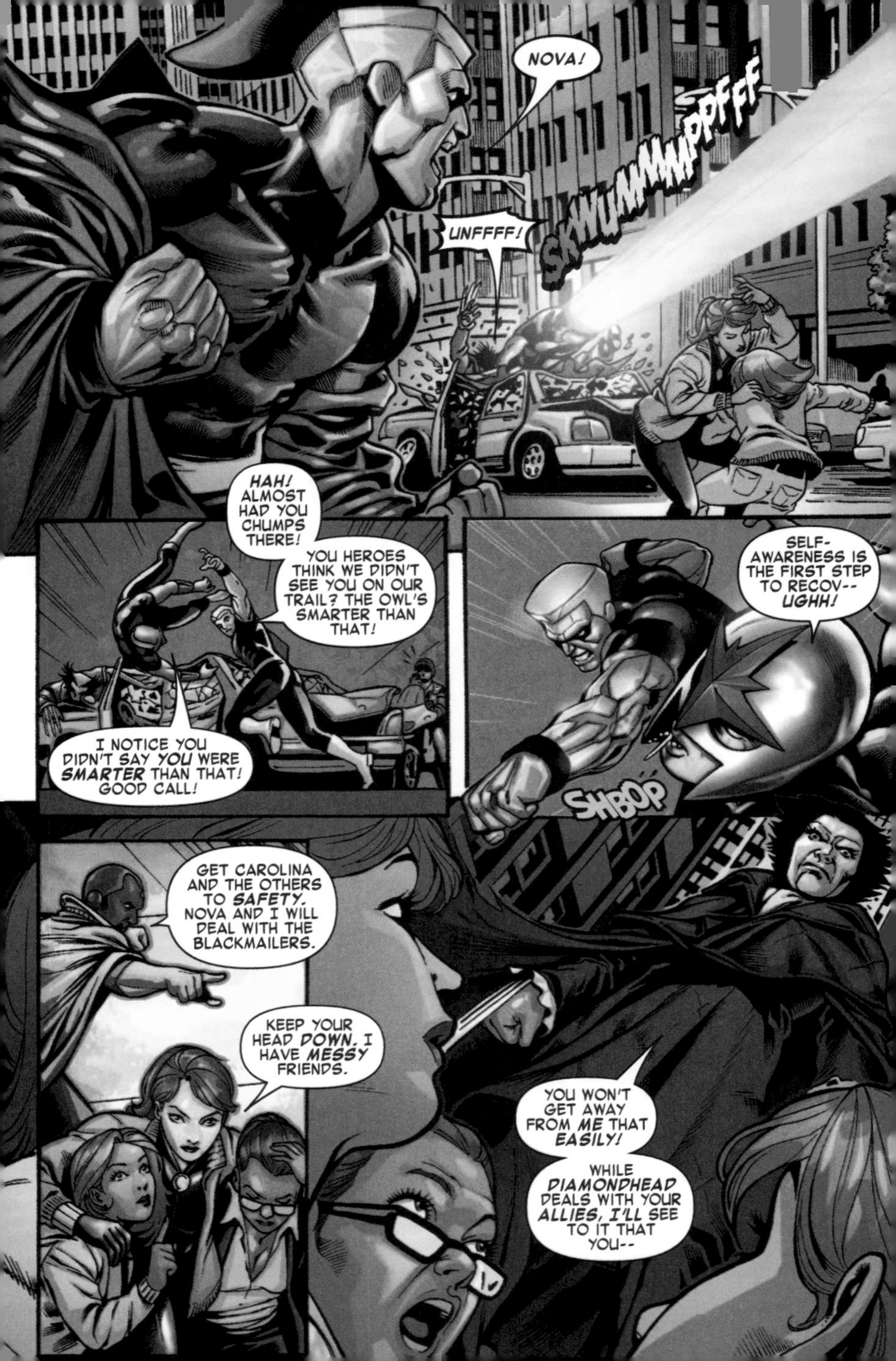
NOVA!
SKWUMMMMPFFFF
UNFFFF!
HAH! ALMOST HAD YOU CHUMPS THERE!
YOU HEROES THINK WE DIDN'T SEE YOU ON OUR TRAIL? THE OWL'S SMARTER THAN THAT!
I NOTICE YOU DIDN'T SAY YOU WERE SMARTER THAN THAT! GOOD CALL!
SELF-AWARENESS IS THE FIRST STEP TO RECOV-- UGHH!
SHBOP
GET CAROLINA AND THE OTHERS TO SAFETY. NOVA AND I WILL DEAL WITH THE BLACKMAILERS.
KEEP YOUR HEAD DOWN. I HAVE MESSY FRIENDS.
YOU WON'T GET AWAY FROM ME THAT EASILY!
WHILE DIAMONDHEAD DEALS WITH YOUR ALLIES, I'LL SEE TO IT THAT YOU--

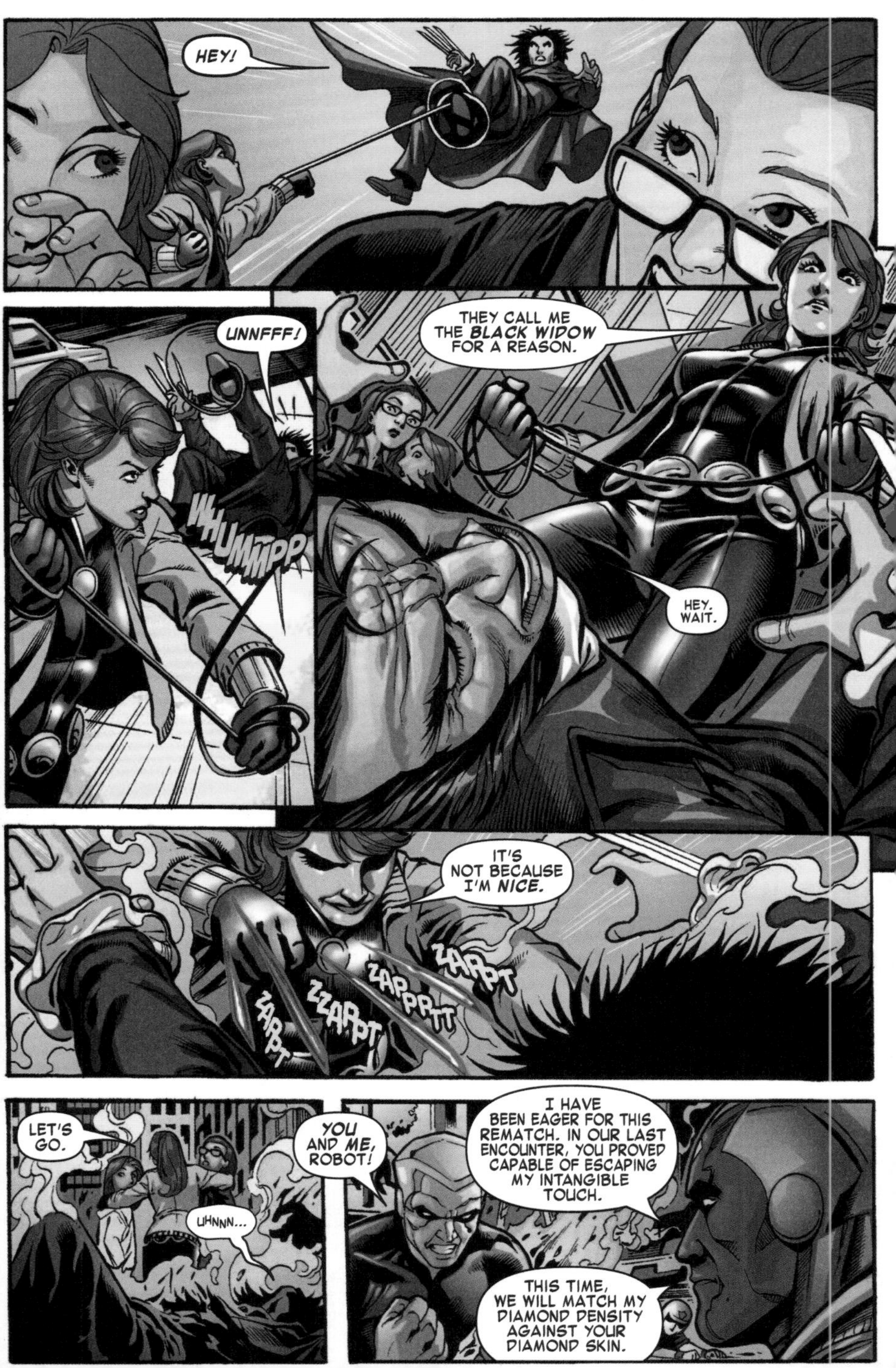
HEY!
UNNFFF!
WHUMMPP
THEY CALL ME THE BLACK WIDOW FOR A REASON.
HEY. WAIT.
IT'S NOT BECAUSE I'M NICE.
ZAPPT
ZAPPRTT
ZZARPT
ZARPT
LET'S GO.
UHNNN...
YOU AND ME, ROBOT!
I HAVE BEEN EAGER FOR THIS REMATCH. IN OUR LAST ENCOUNTER, YOU PROVED CAPABLE OF ESCAPING MY INTANGIBLE TOUCH.
THIS TIME, WE WILL MATCH MY DIAMOND DENSITY AGAINST YOUR DIAMOND SKIN.

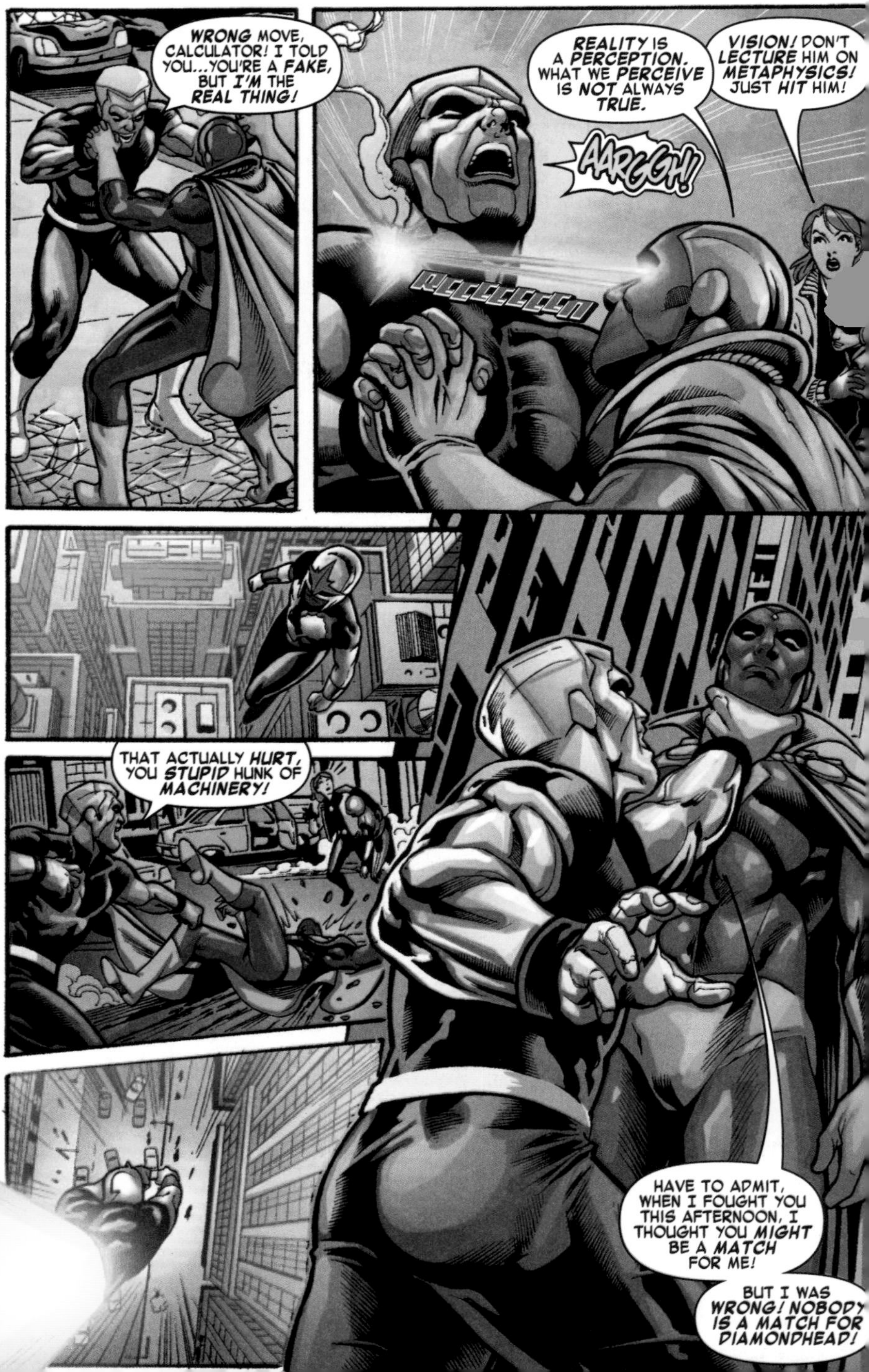
WRONG MOVE, CALCULATOR! I TOLD YOU...YOU'RE A FAKE, BUT I'M THE REAL THING!
REALITY IS A PERCEPTION. WHAT WE PERCEIVE IS NOT ALWAYS TRUE.
VISION! DON'T LECTURE HIM ON METAPHYSICS! JUST HIT HIM!
AARGGH!
THAT ACTUALLY HURT, YOU STUPID HUNK OF MACHINERY!
HAVE TO ADMIT, WHEN I FOUGHT YOU THIS AFTERNOON, I THOUGHT YOU MIGHT BE A MATCH FOR ME!
BUT I WAS WRONG! NOBODY IS A MATCH FOR DIAMONDHEAD!

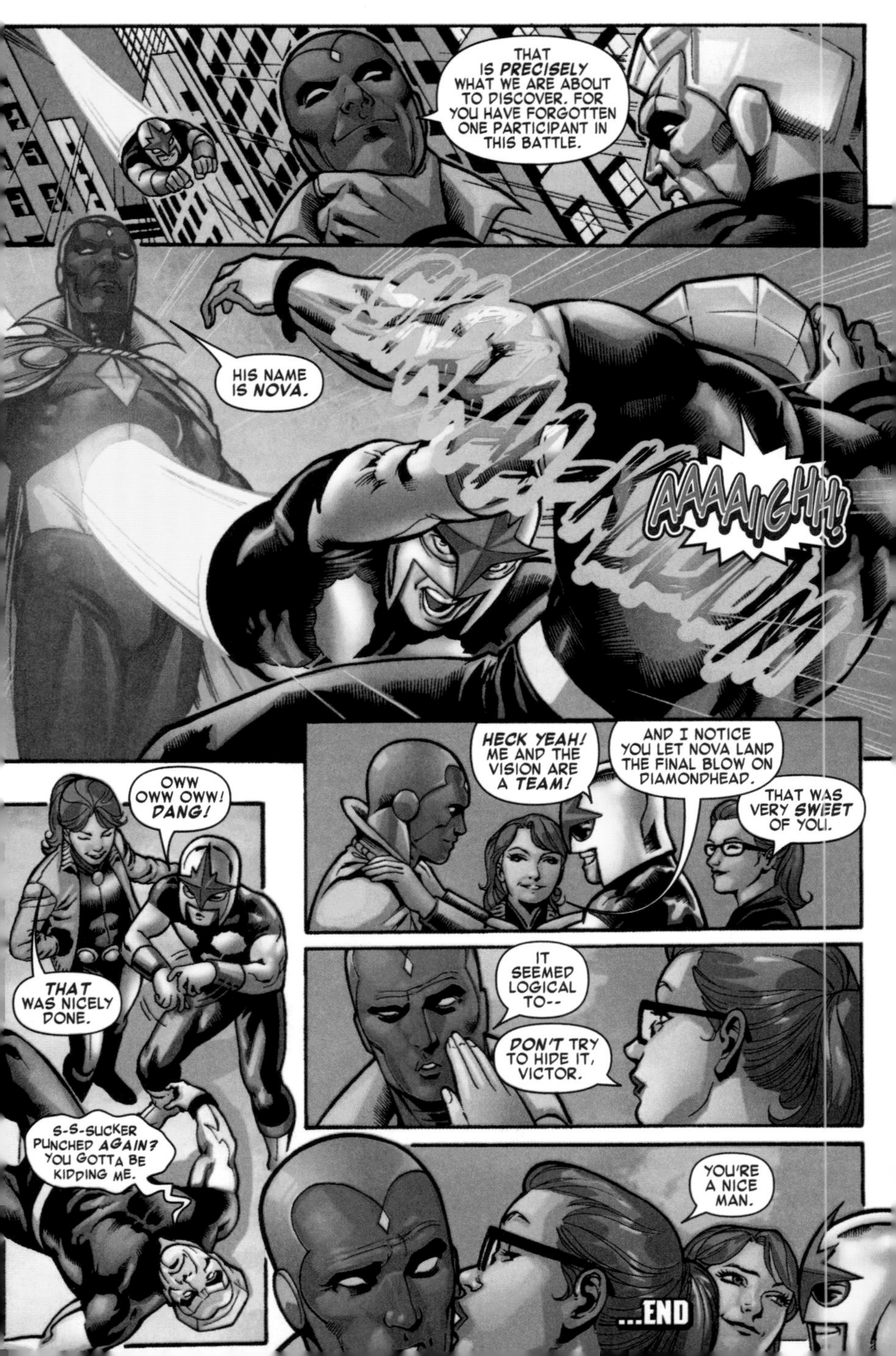
THAT IS PRECISELY WHAT WE ARE ABOUT TO DISCOVER. FOR YOU HAVE FORGOTTEN ONE PARTICIPANT IN THIS BATTLE.
HIS NAME IS NOVA.
AAAAIIGHH!
OWW OWW OWW! DANG!
THAT WAS NICELY DONE.
S-S-SUCKER PUNCHED AGAIN? YOU GOTTA BE KIDDING ME.
HECK YEAH! ME AND THE VISION ARE A TEAM!
AND I NOTICE YOU LET NOVA LAND THE FINAL BLOW ON DIAMONDHEAD.
THAT WAS VERY SWEET OF YOU.
IT SEEMED LOGICAL TO--
DON'T TRY TO HIDE IT, VICTOR.
YOU'RE A NICE MAN.
...END

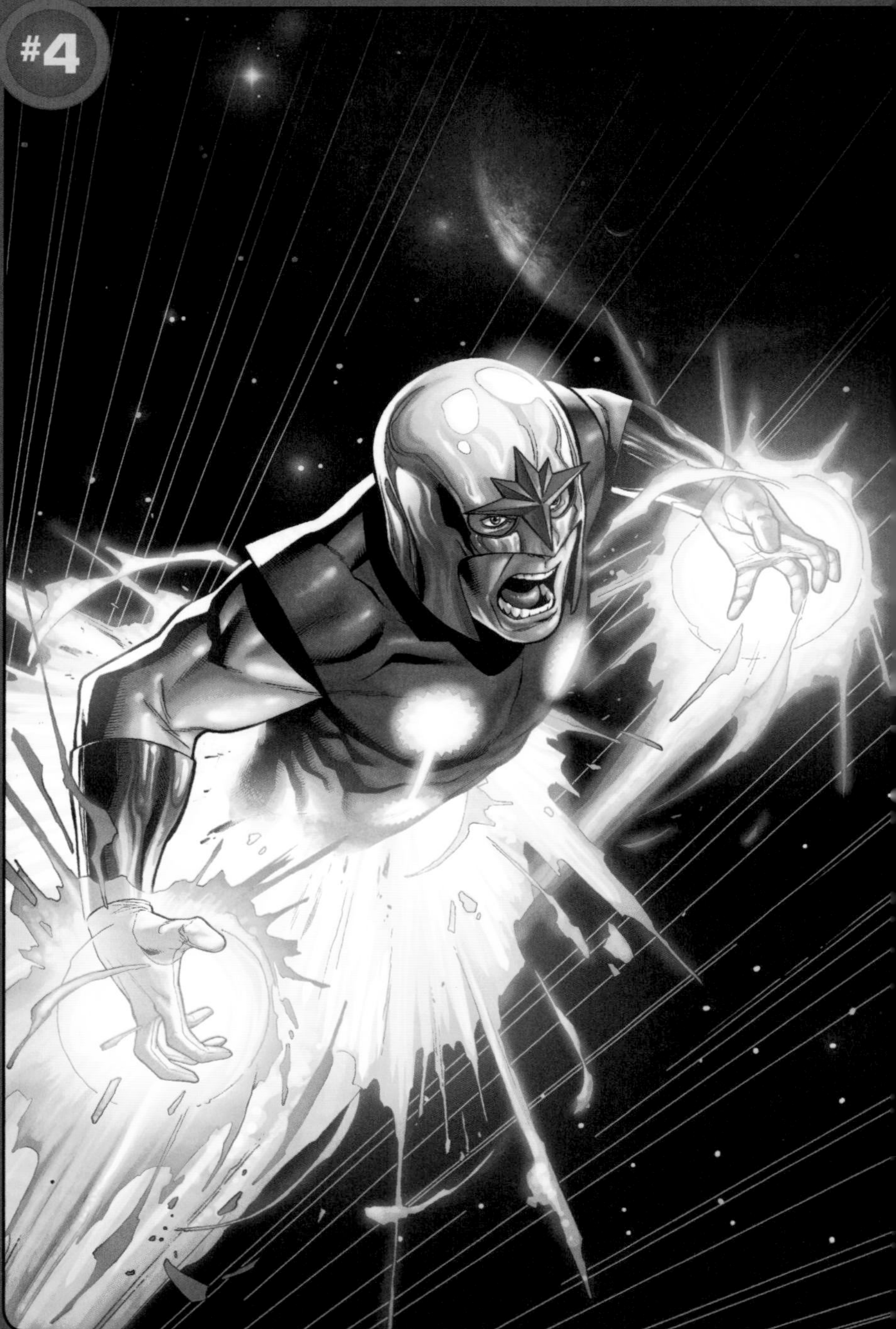
#4

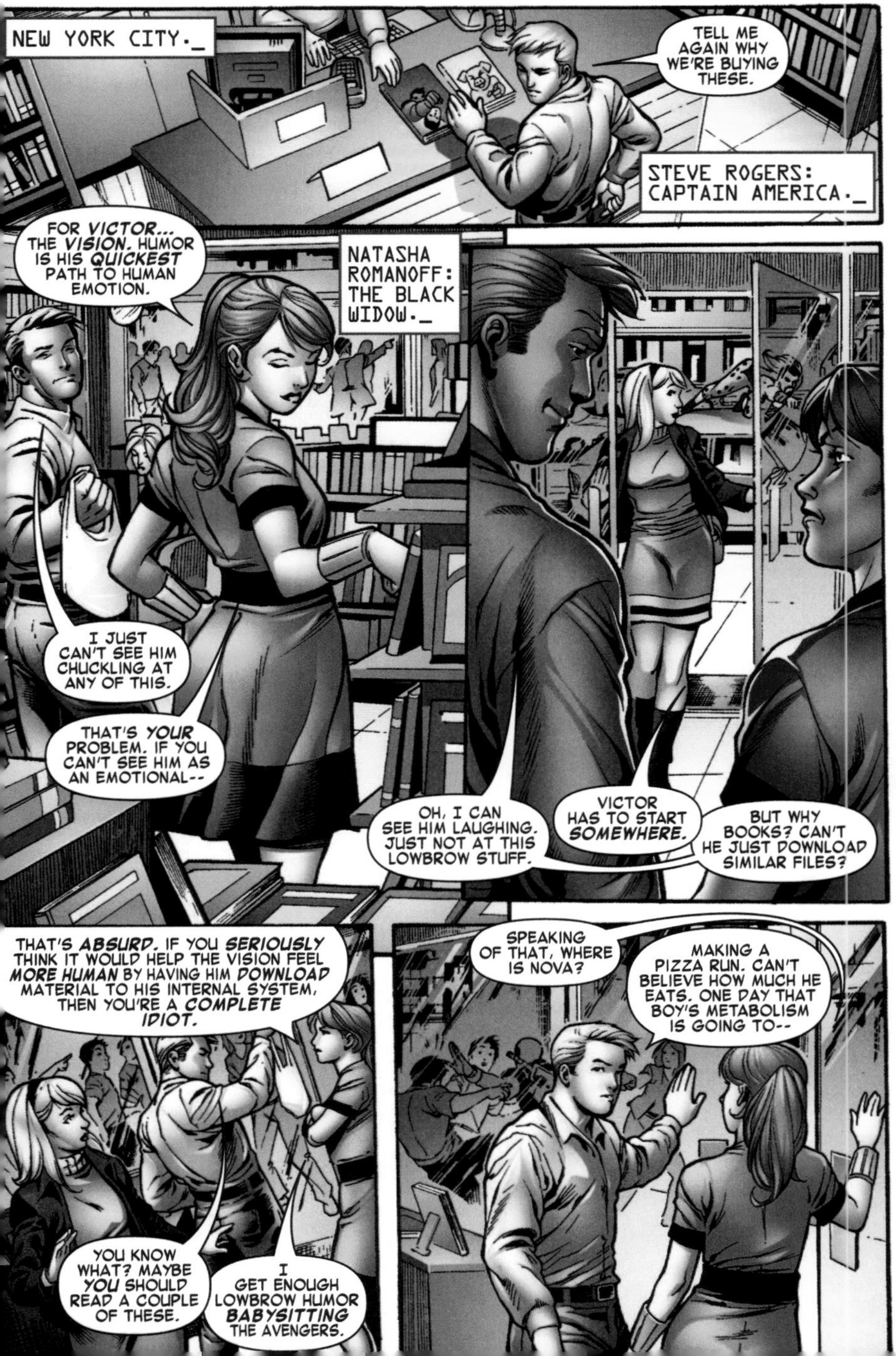
NEW YORK CITY._
TELL ME AGAIN WHY WE'RE BUYING THESE.
STEVE ROGERS: CAPTAIN AMERICA._
FOR VICTOR... THE VISION. HUMOR IS HIS QUICKEST PATH TO HUMAN EMOTION.
NATASHA ROMANOFF: THE BLACK WIDOW._
I JUST CAN'T SEE HIM CHUCKLING AT ANY OF THIS.
THAT'S YOUR PROBLEM. IF YOU CAN'T SEE HIM AS AN EMOTIONAL--
OH, I CAN SEE HIM LAUGHING. JUST NOT AT THIS LOWBROW STUFF.
VICTOR HAS TO START SOMEWHERE.
BUT WHY BOOKS? CAN'T HE JUST DOWNLOAD SIMILAR FILES?
THAT'S ABSURD. IF YOU SERIOUSLY THINK IT WOULD HELP THE VISION FEEL MORE HUMAN BY HAVING HIM DOWNLOAD MATERIAL TO HIS INTERNAL SYSTEM, THEN YOU'RE A COMPLETE IDIOT.
YOU KNOW WHAT? MAYBE YOU SHOULD READ A COUPLE OF THESE.
I GET ENOUGH LOWBROW HUMOR BABYSITTING THE AVENGERS.
SPEAKING OF THAT, WHERE IS NOVA?
MAKING A PIZZA RUN. CAN'T BELIEVE HOW MUCH HE EATS. ONE DAY THAT BOY'S METABOLISM IS GOING TO--

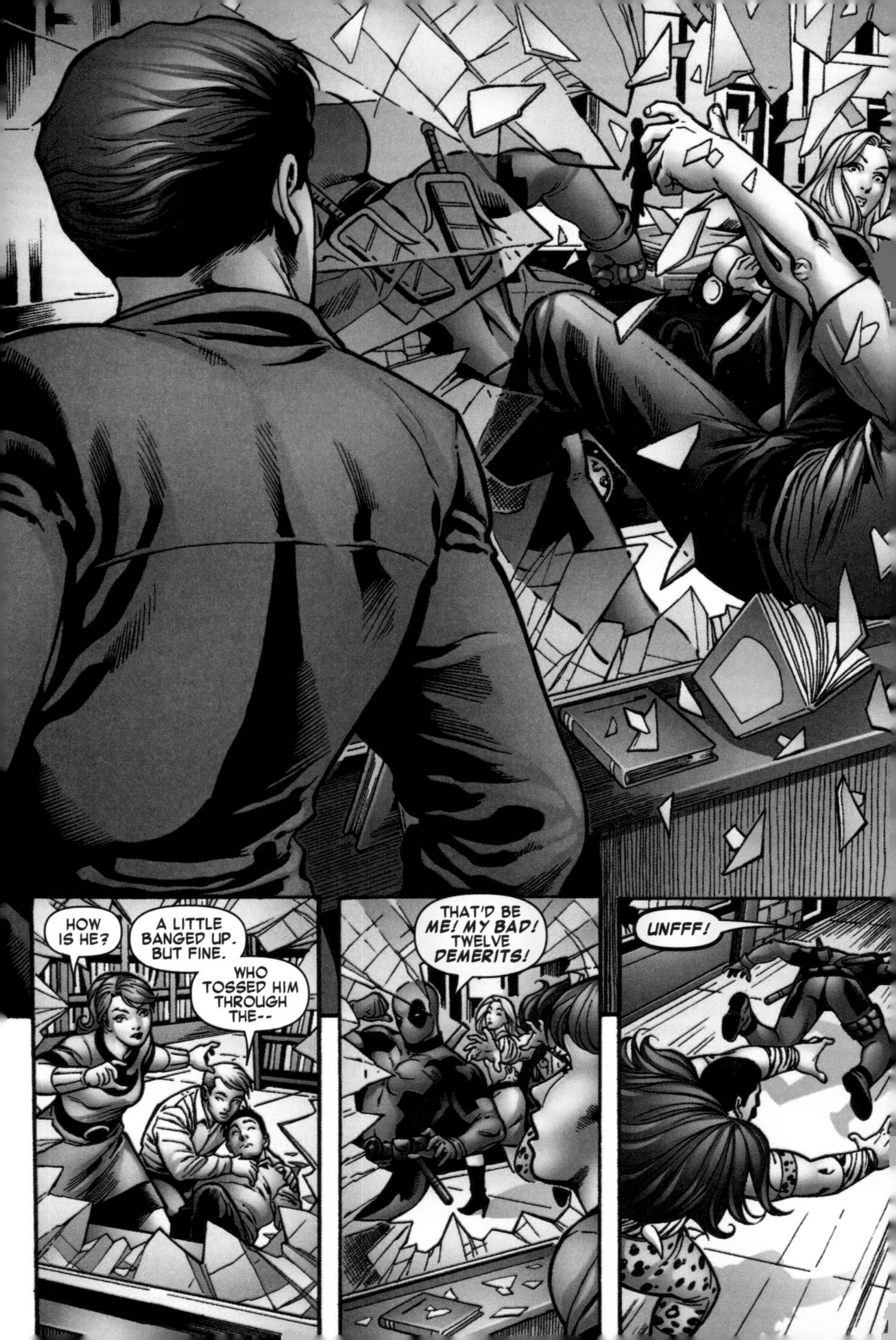
HOW IS HE?
A LITTLE BANGED UP. BUT FINE.
WHO TOSSED HIM THROUGH THE--
THAT'D BE *ME! MY BAD!* TWELVE *DEMERITS!*
UNFFF!

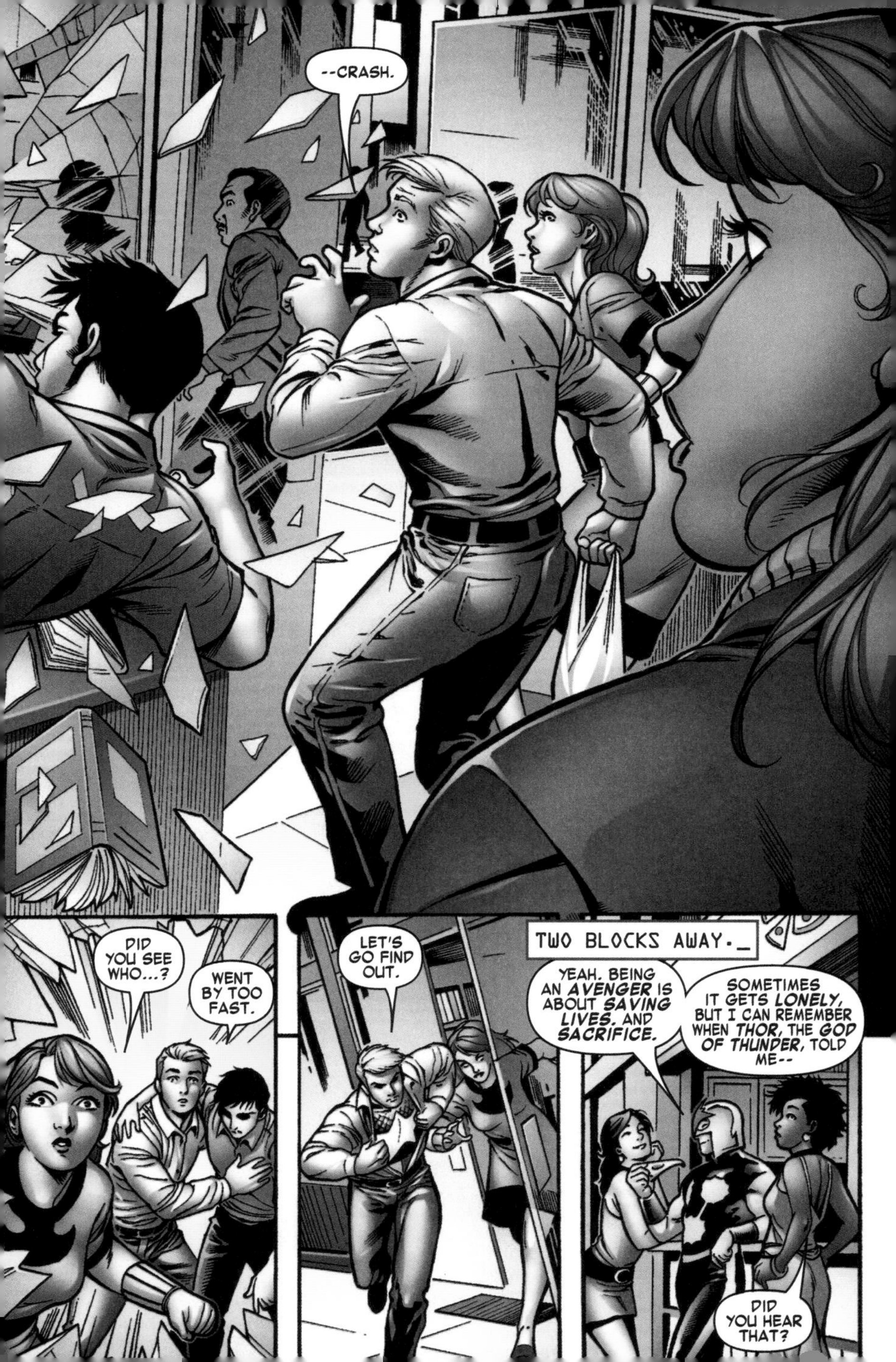
--CRASH.
DID YOU SEE WHO...?
WENT BY TOO FAST.
LET'S GO FIND OUT.
TWO BLOCKS AWAY...
YEAH. BEING AN AVENGER IS ABOUT SAVING LIVES. AND SACRIFICE.
SOMETIMES IT GETS LONELY, BUT I CAN REMEMBER WHEN THOR, THE GOD OF THUNDER, TOLD ME--
DID YOU HEAR THAT?

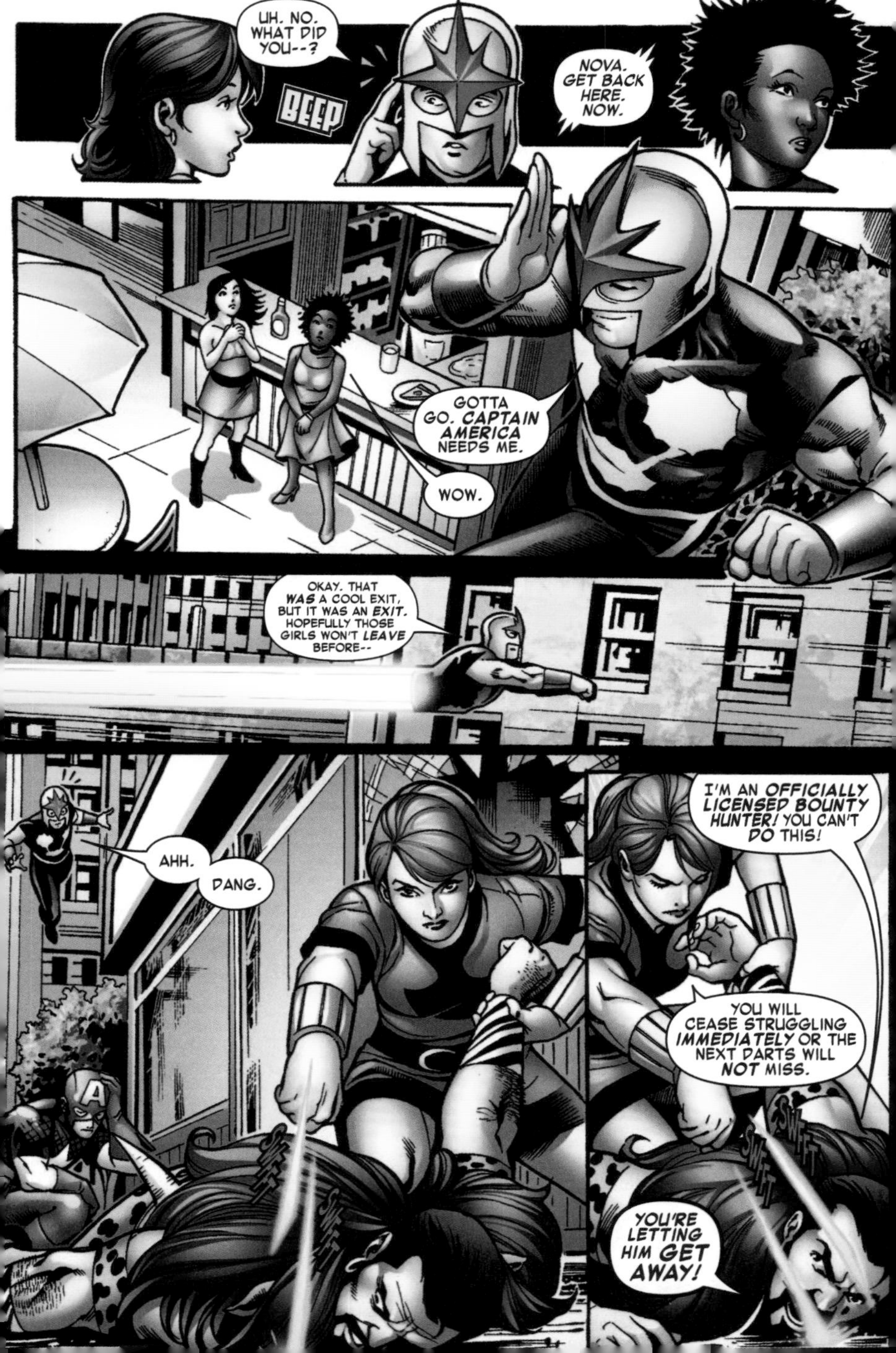
UH. NO. WHAT DID YOU--?
BEEP
NOVA. GET BACK HERE. NOW.
GOTTA GO. CAPTAIN AMERICA NEEDS ME.
WOW.
OKAY. THAT WAS A COOL EXIT, BUT IT WAS AN EXIT. HOPEFULLY THOSE GIRLS WON'T LEAVE BEFORE--
AHH.
DANG.
I'M AN OFFICIALLY LICENSED BOUNTY HUNTER! YOU CAN'T DO THIS!
YOU WILL CEASE STRUGGLING IMMEDIATELY OR THE NEXT DARTS WILL NOT MISS.
YOU'RE LETTING HIM GET AWAY!

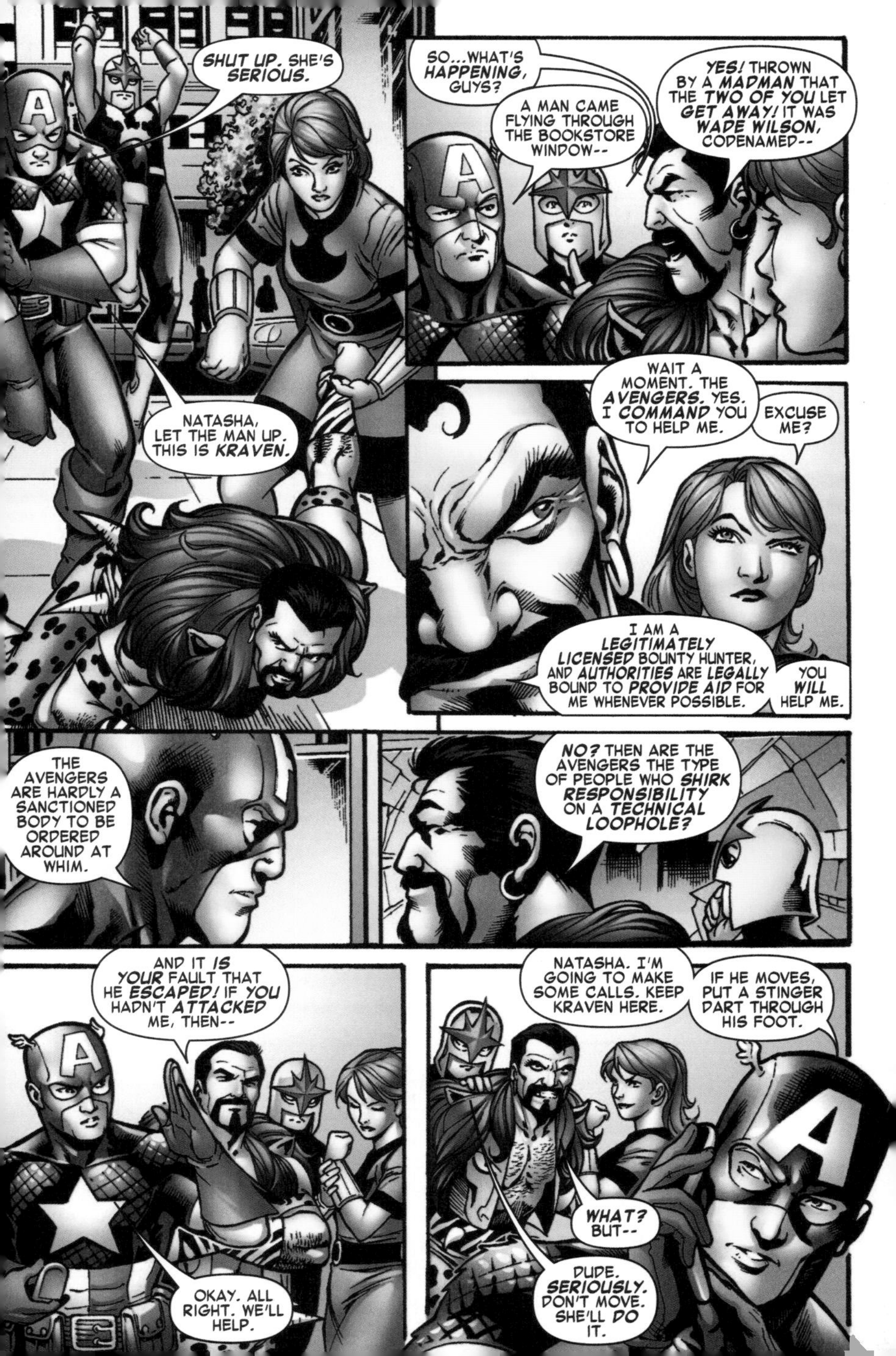
SHUT UP. SHE'S SERIOUS.
NATASHA, LET THE MAN UP. THIS IS KRAVEN.
SO...WHAT'S HAPPENING, GUYS?
A MAN CAME FLYING THROUGH THE BOOKSTORE WINDOW--
YES! THROWN BY A MADMAN THAT THE TWO OF YOU LET GET AWAY! IT WAS WADE WILSON, CODENAMED--
WAIT A MOMENT. THE AVENGERS. YES. I COMMAND YOU TO HELP ME.
EXCUSE ME?
I AM A LEGITIMATELY LICENSED BOUNTY HUNTER, AND AUTHORITIES ARE LEGALLY BOUND TO PROVIDE AID FOR ME WHENEVER POSSIBLE.
YOU WILL HELP ME.
THE AVENGERS ARE HARDLY A SANCTIONED BODY TO BE ORDERED AROUND AT WHIM.
NO? THEN ARE THE AVENGERS THE TYPE OF PEOPLE WHO SHIRK RESPONSIBILITY ON A TECHNICAL LOOPHOLE?
AND IT IS YOUR FAULT THAT HE ESCAPED! IF YOU HADN'T ATTACKED ME, THEN--
OKAY. ALL RIGHT. WE'LL HELP.
NATASHA. I'M GOING TO MAKE SOME CALLS. KEEP KRAVEN HERE.
IF HE MOVES, PUT A STINGER DART THROUGH HIS FOOT.
WHAT? BUT--
DUDE. SERIOUSLY. DON'T MOVE. SHE'LL DO IT.

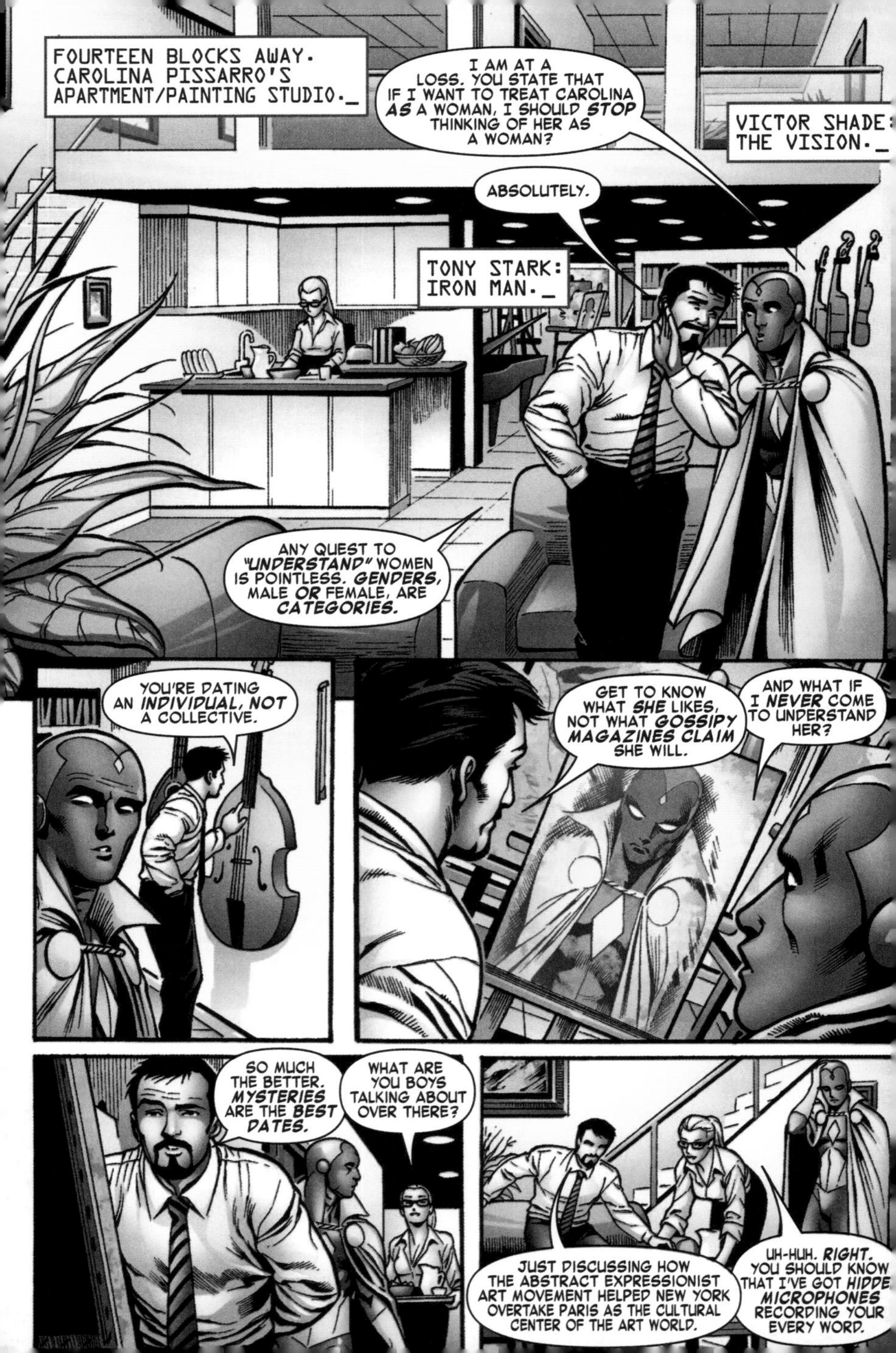
FOURTEEN BLOCKS AWAY. CAROLINA PISSARRO'S APARTMENT/PAINTING STUDIO._
I AM AT A LOSS. YOU STATE THAT IF I WANT TO TREAT CAROLINA AS A WOMAN, I SHOULD STOP THINKING OF HER AS A WOMAN?
VICTOR SHADE: THE VISION._
ABSOLUTELY.
TONY STARK: IRON MAN._
ANY QUEST TO "UNDERSTAND" WOMEN IS POINTLESS. GENDERS, MALE OR FEMALE, ARE CATEGORIES.
YOU'RE DATING AN INDIVIDUAL, NOT A COLLECTIVE.
GET TO KNOW WHAT SHE LIKES, NOT WHAT GOSSIPY MAGAZINES CLAIM SHE WILL.
AND WHAT IF I NEVER COME TO UNDERSTAND HER?
SO MUCH THE BETTER. MYSTERIES ARE THE BEST DATES.
WHAT ARE YOU BOYS TALKING ABOUT OVER THERE?
JUST DISCUSSING HOW THE ABSTRACT EXPRESSIONIST ART MOVEMENT HELPED NEW YORK OVERTAKE PARIS AS THE CULTURAL CENTER OF THE ART WORLD.
UH-HUH. RIGHT. YOU SHOULD KNOW THAT I'VE GOT HIDDE MICROPHONES RECORDING YOUR EVERY WORD.

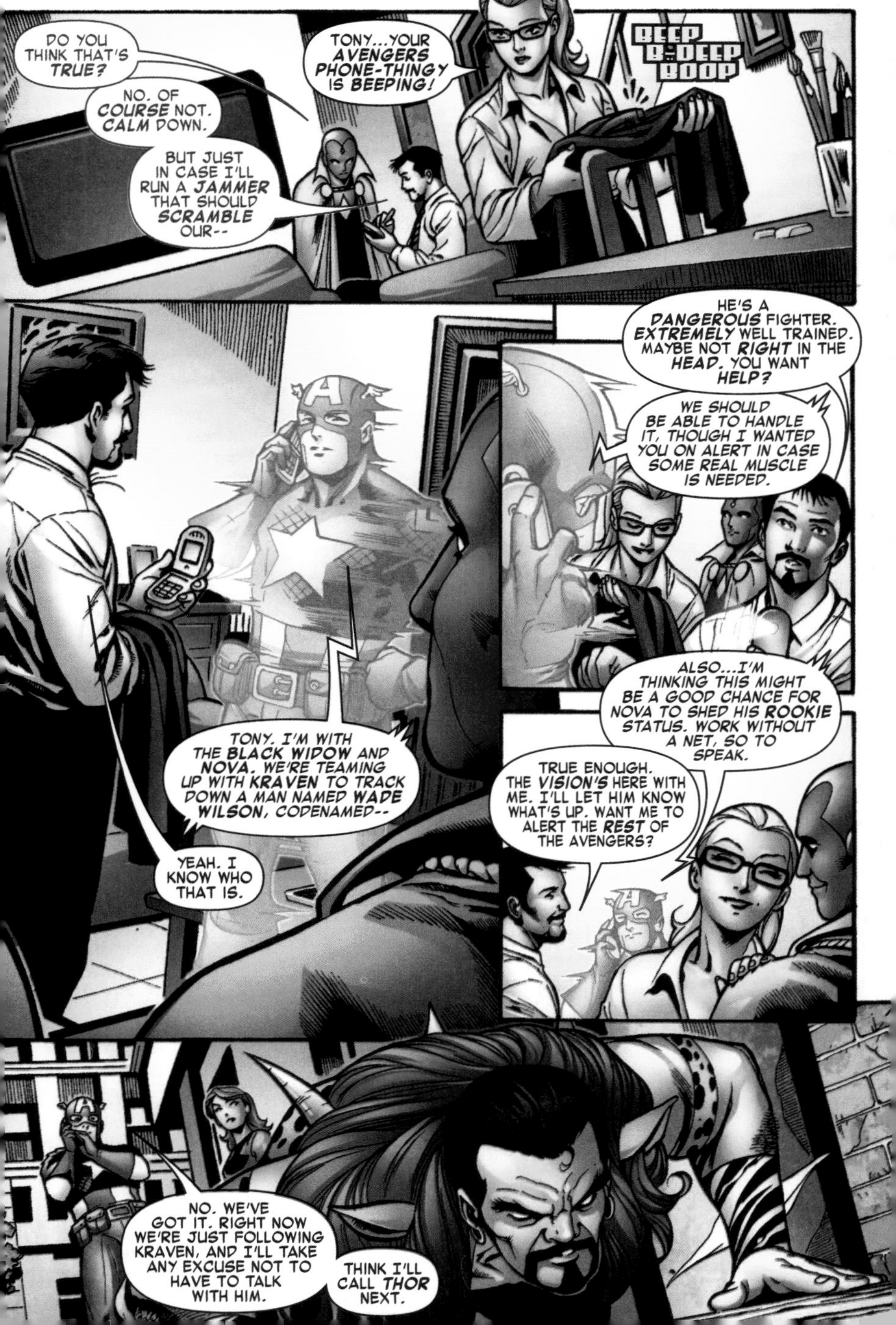
DO YOU THINK THAT'S TRUE?
NO. OF COURSE NOT. CALM DOWN.
TONY...YOUR AVENGERS PHONE-THINGY IS BEEPING!
BEEP B-DEEP BOOP
BUT JUST IN CASE I'LL RUN A JAMMER THAT SHOULD SCRAMBLE OUR--
TONY. I'M WITH THE BLACK WIDOW AND NOVA. WE'RE TEAMING UP WITH KRAVEN TO TRACK DOWN A MAN NAMED WADE WILSON, CODENAMED--
YEAH. I KNOW WHO THAT IS.
HE'S A DANGEROUS FIGHTER. EXTREMELY WELL TRAINED. MAYBE NOT RIGHT IN THE HEAD. YOU WANT HELP?
WE SHOULD BE ABLE TO HANDLE IT, THOUGH I WANTED YOU ON ALERT IN CASE SOME REAL MUSCLE IS NEEDED.
ALSO...I'M THINKING THIS MIGHT BE A GOOD CHANCE FOR NOVA TO SHED HIS ROOKIE STATUS. WORK WITHOUT A NET, SO TO SPEAK.
TRUE ENOUGH. THE VISION'S HERE WITH ME. I'LL LET HIM KNOW WHAT'S UP. WANT ME TO ALERT THE REST OF THE AVENGERS?
NO. WE'VE GOT IT. RIGHT NOW WE'RE JUST FOLLOWING KRAVEN, AND I'LL TAKE ANY EXCUSE NOT TO HAVE TO TALK WITH HIM.
THINK I'LL CALL THOR NEXT.

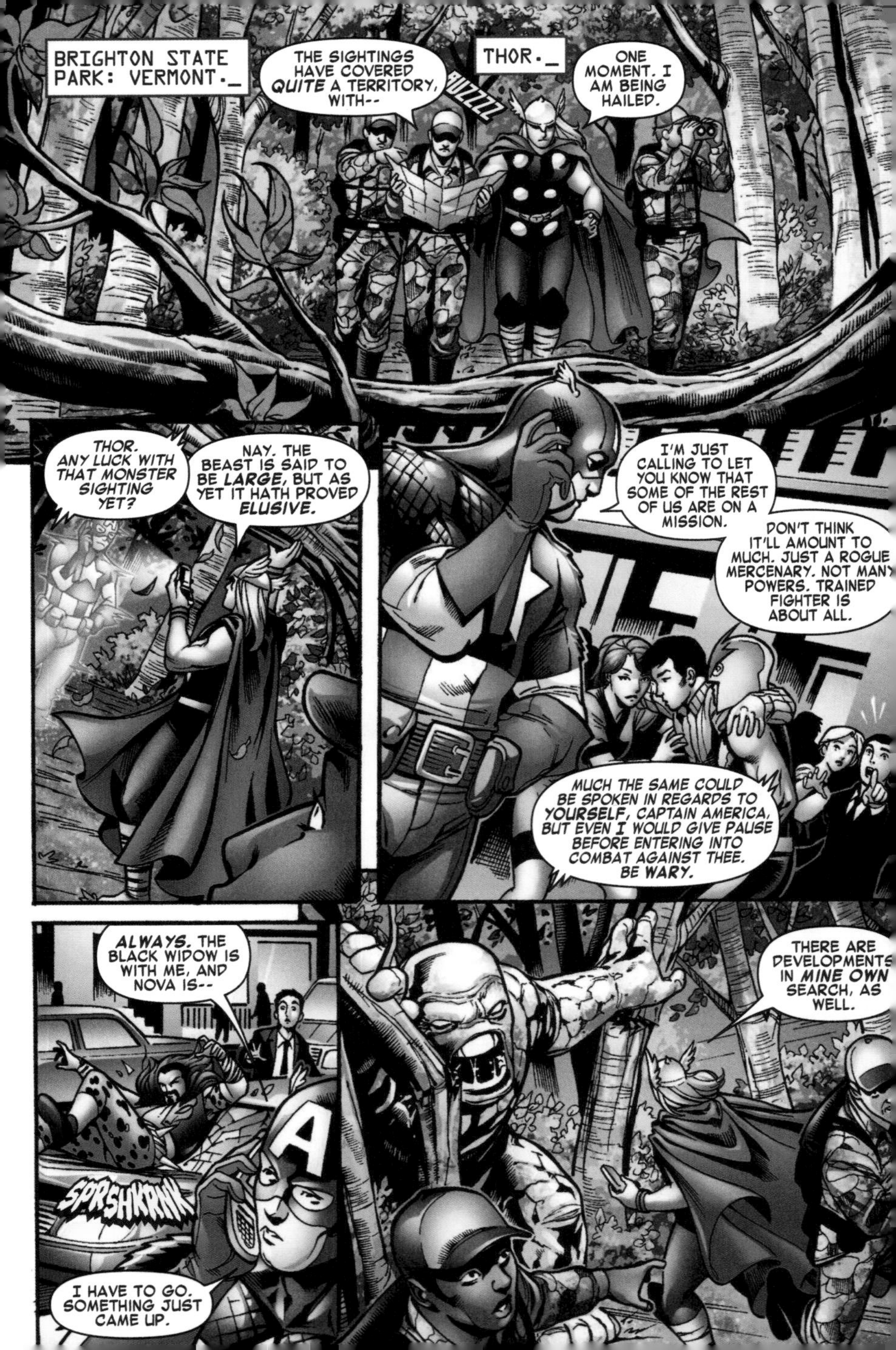
BRIGHTON STATE PARK: VERMONT._
THE SIGHTINGS HAVE COVERED QUITE A TERRITORY, WITH--
BUZZZZ
THOR._
ONE MOMENT. I AM BEING HAILED.
THOR. ANY LUCK WITH THAT MONSTER SIGHTING YET?
NAY. THE BEAST IS SAID TO BE LARGE, BUT AS YET IT HATH PROVED ELUSIVE.
I'M JUST CALLING TO LET YOU KNOW THAT SOME OF THE REST OF US ARE ON A MISSION.
DON'T THINK IT'LL AMOUNT TO MUCH. JUST A ROGUE MERCENARY. NOT MANY POWERS. TRAINED FIGHTER IS ABOUT ALL.
MUCH THE SAME COULD BE SPOKEN IN REGARDS TO YOURSELF, CAPTAIN AMERICA, BUT EVEN I WOULD GIVE PAUSE BEFORE ENTERING INTO COMBAT AGAINST THEE. BE WARY.
ALWAYS. THE BLACK WIDOW IS WITH ME, AND NOVA IS--
SPRSHKRNK
I HAVE TO GO. SOMETHING JUST CAME UP.
THERE ARE DEVELOPMENTS IN MINE OWN SEARCH, AS WELL.

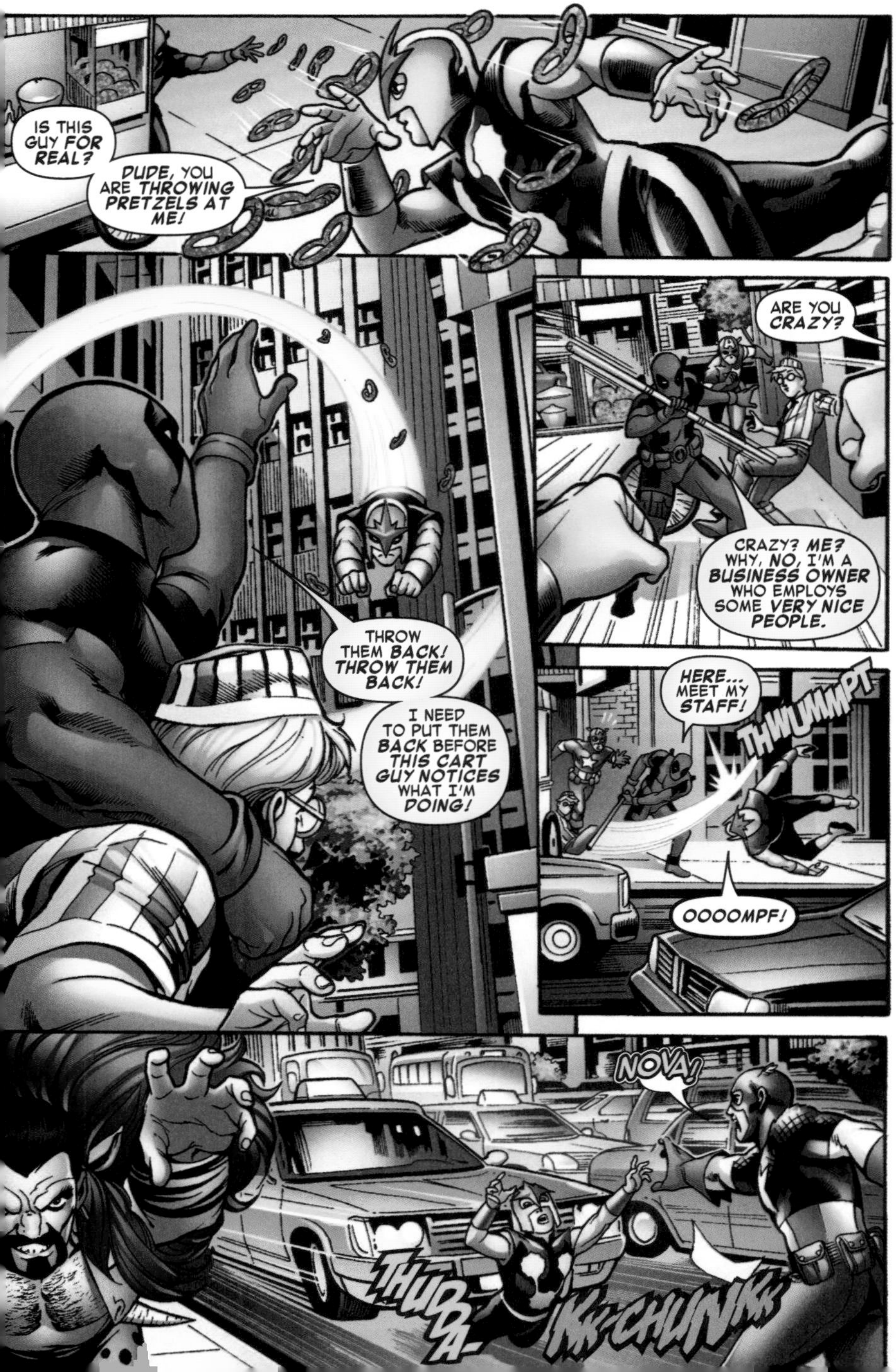

IS THIS GUY FOR REAL?
DUDE, YOU ARE THROWING PRETZELS AT ME!
THROW THEM BACK! THROW THEM BACK!
I NEED TO PUT THEM BACK BEFORE THIS CART GUY NOTICES WHAT I'M DOING!
ARE YOU CRAZY?
CRAZY? ME? WHY, NO, I'M A BUSINESS OWNER WHO EMPLOYS SOME VERY NICE PEOPLE.
HERE... MEET MY STAFF!
THWUMMPT
OOOOMPF!
NOVA!
THUDDA-
KK-CHUNKK

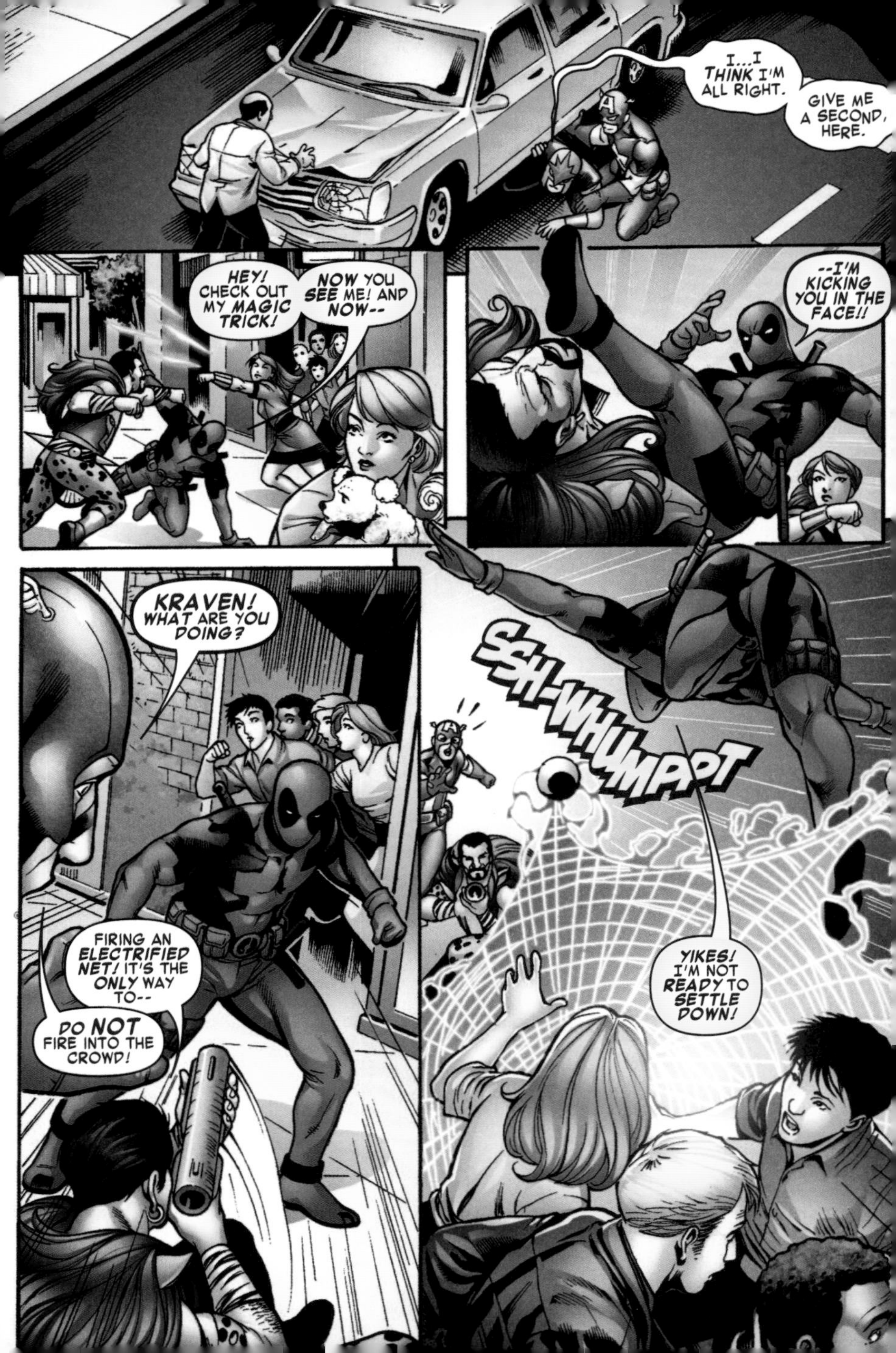
I...I THINK I'M ALL RIGHT.
GIVE ME A SECOND, HERE.
HEY! CHECK OUT MY MAGIC TRICK!
NOW YOU SEE ME! AND NOW--
--I'M KICKING YOU IN THE FACE!!
KRAVEN! WHAT ARE YOU DOING?
FIRING AN ELECTRIFIED NET! IT'S THE ONLY WAY TO--
DO NOT FIRE INTO THE CROWD!
SSH-WHUMPPT
YIKES! I'M NOT READY TO SETTLE DOWN!

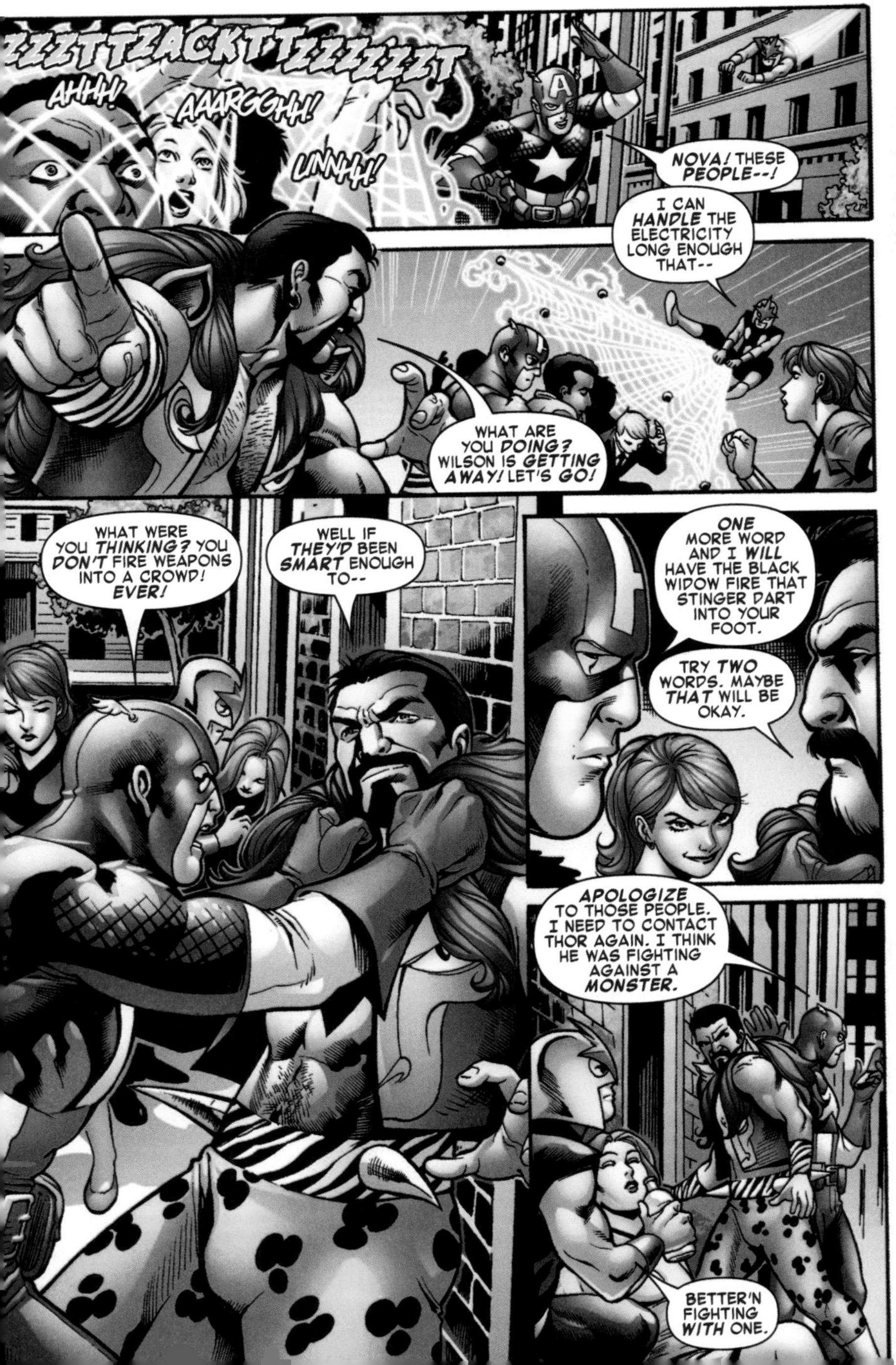
ZZZTTTZACKTTZZZZZZT
AHHH!
AAARGGHH!
UNNHH!
NOVA! THESE PEOPLE--!
I CAN HANDLE THE ELECTRICITY LONG ENOUGH THAT--
WHAT ARE YOU DOING? WILSON IS GETTING AWAY! LET'S GO!
WHAT WERE YOU THINKING? YOU DON'T FIRE WEAPONS INTO A CROWD! EVER!
WELL IF THEY'D BEEN SMART ENOUGH TO--
ONE MORE WORD AND I WILL HAVE THE BLACK WIDOW FIRE THAT STINGER DART INTO YOUR FOOT.
TRY TWO WORDS. MAYBE THAT WILL BE OKAY.
APOLOGIZE TO THOSE PEOPLE. I NEED TO CONTACT THOR AGAIN. I THINK HE WAS FIGHTING AGAINST A MONSTER.
BETTER'N FIGHTING WITH ONE.

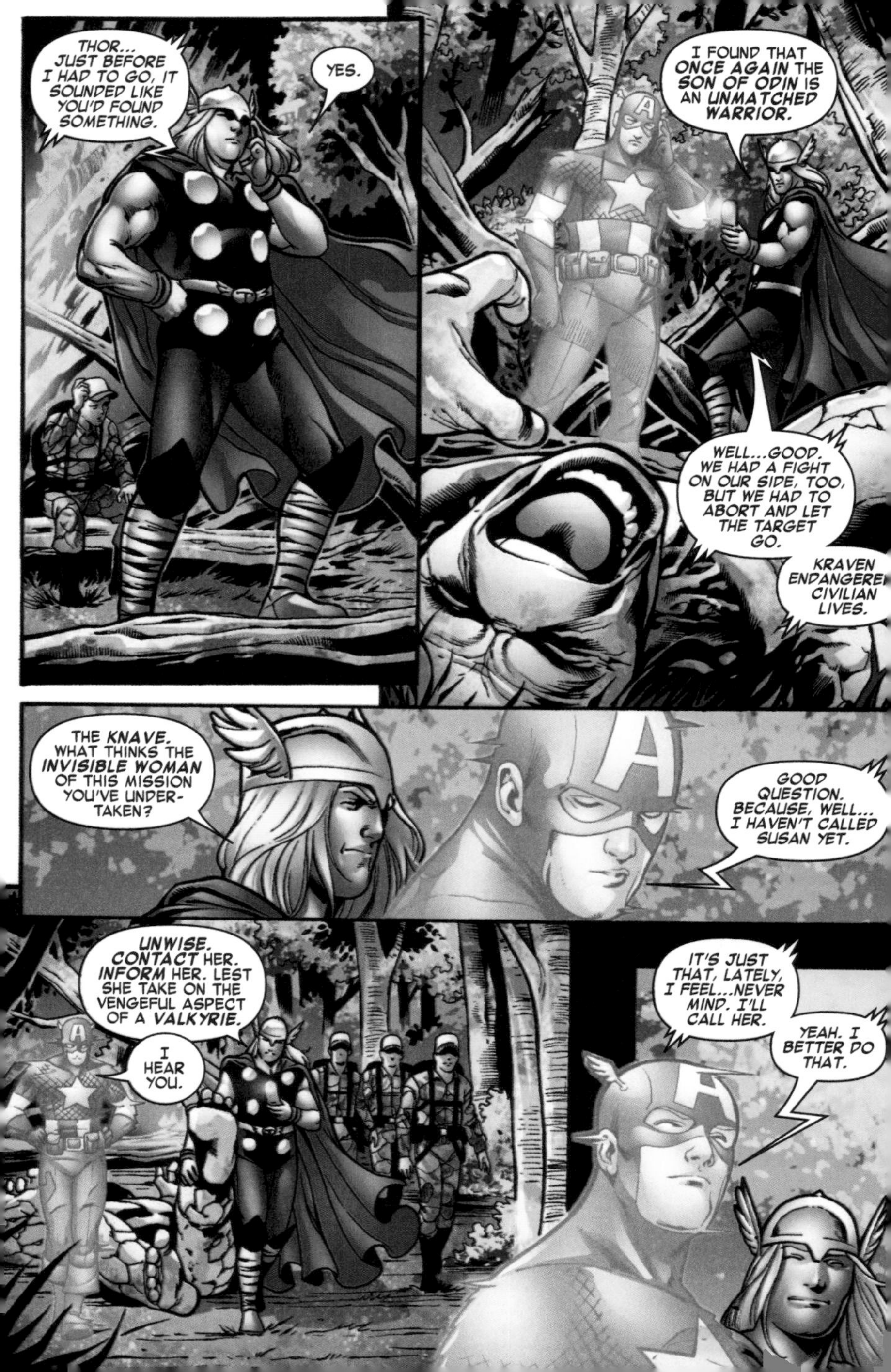
THOR... JUST BEFORE I HAD TO GO, IT SOUNDED LIKE YOU'D FOUND SOMETHING.
YES.
I FOUND THAT ONCE AGAIN THE SON OF ODIN IS AN UNMATCHED WARRIOR.
WELL...GOOD. WE HAD A FIGHT ON OUR SIDE, TOO, BUT WE HAD TO ABORT AND LET THE TARGET GO.
KRAVEN ENDANGERED CIVILIAN LIVES.
THE KNAVE. WHAT THINKS THE INVISIBLE WOMAN OF THIS MISSION YOU'VE UNDER-TAKEN?
GOOD QUESTION. BECAUSE, WELL... I HAVEN'T CALLED SUSAN YET.
UNWISE. CONTACT HER. INFORM HER. LEST SHE TAKE ON THE VENGEFUL ASPECT OF A VALKYRIE.
I HEAR YOU.
IT'S JUST THAT, LATELY, I FEEL...NEVER MIND. I'LL CALL HER.
YEAH. I BETTER DO THAT.

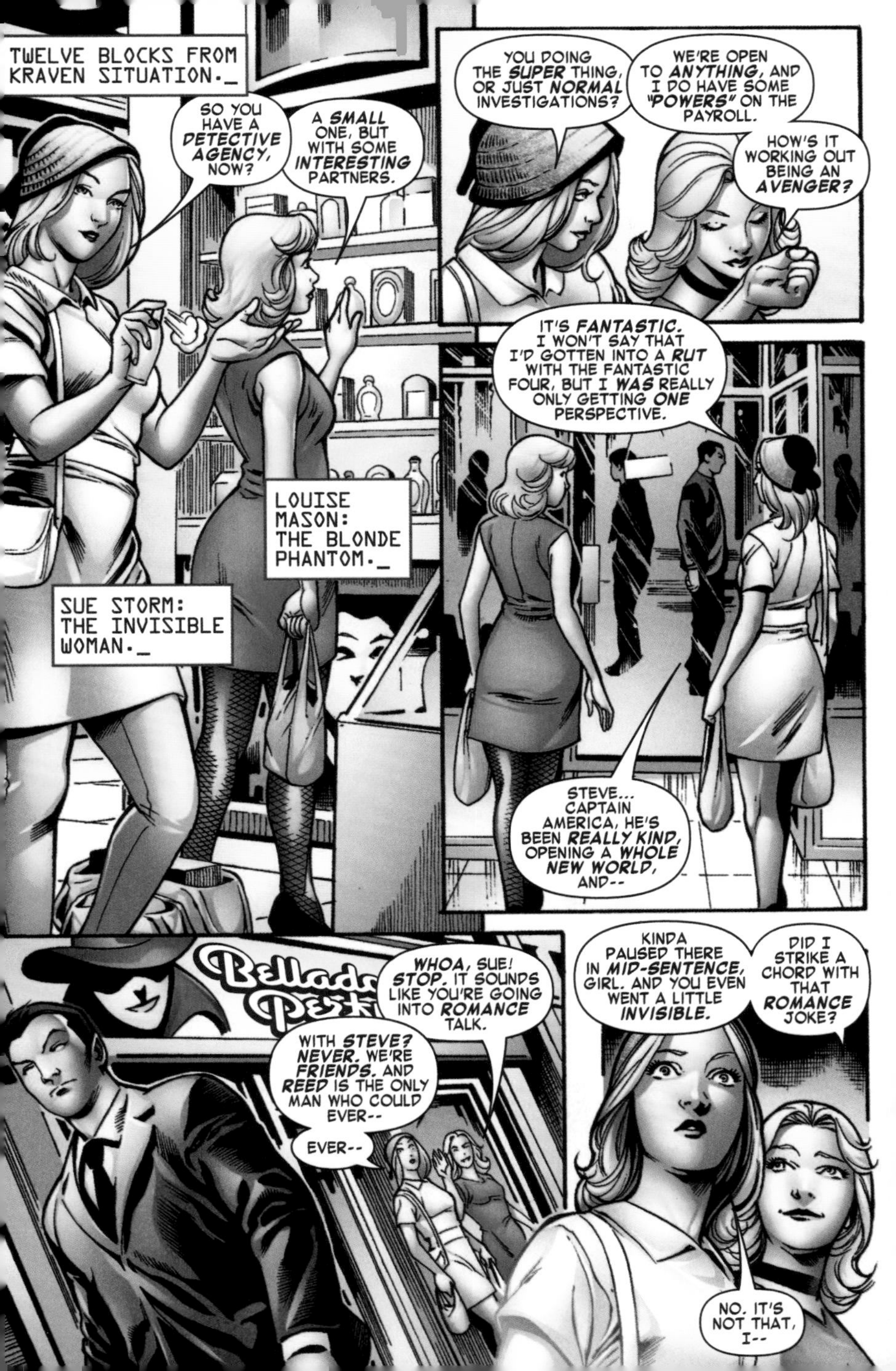
TWELVE BLOCKS FROM KRAVEN SITUATION._
SO YOU HAVE A DETECTIVE AGENCY, NOW?
A SMALL ONE, BUT WITH SOME INTERESTING PARTNERS.
LOUISE MASON: THE BLONDE PHANTOM._
SUE STORM: THE INVISIBLE WOMAN._
YOU DOING THE SUPER THING, OR JUST NORMAL INVESTIGATIONS?
WE'RE OPEN TO ANYTHING, AND I DO HAVE SOME "POWERS" ON THE PAYROLL.
HOW'S IT WORKING OUT BEING AN AVENGER?
IT'S FANTASTIC. I WON'T SAY THAT I'D GOTTEN INTO A RUT WITH THE FANTASTIC FOUR, BUT I WAS REALLY ONLY GETTING ONE PERSPECTIVE.
STEVE... CAPTAIN AMERICA, HE'S BEEN REALLY KIND, OPENING A WHOLE NEW WORLD, AND--
WHOA, SUE! STOP. IT SOUNDS LIKE YOU'RE GOING INTO ROMANCE TALK.
WITH STEVE? NEVER. WE'RE FRIENDS. AND REED IS THE ONLY MAN WHO COULD EVER--
EVER--
KINDA PAUSED THERE IN MID-SENTENCE, GIRL. AND YOU EVEN WENT A LITTLE INVISIBLE.
DID I STRIKE A CHORD WITH THAT ROMANCE JOKE?
NO. IT'S NOT THAT, I--

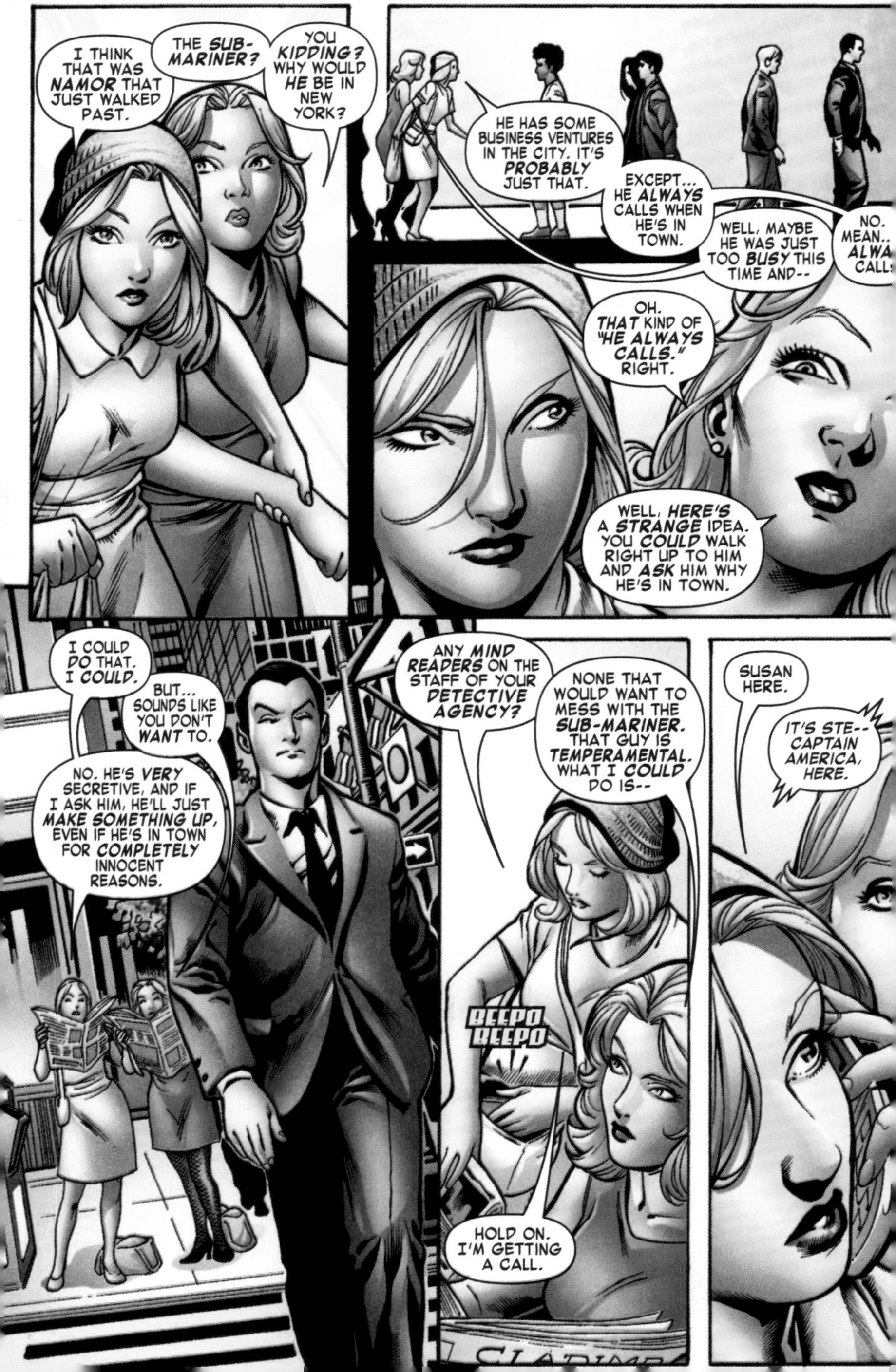
I THINK THAT WAS NAMOR THAT JUST WALKED PAST.
THE SUB-MARINER?
YOU KIDDING? WHY WOULD HE BE IN NEW YORK?
HE HAS SOME BUSINESS VENTURES IN THE CITY. IT'S PROBABLY JUST THAT.
EXCEPT... HE ALWAYS CALLS WHEN HE'S IN TOWN.
WELL, MAYBE HE WAS JUST TOO BUSY THIS TIME AND--
NO. MEAN.. ALWA CALL
OH. THAT KIND OF "HE ALWAYS CALLS." RIGHT.
WELL, HERE'S A STRANGE IDEA. YOU COULD WALK RIGHT UP TO HIM AND ASK HIM WHY HE'S IN TOWN.
I COULD DO THAT. I COULD.
BUT... SOUNDS LIKE YOU DON'T WANT TO.
NO. HE'S VERY SECRETIVE, AND IF I ASK HIM, HE'LL JUST MAKE SOMETHING UP, EVEN IF HE'S IN TOWN FOR COMPLETELY INNOCENT REASONS.
ANY MIND READERS ON THE STAFF OF YOUR DETECTIVE AGENCY?
NONE THAT WOULD WANT TO MESS WITH THE SUB-MARINER. THAT GUY IS TEMPERAMENTAL. WHAT I COULD DO IS--
BEEPO BEEPO
HOLD ON. I'M GETTING A CALL.
SUSAN HERE.
IT'S STE-- CAPTAIN AMERICA, HERE.

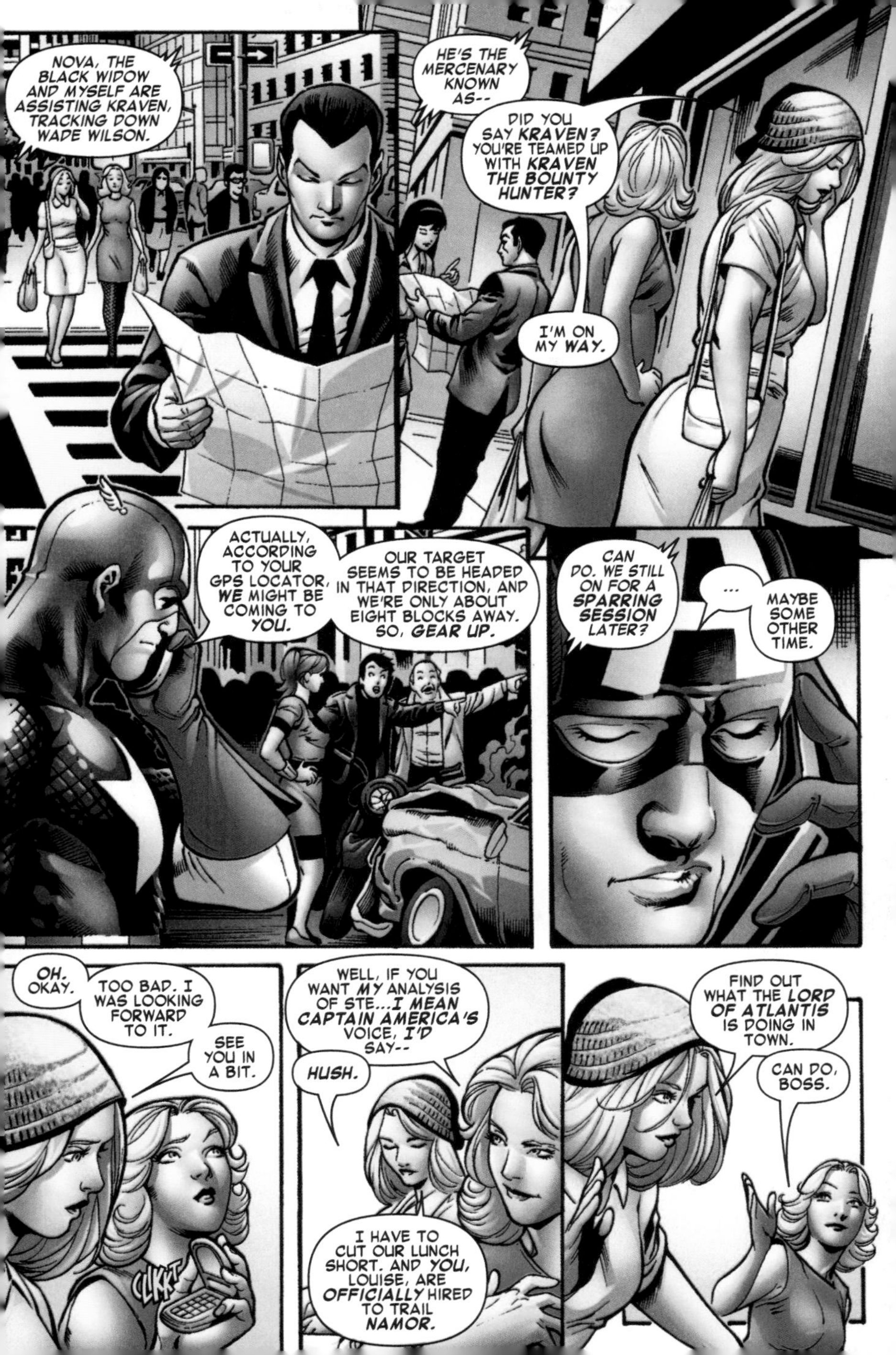
NOVA, THE BLACK WIDOW AND MYSELF ARE ASSISTING KRAVEN, TRACKING DOWN WADE WILSON.
HE'S THE MERCENARY KNOWN AS--
DID YOU SAY KRAVEN? YOU'RE TEAMED UP WITH KRAVEN THE BOUNTY HUNTER?
I'M ON MY WAY.
ACTUALLY, ACCORDING TO YOUR GPS LOCATOR, WE MIGHT BE COMING TO YOU.
OUR TARGET SEEMS TO BE HEADED IN THAT DIRECTION, AND WE'RE ONLY ABOUT EIGHT BLOCKS AWAY. SO, GEAR UP.
CAN DO. WE STILL ON FOR A SPARRING SESSION LATER?
...
MAYBE SOME OTHER TIME.
OH. OKAY.
TOO BAD. I WAS LOOKING FORWARD TO IT.
SEE YOU IN A BIT.
CLIKKT
WELL, IF YOU WANT MY ANALYSIS OF STE...I MEAN CAPTAIN AMERICA'S VOICE, I'D SAY--
HUSH.
I HAVE TO CUT OUR LUNCH SHORT. AND YOU, LOUISE, ARE OFFICIALLY HIRED TO TRAIL NAMOR.
FIND OUT WHAT THE LORD OF ATLANTIS IS DOING IN TOWN.
CAN DO, BOSS.

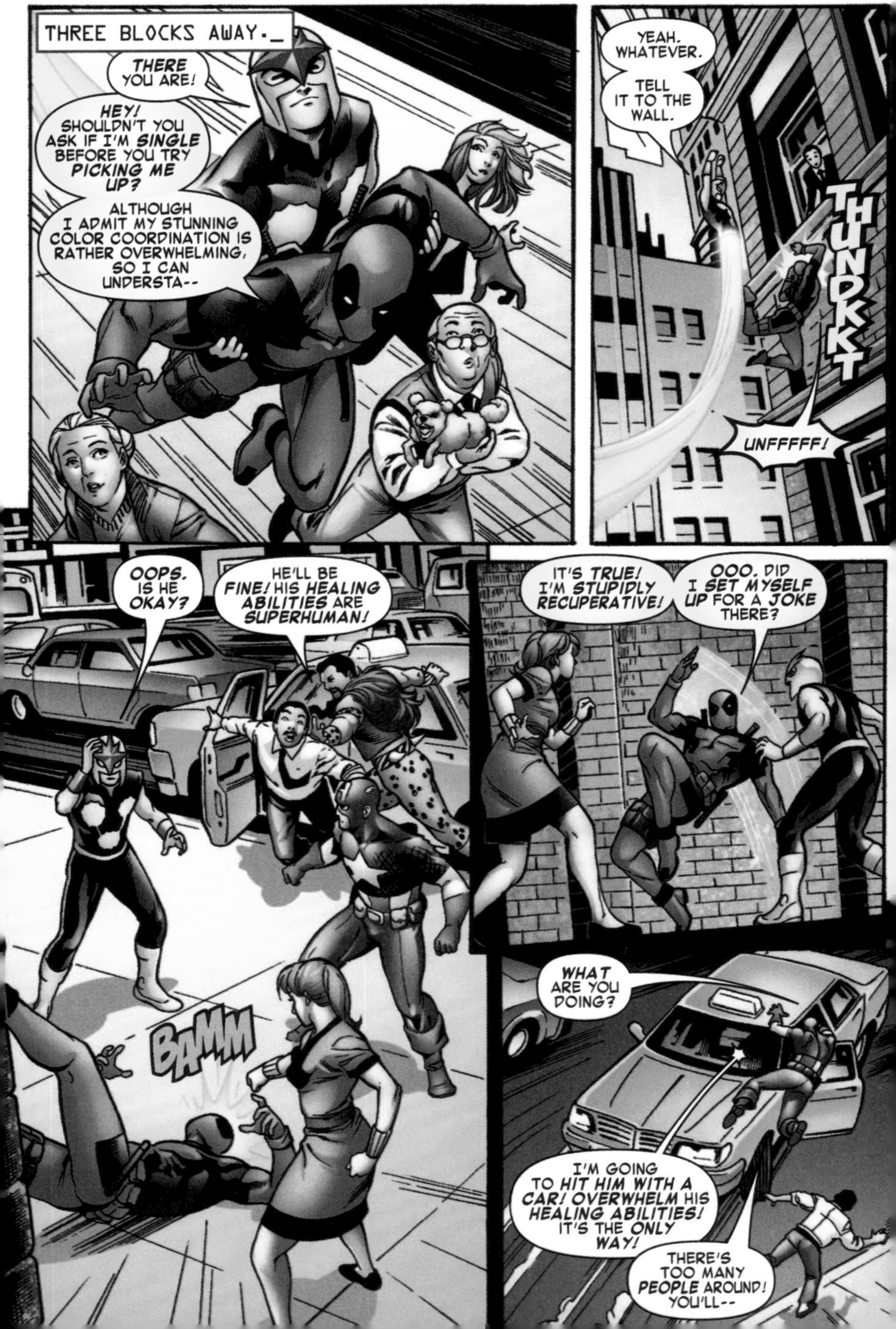
THREE BLOCKS AWAY._
THERE YOU ARE!
HEY! SHOULDN'T YOU ASK IF I'M SINGLE BEFORE YOU TRY PICKING ME UP?
ALTHOUGH I ADMIT MY STUNNING COLOR COORDINATION IS RATHER OVERWHELMING, SO I CAN UNDERSTA--
YEAH. WHATEVER.
TELL IT TO THE WALL.
THUNDKT
UNFFFFF!
OOPS. IS HE OKAY?
HE'LL BE FINE! HIS HEALING ABILITIES ARE SUPERHUMAN!
BAMM
IT'S TRUE! I'M STUPIDLY RECUPERATIVE!
OOO. DID I SET MYSELF UP FOR A JOKE THERE?
WHAT ARE YOU DOING?
I'M GOING TO HIT HIM WITH A CAR! OVERWHELM HIS HEALING ABILITIES! IT'S THE ONLY WAY!
THERE'S TOO MANY PEOPLE AROUND! YOU'LL--

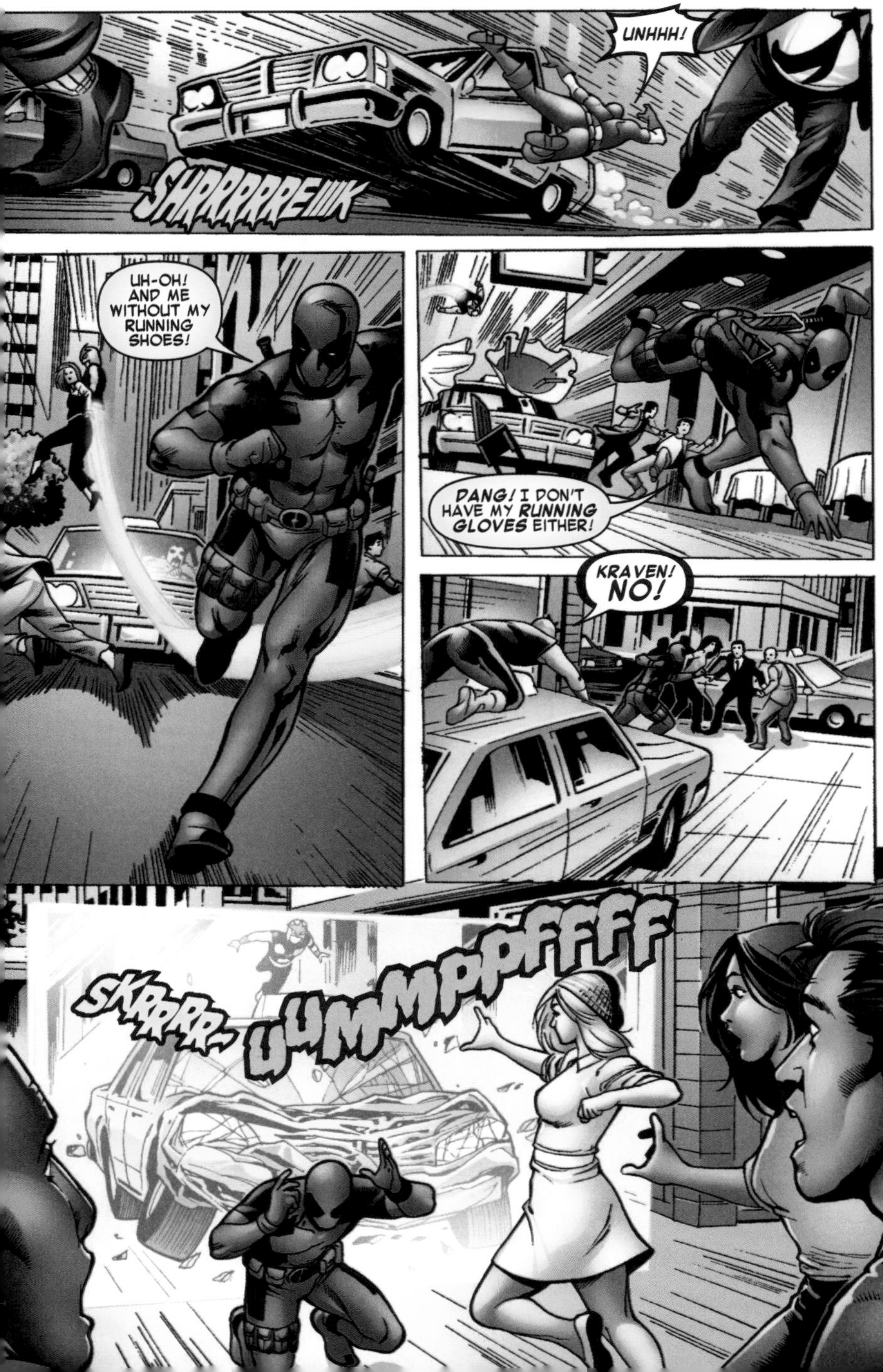
UNHHH!
SHRRRRREIIIK
UH-OH! AND ME WITHOUT MY RUNNING SHOES!
DANG! I DON'T HAVE MY RUNNING GLOVES EITHER!
KRAVEN! NO!
SKRRRR-UUMMPPFFFFF

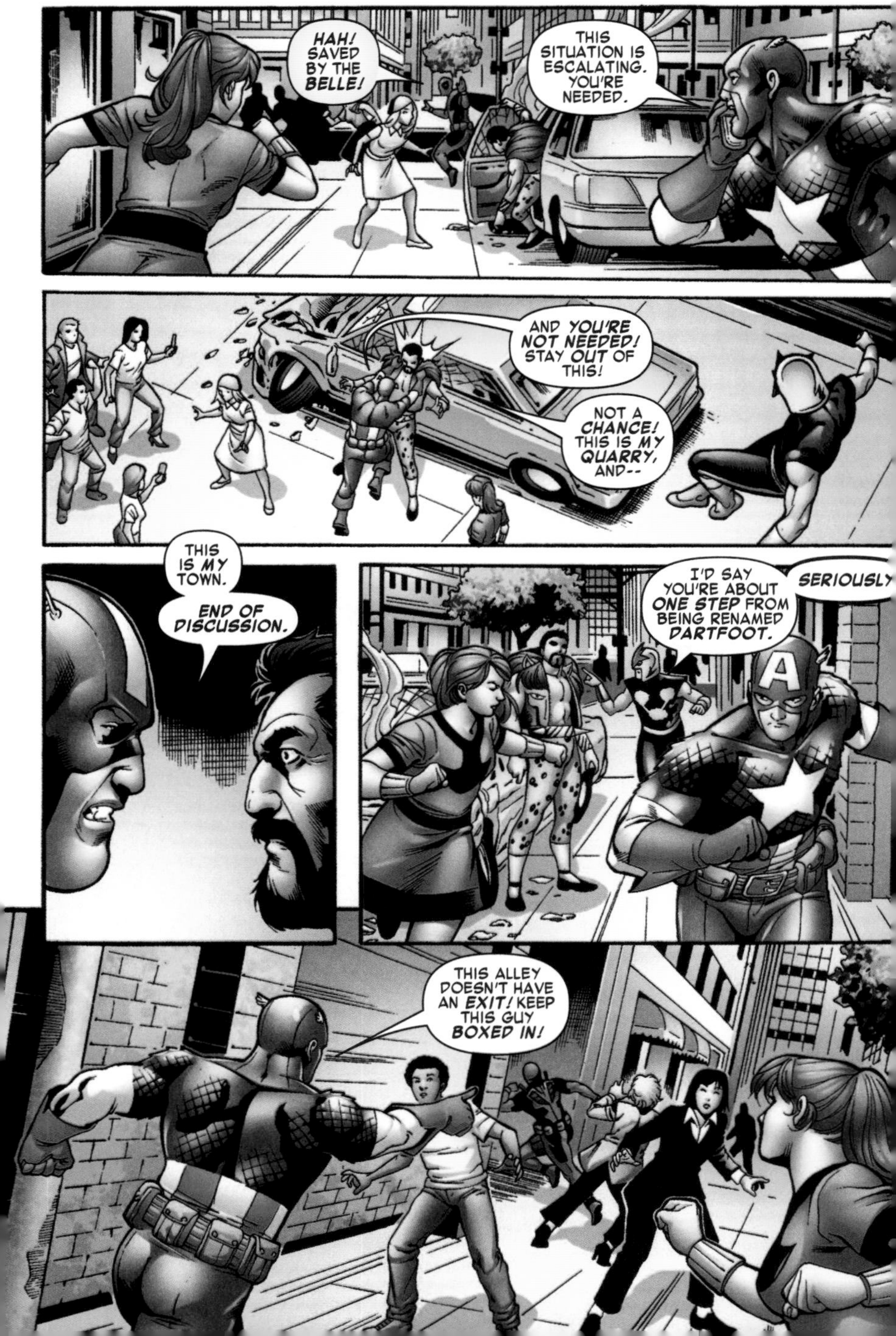
HAH! SAVED BY THE BELLE!
THIS SITUATION IS ESCALATING. YOU'RE NEEDED.
AND YOU'RE NOT NEEDED! STAY OUT OF THIS!
NOT A CHANCE! THIS IS MY QUARRY, AND--
THIS IS MY TOWN.
END OF DISCUSSION.
I'D SAY YOU'RE ABOUT ONE STEP FROM BEING RENAMED DARTFOOT.
SERIOUSLY
THIS ALLEY DOESN'T HAVE AN EXIT! KEEP THIS GUY BOXED IN!

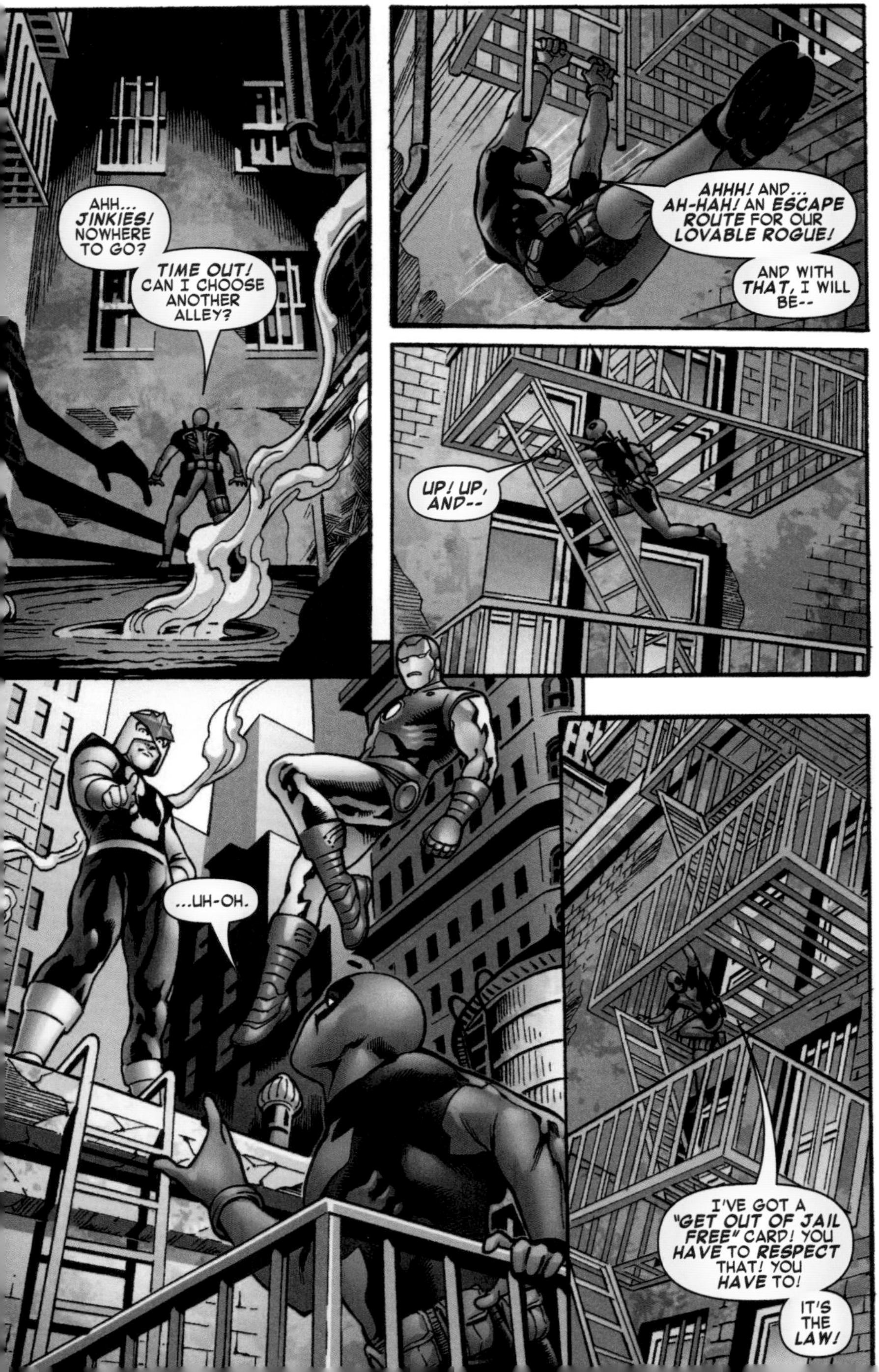

AHH... JINKIES! NOWHERE TO GO?
TIME OUT! CAN I CHOOSE ANOTHER ALLEY?
AHHH! AND... AH-HAH! AN ESCAPE ROUTE FOR OUR LOVABLE ROGUE!
AND WITH THAT, I WILL BE--
UP! UP, AND--
...UH-OH.
I'VE GOT A "GET OUT OF JAIL FREE" CARD! YOU HAVE TO RESPECT THAT! YOU HAVE TO!
IT'S THE LAW!

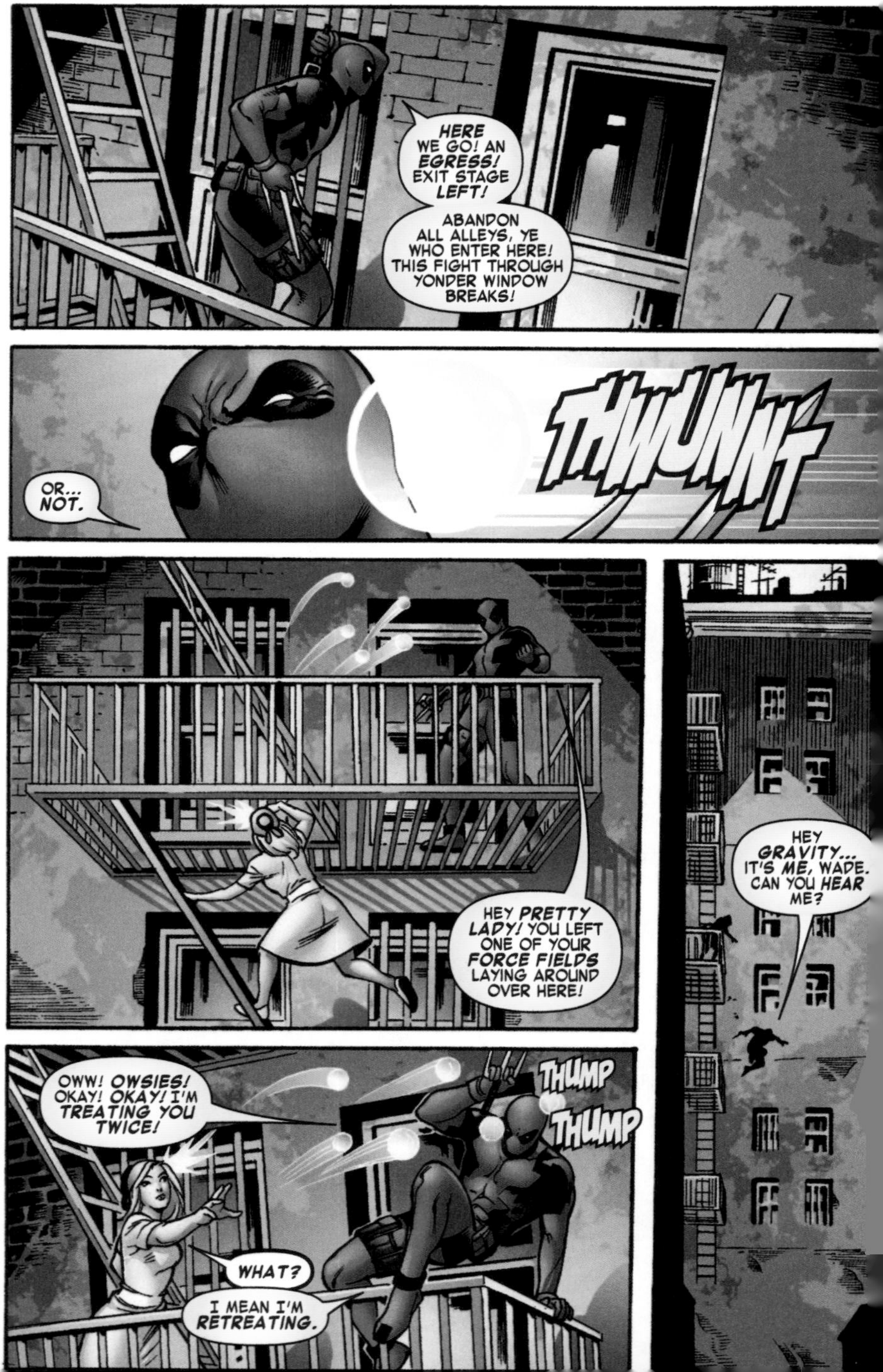

HERE WE GO! AN EGRESS! EXIT STAGE LEFT!
ABANDON ALL ALLEYS, YE WHO ENTER HERE! THIS FIGHT THROUGH YONDER WINDOW BREAKS!
THWUNNT
OR... NOT.
HEY PRETTY LADY! YOU LEFT ONE OF YOUR FORCE FIELDS LAYING AROUND OVER HERE!
OWW! OWSIES! OKAY! OKAY! I'M TREATING YOU TWICE!
THUMP
THUMP
WHAT?
I MEAN I'M RETREATING.
HEY GRAVITY... IT'S ME, WADE. CAN YOU HEAR ME?

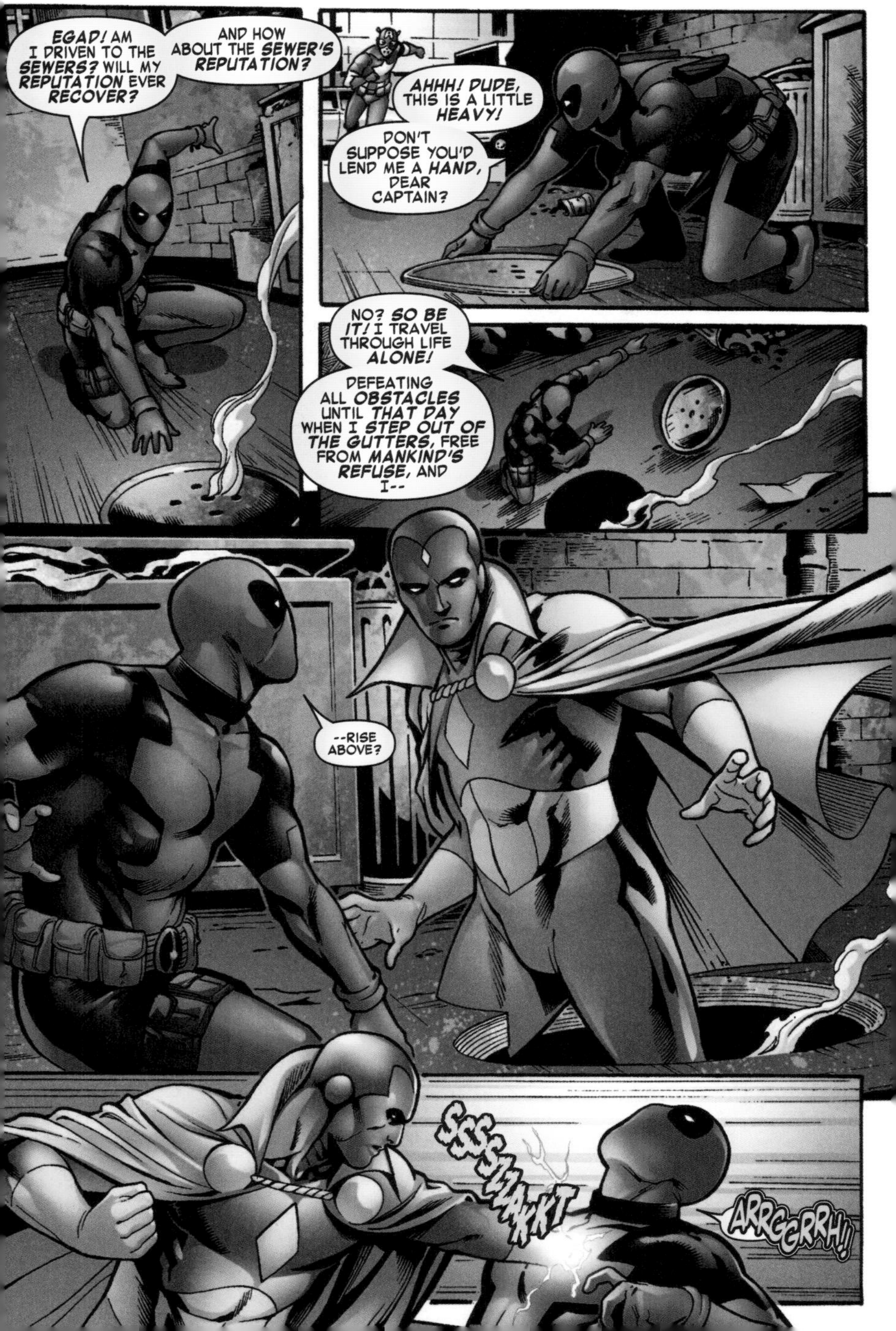

EGAD! AM I DRIVEN TO THE SEWERS? WILL MY REPUTATION EVER RECOVER?
AND HOW ABOUT THE SEWER'S REPUTATION?
AHHH! DUDE, THIS IS A LITTLE HEAVY!
DON'T SUPPOSE YOU'D LEND ME A HAND, DEAR CAPTAIN?
NO? SO BE IT! I TRAVEL THROUGH LIFE ALONE!
DEFEATING ALL OBSTACLES UNTIL THAT DAY WHEN I STEP OUT OF THE GUTTERS, FREE FROM MANKIND'S REFUSE, AND I--
--RISE ABOVE?
SSSSZZAKKT
ARRGGRRH!!

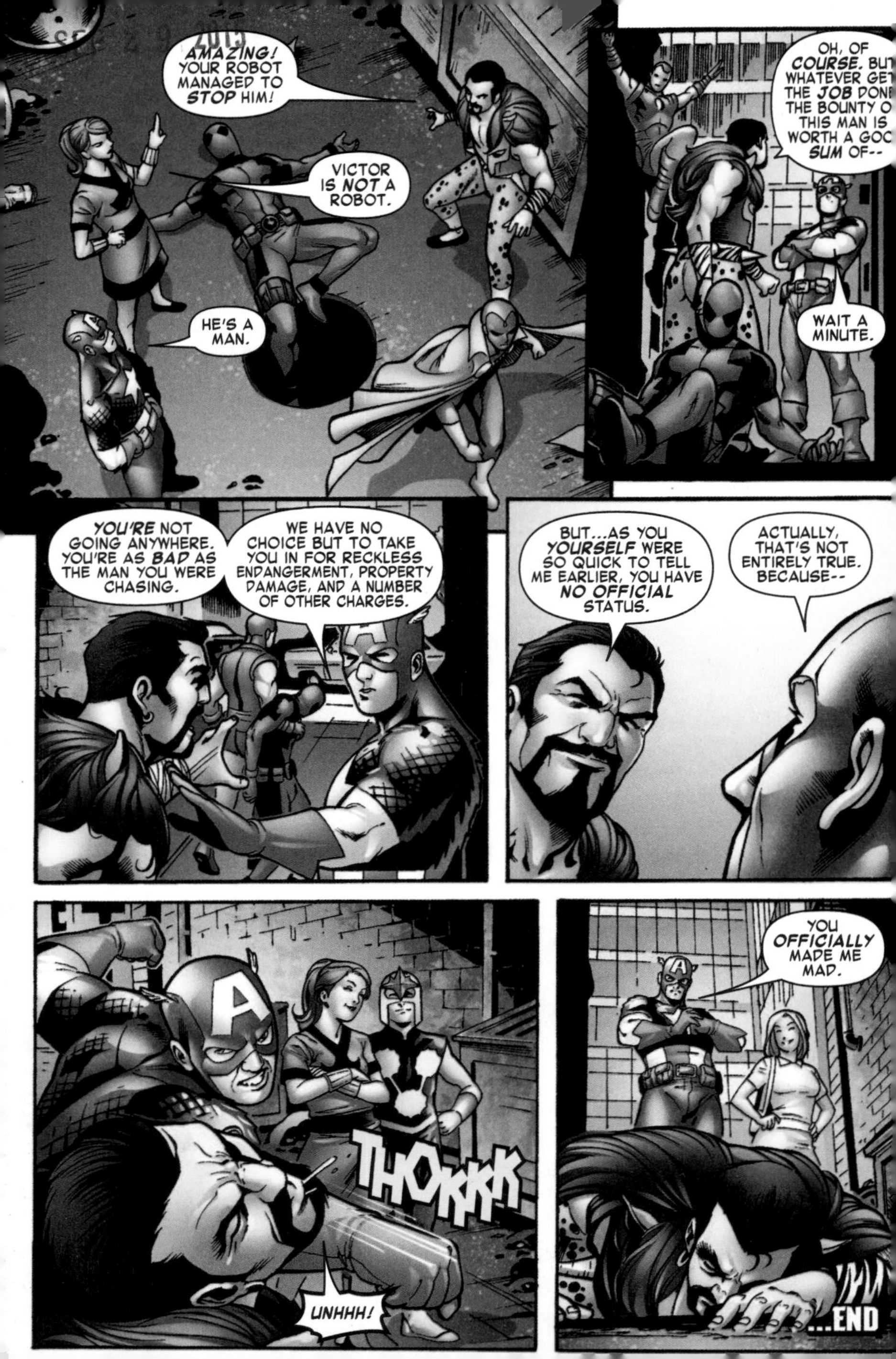
AMAZING! YOUR ROBOT MANAGED TO STOP HIM!
VICTOR IS NOT A ROBOT.
HE'S A MAN.
OH, OF COURSE. BU WHATEVER GE THE JOB DON THE BOUNTY O THIS MAN IS WORTH A GOO SUM OF--
WAIT A MINUTE.
YOU'RE NOT GOING ANYWHERE. YOU'RE AS BAD AS THE MAN YOU WERE CHASING.
WE HAVE NO CHOICE BUT TO TAKE YOU IN FOR RECKLESS ENDANGERMENT, PROPERTY DAMAGE, AND A NUMBER OF OTHER CHARGES.
BUT...AS YOU YOURSELF WERE SO QUICK TO TELL ME EARLIER, YOU HAVE NO OFFICIAL STATUS.
ACTUALLY, THAT'S NOT ENTIRELY TRUE. BECAUSE--
THOKKK
UNHHH!
YOU OFFICIALLY MADE ME MAD.
...END